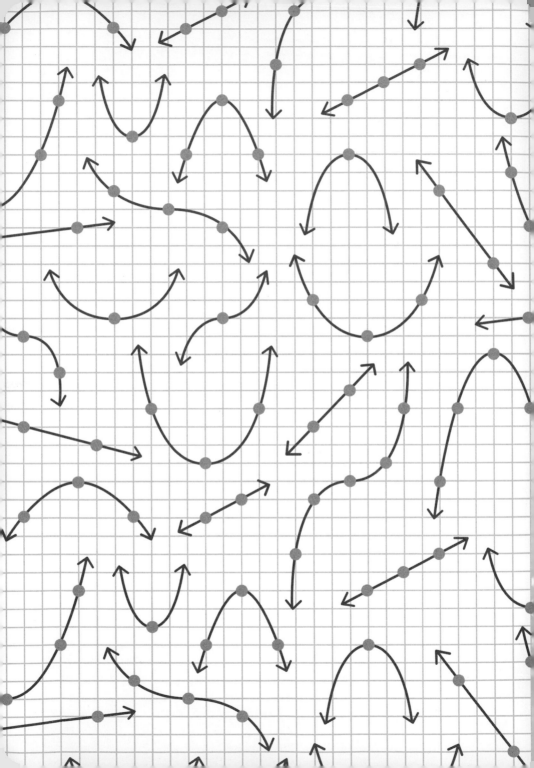

PRE-ALGEBRA & ALGEBRA 1

Library of Congress Cataloging-in-Publication Data is available.

ISBN: 978-1-5235-0438-1

Writer: Jason Wang   Reviewer: Debra Calvino
Illustrator: Kim Ku
Designer: Abby Dening
Concept by Raquel Jaramillo

SPECIAL DISCOUNT FOR EDUCATORS:
The Big Fat Notebooks are available at special discounts when purchased in bulk for premiums and sales promotions as well as for fundraising or educational use. Special editions or book excerpts can also be created to specification. For details, please contact special.markets@hbgusa.com.

Workman Publishing Co., Inc., a subsidiary of Hachette Book Group, Inc.
1290 Avenue of the Americas
New York, NY 10104
workman.com

Distributed in Europe by Hachette Livre, 58 rue Jean Bleuzen, 92 178 Vanves Cedex, France. Distributed in the United Kingdom by Hachette Book Group, UK, Carmelite House, 50 Victoria Embankment, London EC4Y 0DZ.

WORKMAN, BRAIN QUEST, and BIG FAT NOTE-BOOK are registered trademarks of Workman Publishing Co., Inc., a subsidiary of Hachette Book Group, Inc.

Printed in China on responsibly sourced paper.

First printing July 2021

10 9 8 7 6 5 4 3

THE **COMPLETE** HIGH SCHOOL STUDY GUIDE

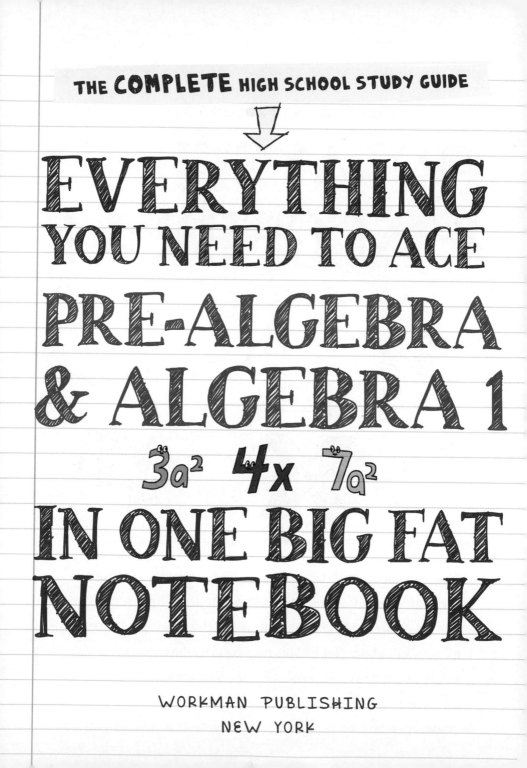

EVERYTHING YOU NEED TO ACE

PRE-ALGEBRA & ALGEBRA 1

$3a^2$ $4x$ $7a^2$

IN ONE BIG FAT NOTEBOOK

WORKMAN PUBLISHING
NEW YORK

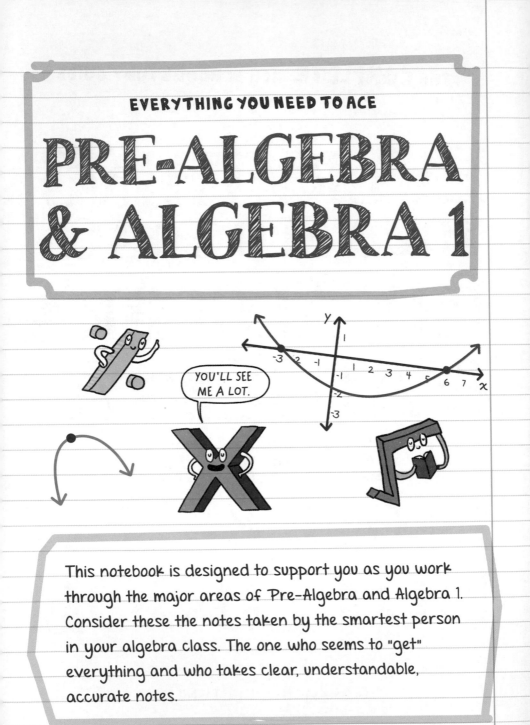

EVERYTHING YOU NEED TO ACE

PRE-ALGEBRA & ALGEBRA 1

YOU'LL SEE ME A LOT.

This notebook is designed to support you as you work through the major areas of Pre-Algebra and Algebra 1. Consider these the notes taken by the smartest person in your algebra class. The one who seems to "get" everything and who takes clear, understandable, accurate notes.

Within these chapters you'll find important concepts presented in an accessible, relatable way. Linear equations and inequalities, statistics and probability, functions, factoring polynomials, and solving and graphing quadratic equations are all presented as notes you can easily understand. It's algebra for the regular person.

Notes are presented in an organized way:

- Important vocabulary words are highlighted in **YELLOW**.
- All vocabulary words are clearly defined.
- Related terms and concepts are written in BLUE PEN.
- Clear step-by-step examples and calculations are supported by explanations, color coding, illustrations, and charts.

If you want something to use as a companion to your textbook that's fun and easy to understand, and you're not so great at taking notes in class, this notebook will help. It hits all the key concepts you'll learn in Pre-Algebra and Algebra 1.

CONTENTS

UNIT 3:
RATIOS, PROPORTIONS, AND PERCENT 75

UNIT 4:
EXPONENTS AND ALGEBRAIC EXPRESSIONS 141

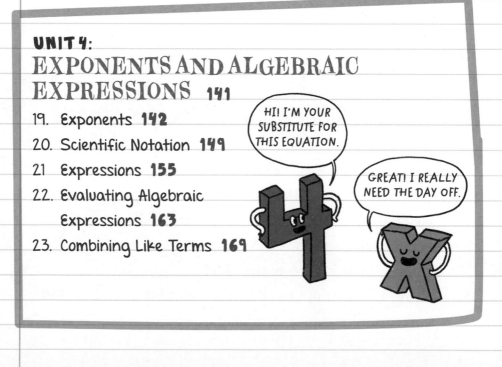

UNIT 13:
QUADRATIC FUNCTIONS 587

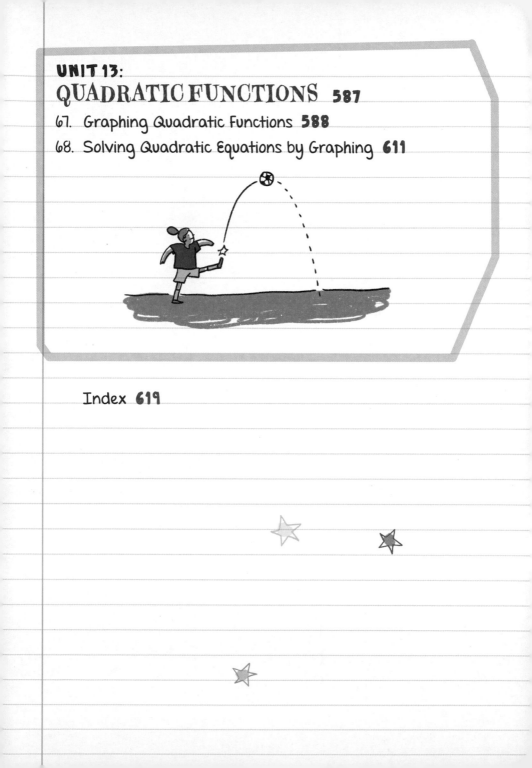

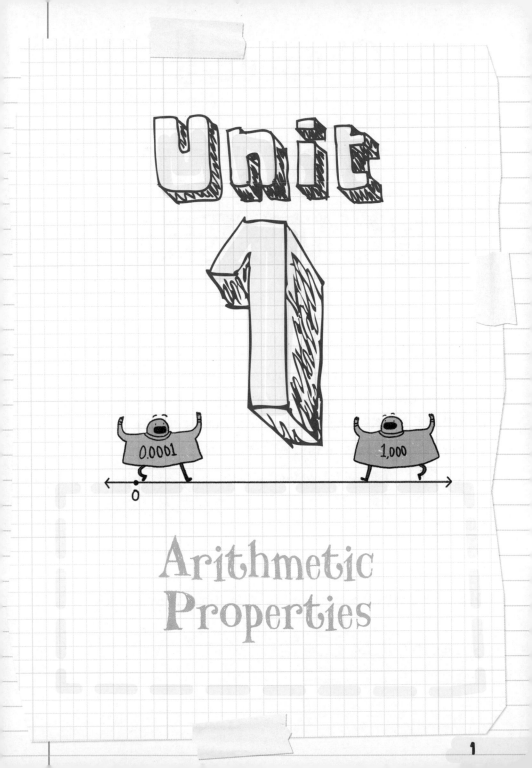

Unit

1

0.0001

1,000

0

Arithmetic
Properties

Chapter 1

TYPES OF NUMBERS

All numbers can be classified into various categories. Here are the categories that are most often used in mathematics:

NATURAL NUMBERS or Counting Numbers: The set of all positive numbers starting at 1 that have no fractional or decimal part; also called whole numbers.

Examples: 1, 2, 3, 4, 5, . . .

WHOLE NUMBERS: The set of all natural numbers and 0.

Examples: 0, 1, 2, 3, 4, 5, . . .

INTEGERS: The set of all whole numbers, including negative natural numbers.

Examples: . . . –5, –4, –3, –2, –1, 0, 1, 2, 3, 4, 5, . . .

RATIONAL NUMBERS: The set of all numbers that can be written by dividing one integer by another. These include any number that can be written as a fraction or ratio.

Note: You cannot have 0 in the denominator of a fraction.

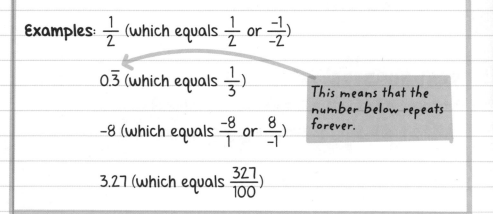

Examples: $\frac{1}{2}$ (which equals $\frac{1}{2}$ or $\frac{-1}{-2}$)

$0.\overline{3}$ (which equals $\frac{1}{3}$)

This means that the number below repeats forever.

–8 (which equals $\frac{-8}{1}$ or $\frac{8}{-1}$)

3.27 (which equals $\frac{327}{100}$)

Natural numbers, whole numbers, and integers are all rational numbers.

IRRATIONAL NUMBERS: The set of all numbers that are *not* rational numbers. These are numbers that cannot be written by dividing one integer by another. When we write an irrational number as a decimal, it goes on forever, without repeating itself.

"..." means that the number continues on forever.

Examples: $\sqrt{5}$ = 2.2360679774997... $\qquad$ π = 3.141592653...

0.25 is NOT irrational because it terminates or ends.

0.347115715715715... is NOT irrational because the digits repeat themselves.

REAL NUMBERS: The set of all numbers on a number line. Real numbers include all rational and irrational numbers. This can be zero, positive or negative integers, decimals, fractions, etc.

Examples: $8, -19, 0, \dfrac{3}{2}, \sqrt{47}, \sqrt{25}, \pi, \ldots$

Numbers less than zero are located to the left of 0 on the number line.

YOU'RE SO FAR AWAY!

Numbers greater than 0 are located to the right of 0 on the number line.

0.0001

1,000

0

Here's how all the types of numbers fit together in our number system.

Example: -2 is an integer, a rational number, and a real number

Some other examples:

24 is natural, whole, an integer, rational, and real.

0 is whole, an integer, rational, and real.

$\frac{2}{3}$ is rational and real.

6.675 is rational and real.

$\sqrt{5}$ = 2.2360679774997 . . . is irrational and real.

SOME IMPORTANT POINTS ABOUT DECIMALS

1. **Terminating decimals** are decimals that have no repeating digit or group of digits.

   All terminating decimals are rational numbers.

   > To **terminate** means to end.

   Example: 0.25 ← the decimal ends

2. **Repeating decimals** are decimals that go on infinitely, but one or more digits repeat themselves. All repeating decimals are rational numbers.

   Examples: $\frac{1}{3} = 0.\overline{3}$ or $\frac{9}{7} = 1.\overline{285714}$

   $\frac{9}{7} = 1.285714285714\ldots$

   The bar over the digits "285714" means that all of those digits repeat infinitely.

3.1415926535...

CHECK YOUR KNOWLEDGE

For questions 1 through 10, classify each number in as many categories as possible.

1. 62

2. $\dfrac{8}{10}$

3. 9.28519692714385 . . .

4. 0

5. 3.7

6. –260

7. $-\dfrac{5}{2}$

8. π

9. $3.25\overline{197}$

10. $\sqrt{49}$

1. natural, whole, integer, rational number, real number

2. rational, real

3. irrational, real

4. whole, integer, rational, real

5. rational, real

6. integer, rational, real

7. rational, real

8. irrational, real

9. rational, real

10. Since $\sqrt{49}$ is equal to 7, it is a natural number, whole number, integer, rational number, and real number.

Chapter 2

ALGEBRAIC PROPERTIES

BASIC PROPERTIES

The **Commutative Property of Addition** and the **Commutative PROPERTY OF MULTIPLICATION** tell us that when we are adding two numbers or multiplying two numbers, the order of the numbers does not matter to get a correct calculation.

> **Think:** To commute means to move around. So we can move the order of numbers around and not affect the result.

The **COMMUTATIVE PROPERTY OF ADDITION** states that for any two numbers a and b: $a + b = b + a$.

These are **equivalent numerical expressions**. This means that both sides of the math equation have equal value.

Example: $1 + 2 = 2 + 1$ ■ □ □   □ □ ■

$$3\frac{2}{7} + 1\frac{5}{6} = 1\frac{5}{6} + 3\frac{2}{7}$$

The **COMMUTATIVE PROPERTY OF MULTIPLICATION** states that for any two numbers x and y: $x \cdot y = y \cdot x$.

Example: $5 \cdot 3 = 3 \cdot 5$

The Commutative Properties work **only** with addition and multiplication; they do not work with subtraction and division.

The **Associative Property of Addition** and the **Associative Property of Multiplication** tell us that when we are adding three numbers or multiplying three numbers, the order in which we group the numbers does not matter.

The **ASSOCIATIVE PROPERTY OF ADDITION** states that for any three numbers a, b, and c: $(a + b) + c = a + (b + c)$.

For example, $1 + 2 + 5$ can be calculated either as:

$(1 + 2) + 5 = 3 + 5 = 8$

or

$1 + (2 + 5) = 1 + 7 = 8$

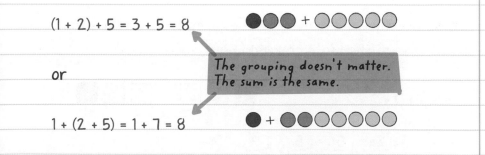

The grouping doesn't matter. The sum is the same.

The **ASSOCIATIVE PROPERTY OF MULTIPLICATION** states that for any three numbers a, b, and c:
$(a \cdot b) \cdot c = a \cdot (b \cdot c)$.

For example, $2 \cdot 3 \cdot 5$ can be calculated either as:

$(2 \cdot 3) \cdot 5 = 6 \cdot 5 = 30$

or

Grouping doesn't matter. The product is the same.

$2 \cdot (3 \cdot 5) = 2 \cdot 15 = 30$

The Associative Properties work **only** with addition and multiplication; they do not work with subtraction and division.

What's the difference between commutative properties and associative properties?

Commutative relates to the order of the numbers.

Associative relates to the grouping of the numbers.

The **DISTRIBUTIVE PROPERTY OF MULTIPLICATION OVER ADDITION**

Think: Distributive means to share or give out.

says that we get the same number when we multiply a group of numbers added together or when we multiply each number separately and then add them.

- The Distributive Property can be used when multiplying a number by the sum of two numbers:

Given three numbers a, b, and c: $a(b + c) = (a \cdot b) + (a \cdot c)$.

$a(b + c) = a \cdot b + a \cdot c$ We are **DISTRIBUTING** the term a to each of the terms b and c.

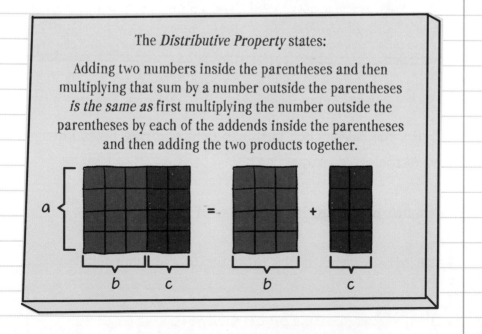

The *Distributive Property* states:

Adding two numbers inside the parentheses and then multiplying that sum by a number outside the parentheses *is the same as* first multiplying the number outside the parentheses by each of the addends inside the parentheses and then adding the two products together.

EXAMPLE: Use the Distributive Property to expand and then simplify $3(6 + 8)$.

$3(6 + 8) = 3 \cdot 6 + 3 \cdot 8$ expand
$\qquad\quad = 18 + 24 = 42$ simplify

The **DISTRIBUTIVE PROPERTY OF MULTIPLICATION OVER SUBTRACTION** says that we get the same number when we multiply a group of numbers subtracted together or when we multiply each number separately and subtract them.

Given three numbers a, b, and c: $a(b - c) = (a \cdot b) - (a \cdot c)$.

So, $a(b - c) = a \cdot b - a \cdot c$

EXAMPLE: Use the Distributive Property to expand and then simplify $2(10 - 7)$.

$2(10 - 7) = 2 \cdot 10 - 2 \cdot 7 = 20 - 14 = 6$

- The Distributive Property can also be used for expressions with multiple terms.

To expand $a(b + c - d)$:

$$a(b + c - d) = a \cdot b + a \cdot c - a \cdot d = ab + ac - ad$$

EXAMPLE: Use the Distributive Property to expand and simplify $6(2 - 1 + 5)$.

$$6(2 - 1 + 5) = 6(2) - 6(1) + 6(5)$$
$$= 12 - 6 + 30 = 36$$

Note: The Distributive Property does **NOT** work for division!

Examples:

$$a \div (b + c) \neq a \div b + a \div c$$
$$40 \div (8 + 2) \neq 40 \div 8 + 40 \div 2$$

CHECK YOUR KNOWLEDGE

For questions 1 through 4, state the property used.

1. $3 \cdot 5 = 5 \cdot 3$

2. $(a + b) + \frac{1}{2} = a + (b + \frac{1}{2})$

3. $\frac{1}{2} \cdot (5 \cdot \frac{4}{3}) = (\frac{1}{2} \cdot 5) \cdot \frac{4}{3}$

4. $0 + 5 = 5 + 0$

For problems 5 through 6, state whether or not the property is being applied correctly.

5. Use the Associative Property to state: $\frac{1}{2} \div 7 = 7 \div \frac{1}{2}$

6. Use the Associative Property to state: $7 + 3 - 1$ can be calculated either as:
$(10 - 3) - 1$ or $10 - (3 - 1)$

For questions 7 through 10, use the Distributive Property to expand each expression, then simplify your answer.

7. $2(3 + 8)$

8. $m(n) - m(12) = mn - 12m$

9. $4(10 - 2 + 5)$

10. $x(y) - x(z) + x(3) = xy - xz + 3x$

CHECK YOUR ANSWERS

1. Commutative Property of Multiplication

2. Associative Property of Addition

3. Associative Property of Multiplication

4. Commutative Property of Addition

5. Not correct. The Associative and Commutative Properties cannot be used for division.

6. Not correct. The expression results in different answers.

7. $2(3) + 2(8) = 6 + 16 = 22$

8. $mn - 12m$

9. $4(10) - 4(2) + 4(5) = 40 - 8 + 20 = 52$

10. $xy - xz + 3x$

Chapter 3

ORDER OF OPERATIONS

The order of operations is an order agreed upon by mathematicians. It directs us to perform mathematical calculation in the following order:

1ST Any calculations inside parentheses or brackets

2ND Exponents, roots, and absolute value are calculated left to right

3RD Multiplication and division—whichever comes first when you calculate left to right

4TH Addition and subtraction—whichever comes first when you calculate left to right

You can use the mnemonic "**Please Excuse My Dear Aunt Sally**" for the acronym **PEMDAS** (Parentheses, Exponents, Multiplication, Division, Addition, and Subtraction) to remember the order of operations, but it can be VERY misleading.

This is because you can do division before multiplication or subtraction before addition, as long as you are calculating **from left to right**.

Also, because other calculations like roots and absolute value aren't included, PEMDAS isn't totally foolproof.

EXAMPLE: Simplify the expression: 7 – 4 + 1

= $\boxed{7 - 4}$ + 1

= 3 + 1

= 4

First, do subtraction or addition, whatever comes first, left to right.

PARENTHESES

EXPONENTS

MULTIPLICATION (left to right)

DIVISION (left to right)

ADDITION (left to right)

SUBTRACTION (left to right)

EXAMPLE: Simplify the expression: 10 − 3 × 2

= 10 − $\boxed{3 \times 2}$ ⟵ First, do multiplication.
= 10 − 6   (PEMDAS: multiplication before subtraction)
= 4

EXAMPLE: Simplify the expression: (9 + 3) ÷ 1.5

= $\boxed{(9 + 3)}$ ÷ 1.5 ⟵ First, do the operation inside the parentheses.
= 12 ÷ 1.5 or $\frac{12}{1.5}$
= 8

EXAMPLE: Simplify the expression: 84 − 72 ÷ 6 × 2 + 1

= 84 − $\boxed{72 \div 6}$ × 2 + 1   Note: Another way to think of this
= 84 − $\boxed{12 \times 2}$ + 1   problem is by using a fraction bar: $\frac{72}{6}$
= $\boxed{84 - 24}$ + 1
= 60 + 1
= 61

Since both division and multiplication appear
in this expression start with whichever of
the two is first, from left to right.

EXAMPLE: Alice's basketball team makes 8 regular two-point shots and 4 three-point shots. Bob's basketball team makes 10 two-point and 2 three-point shots. How many more total points did Alice's team score than Bob's team?

Calculate the total points Alice's team made:

$[(8 \cdot 2) + (4 \cdot 3)]$

Calculate the total points Bob's team made:

$[(10 \cdot 2) + (2 \cdot 3)]$

Subtract the two scores:

$= [(8 \cdot 2) + (4 \cdot 3)] - [(10 \cdot 2) + (2 \cdot 3)]$
$= (16 + 12) - [(10 \cdot 2) + (2 \cdot 3)]$
$= 28 - [(10 \cdot 2) + (2 \cdot 3)]$
$= 28 - (20 + 6)$
$= 28 - 26$
$= 2$

Alice's team scored 2 more points than Bob's team.

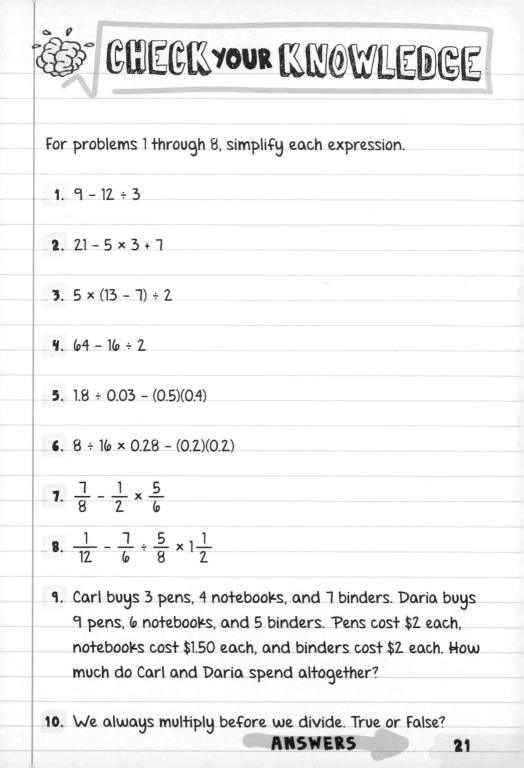

CHECK YOUR KNOWLEDGE

For problems 1 through 8, simplify each expression.

1. $9 - 12 \div 3$

2. $21 - 5 \times 3 + 7$

3. $5 \times (13 - 7) \div 2$

4. $64 - 16 \div 2$

5. $1.8 \div 0.03 - (0.5)(0.4)$

6. $8 \div 16 \times 0.28 - (0.2)(0.2)$

7. $\dfrac{7}{8} - \dfrac{1}{2} \times \dfrac{5}{6}$

8. $\dfrac{1}{12} - \dfrac{7}{6} \div \dfrac{5}{8} \times 1\dfrac{1}{2}$

9. Carl buys 3 pens, 4 notebooks, and 7 binders. Daria buys 9 pens, 6 notebooks, and 5 binders. Pens cost $2 each, notebooks cost $1.50 each, and binders cost $2 each. How much do Carl and Daria spend altogether?

10. We always multiply before we divide. True or False?

ANSWERS

21

CHECK YOUR KNOWLEDGE

1. 5

2. 13

3. 15

4. 56

5. 59.8

6. 0.1

7. $\dfrac{11}{24}$

8. $-2\dfrac{43}{60}$

9. $63

10. False. We choose whether to multiply or divide first based on which comes first, left to right.

Unit 2

The Number System

Chapter 4

ADDING
POSITIVE AND NEGATIVE
WHOLE NUMBERS

POSITIVE NUMBERS describe quantities greater than zero. Positive numbers are shown with and without the positive sign. For example, +2 and 2.

NEGATIVE NUMBERS describe quantities less than zero. All negative numbers have a negative sign in front of them. For example, −6.

There are various ways to add positive and negative numbers.

METHOD #1:

USE A NUMBER LINE

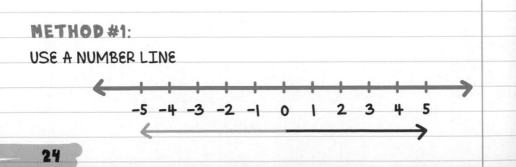

Draw a number line. Begin at zero.

For a POSITIVE (+) number, x, move x units to the right.
For a NEGATIVE (–) number, –y, move y units to the left.

Whichever position you end up at is the answer.

EXAMPLE: Find the sum: 5 + (–3).

1. Begin at zero. Since 5 is a positive number, move 5 units to the right.

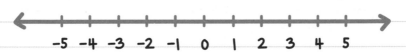

2. Begin where you left off with the first number. Since –3 is a negative number, start at 5 and move 3 units to the left.

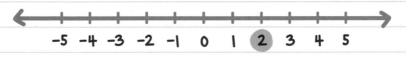

We end up at 2.

The sum of 5 and –3 is 2.

EXAMPLE: Find the sum: (–1) + (–4).

1. Begin at zero. Since –1 is a negative number, move 1 unit to the left.

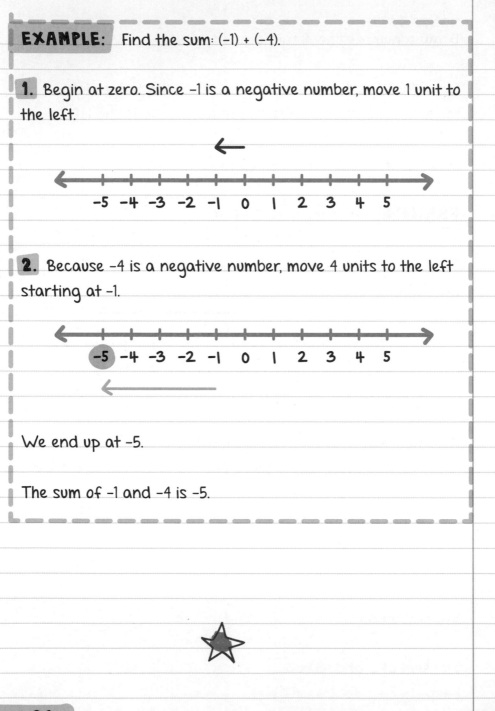

2. Because –4 is a negative number, move 4 units to the left starting at –1.

We end up at –5.

The sum of –1 and –4 is –5.

EXAMPLE: Find the sum: 5 + (–7).

Move 5 units to the right. Then move 7 units to the left.

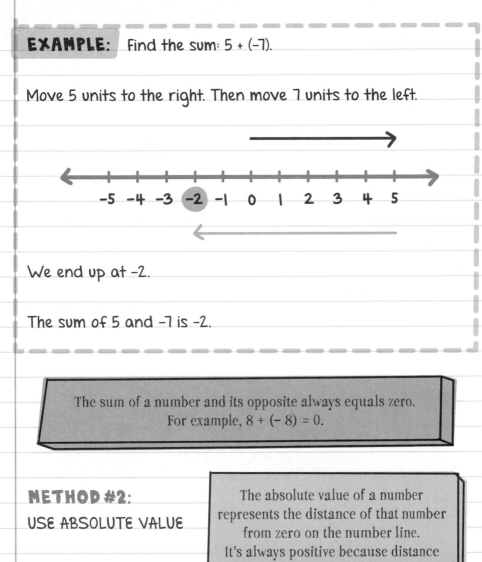

We end up at –2.

The sum of 5 and –7 is –2.

The sum of a number and its opposite always equals zero.
For example, 8 + (– 8) = 0.

METHOD #2:
USE ABSOLUTE VALUE

The absolute value of a number represents the distance of that number from zero on the number line.
It's always positive because distance is always positive!

If the signs of the addends are the same, it means that they move in the same direction on the number line. This means that you can add those two numbers together and keep the sign that they share.

If the signs of the addends are different, it means that they move in opposite directions on the number line. This means you can subtract the absolute value of each of the two numbers. The answer will have the same sign as the number with the greater absolute value.

EXAMPLE: Find the sum: (−11) + 5.

−11 and 5 have different signs, so subtract the absolute value of −11 and the absolute value of 5:

$|-11| - |5| = 11 - 5 = 6$

LOOKS LIKE YOU'RE UP.

−11 has the greater absolute value, so the answer is also negative: -6.

EXAMPLE: An archaeologist is studying ancient ruins. She brings a ladder to study some artifacts found above ground level and some found below ground level. The archaeologist first climbs the ladder to 5 feet above ground level to study artifacts found in a wall. She then climbs the ladder another 2 feet higher. Finally, the archaeologist climbs down the ladder 11 feet. Where does the archaeologist end up?

First, assign integers to the archaeologist's movements.

Climbs 5 feet above ground level: +5

Climbs another 2 feet above: +2

Climbs down 11 feet: –11

Write an equation to show the archaeologist's movements.

$= 5 + 2 + |-11|$
$= 7 + |-11|$
$= -4$

The archaeologist ends up 4 feet below ground level.

CHECK YOUR KNOWLEDGE

For problems 1 through 7, find the sum of each expression.

1. 8 + (–3)

2. –7 + 3

3. –6 + (–8)

4. –7 + 9

5. –10 + (–9)

6. (–5) + (–8)

7. 9 + (–14)

8. A hiker is currently in a valley that is at an elevation of 50 feet below sea level. She hikes up a hill and increases her elevation 300 feet. What is the new elevation of the hiker?

9. A submarine pilot is currently at a depth of 75 feet below sea level. He then pilots his submarine 350 feet lower. What is the new depth of the pilot?

For problem 10, state whether the statement is true or false.

10. Kris is asked to find the sum of (–8) + 5. Kris says: "Since the numbers have opposite signs, we subtract the absolute value of the numbers: $|-8| - |5| = 8 - 5 = 3$. Therefore, the answer is: 3."

CHECK YOUR ANSWERS

1. 5

2. −4

3. −14

4. 2

5. −19

6. −13

7. −5

8. 250 feet above sea level

9. 425 feet below sea level

10. False. Since −8 has the larger absolute value, the answer is negative.

Chapter 5

SUBTRACTING POSITIVE AND NEGATIVE WHOLE NUMBERS

Subtraction and addition are inverse operations. To solve a subtraction problem we can change it to an addition problem by using the **ADDITIVE INVERSE**.

> **ADDITIVE INVERSE**
> the number you add to a given number to get zero

EXAMPLE: Find the difference: 7 − 3.

= 7 − 3

= 7 + (−3)   Change the subtraction problem into an addition problem. Add the additive inverse.

= 4

EXAMPLE: Find the difference: –3 – 5.

= –3 – 5

= –3 + (–5)   Change the subtraction problem into an addition problem. –5 is the additive inverse of 5.

= –8

EXAMPLE: Find the difference: –7 – (–6).

= –7 – (–6)

= –7 + (6)   Change the subtraction problem into an addition problem. 6 is the additive inverse of -6.

= –1

EXAMPLE: The temperature in North Dakota was 5°F in the afternoon. By night, the temperature had decreased by 12 degrees. What was the temperature at night?

Since the temperature decreased, we use subtraction to find the answer:

= 5 – 12

= 5 + (–12)

= –7

The temperature at night was –7°F.

°F

CHECK YOUR KNOWLEDGE

For problems 1 through 8, find the difference for each expression.

1. 3 – 9

2. 5 – 7

3. –2 – 5

4. –10 – 4

5. 8 – (–5)

6. –7 – (10)

7. 9 – (–20)

8. (–12) – (–15)

For 9 through 10, answer each problem using the subtraction of integers.

9. Sam guesses that his store's average profit is $17 per hour. However, his store's actual average profit is –$6 per hour. How far apart is the error in his analysis?

10. A window washer is 110 feet above sea level. A diver is 70 feet below sea level. How many feet apart are the window washer and the diver?

ANSWERS

1. −6

2. −2

3. −7

4. −14

5. 13

6. −17

7. 29

8. 3

9. The error is $23 apart.

10. The window washer and the diver are 180 feet apart.

Chapter 6

MULTIPLYING AND DIVIDING POSITIVE AND NEGATIVE WHOLE NUMBERS

When multiplying or dividing positive and negative numbers:
First, count the number of negative signs. Then multiply or divide the numbers.

If there is an **ODD NUMBER** of negative signs, then the answer is **NEGATIVE**.

If there is an **EVEN NUMBER** of negative signs, then the answer is **POSITIVE**.

There is an odd number (1) of negative signs, so the answer is negative.

$(+) \times (-) = (-)$

$(-) \div (+) = (-)$

There is an odd number (1) of negative signs, so the answer is negative.

There are an even number (2) of negative signs, so the answer is positive.

$(-) \times (-) = (+)$

EXAMPLES:

Calculate the product of 4 × (−5).

= 4 × (−5)

= −(4 × 5)   There is 1 negative sign. So, the answer is negative.

= −20

Calculate the quotient of (−91) ÷ (−7).

= (−91) ÷ (−7)   There are 2 negative signs. So, the answer is positive.

= (91 ÷ 7)   Divide 91 by 7.

= 13

Ray's credit card balance decreases by $14 each month. How much will his balance decrease by after 9 months?

9 × (−14)   Ray's credit card balance will have decreased by

−(9 × 14) = −126 $126 after nine months.

There are 2 negative signs, so the answer is positive.

$$(+) \div (-) \div (-) = (+)$$

$$(-) \times (+) \div (-) \times (-) \times (-) \div (+) \div (-) = (-)$$

There are 5 negative signs, so the answer is negative.

The same rule applies when multiplication and division are in the same expression.

EXAMPLE:

Simplify $20 \div (-5) \times (-2)$.

$= 20 \div (-5) \times (-2)$ — There are 2 negative signs. So, the answer is positive.

$= (20 \div 5 \times 2)$ — Multiply or divide—whatever comes first—left to right. So divide!

$= (4 \times 2)$

$= 8$

CHECK YOUR KNOWLEDGE

For questions 1 through 8, simplify each expression.

1. $7 \times (-12)$

2. $(-84) \div (-12)$

3. $2 \times (-1) \times (-7)$

4. $(-5)(-2)(-3)(0)(-8)$

5. $(-42) \div (-3)$

6. $(-84) \div (-7) \div (-3)$

7. $(-80) \div (-5) \div (-2) \div (-1) \div (-4)$

8. $(-32) \div (-8) \div (-2)$

For questions 9 and 10, answer each problem using the multiplication or division of integers.

9. Mary drops a penny into a pond. The penny drops 1.5 inches every second. How many inches below the surface will it be after 8 seconds?

10. Patricia randomly picks a negative number. She then decides to multiply that negative number by itself over and over, for a total of 327 times. What sign will the final answer have?

CHECK YOUR ANSWERS

1. −84

2. 7

3. 14

4. 0

5. 14

6. −4

7. −2

8. −2

9. The penny will be 12 inches below the surface.

10. The answer will be negative.

Chapter 7

MULTIPLYING AND DIVIDING POSITIVE AND NEGATIVE FRACTIONS

Multiplying and dividing positive and negative fractions uses the same method that we used with whole numbers:

1. First, count the number of negative signs to determine the sign of the product or quotient.

2. Convert any mixed numbers into improper fractions.

3. Last, multiply or divide the fractions without the negative sign.

When multiplying fractions, you sometimes might see that one fraction's numerator and another fraction's denominator have common factors.

You can simplify those numbers in the same way that fractions are simplified, by dividing both numbers by the Greatest Common Factor (GCF).

This is called CROSS-REDUCING or CROSS-CANCELING.

EXAMPLE: Find the product:

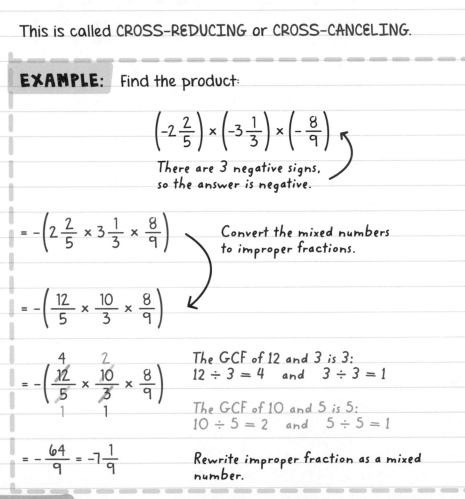

$$\left(-2\frac{2}{5}\right) \times \left(-3\frac{1}{3}\right) \times \left(-\frac{8}{9}\right)$$

There are 3 negative signs, so the answer is negative.

$$= -\left(2\frac{2}{5} \times 3\frac{1}{3} \times \frac{8}{9}\right)$$

Convert the mixed numbers to improper fractions.

$$= -\left(\frac{12}{5} \times \frac{10}{3} \times \frac{8}{9}\right)$$

$$= -\left(\frac{\overset{4}{\cancel{12}}}{5} \times \frac{\overset{2}{\cancel{10}}}{\underset{1}{\cancel{3}}} \times \frac{8}{9}\right)$$

The GCF of 12 and 3 is 3:
$12 \div 3 = 4$ and $3 \div 3 = 1$

The GCF of 10 and 5 is 5:
$10 \div 5 = 2$ and $5 \div 5 = 1$

$$= -\frac{64}{9} = -7\frac{1}{9}$$

Rewrite improper fraction as a mixed number.

EXAMPLE: Zoe needs $3\frac{1}{5}$ feet of fabric to make a tall hat.

If Zoe wants enough fabric to make $2\frac{1}{2}$ tall hats, how much fabric will Zoe need?

$= 3\frac{1}{5} \times 2\frac{1}{2}$

Change the mixed numbers to improper fractions.

$= \frac{16}{5} \times \frac{5}{2}$

$= \frac{\overset{8}{\cancel{16}}}{\underset{1}{\cancel{5}}} \times \frac{\overset{1}{\cancel{5}}}{\underset{1}{\cancel{2}}}$

The GCF of 16 and 2 is 2:
$16 \div 2 = 8$ and $2 \div 2 = 1$

$= 8$

Zoe will need 8 feet of fabric.

DIVIDING POSITIVE AND NEGATIVE FRACTIONS

When dividing fractions, rewrite the division problem as a multiplication problem by finding the reciprocal of the second number.

When a number is multiplied by its **RECIPROCAL**, the resulting product is 1. For example, the reciprocal of 8 is $\frac{1}{8}$. If you multiply the two numbers, you get 1.

$$\frac{8}{1} \times \frac{1}{8} = 1$$

EXAMPLE: Calculate the quotient of $\frac{6}{7} \div \frac{8}{11}$.

$= \frac{6}{7} \times \frac{11}{8}$ Rewrite the division problem as a multiplication problem by finding the reciprocal of $\frac{8}{11}$, which is $\frac{11}{8}$.

$= \frac{\overset{3}{\cancel{6}}}{7} \times \frac{11}{\underset{4}{\cancel{8}}}$ Simplify by cross-canceling.
The GCF of 6 and 8 is 2:
    $6 \div 2 = 3$ and $8 \div 2 = 4$

$= \frac{33}{28} = 1\frac{5}{28}$

EXAMPLE: Jay's landscaping has a few gas cans that can hold up to $5\frac{1}{4}$ gallons of gasoline to be used for their lawn mowers.

If the owner has a total of $12\frac{5}{6}$ gallons of gasoline, how many gas cans can he fill?

$= 12\frac{5}{6} \div 5\frac{1}{4}$

$= \frac{77}{6} \div \frac{21}{4}$

$= \frac{77}{6} \times \frac{4}{21}$

Remember, in order to find the quotient you must first convert any mixed numbers to improper fractions.

$= \frac{\overset{11}{\cancel{77}}}{\underset{3}{\cancel{6}}} \times \frac{\overset{2}{\cancel{4}}}{\underset{3}{\cancel{21}}}$

$= \frac{22}{9} = 2\frac{4}{9}$

The owner can fill $2\frac{4}{9}$ gas cans.

Calculate the product or quotient.

1. $\dfrac{5}{8} \times \dfrac{14}{15}$

2. $\left(-1\dfrac{2}{7}\right) \times 1\dfrac{5}{9}$

3. $\left(-\dfrac{6}{11}\right) \times \left(-\dfrac{2}{3}\right)$

4. $\dfrac{2}{3} \div \dfrac{4}{5}$

5. $\left(-\dfrac{7}{4}\right) \div 4\dfrac{2}{3}$

6. $(-5) \div \left(-3\dfrac{1}{3}\right) \div \left(-\dfrac{1}{8}\right)$

7. $2\dfrac{4}{7} \times \dfrac{11}{12} \div \left(-1\dfrac{1}{21}\right)$

Choose the correct method to find the answer.

8. $\dfrac{1}{3} \div \dfrac{6}{11}$

   A. $\dfrac{1}{3} \times \dfrac{6}{11}$ C. $\dfrac{1}{3} \div \dfrac{11}{6}$

   B. $\dfrac{3}{1} \times \dfrac{11}{6}$ D. $\dfrac{1}{3} \times \dfrac{11}{6}$

CHECK YOUR ANSWERS

1. $\dfrac{7}{12}$

2. -2

3. $\dfrac{4}{11}$

4. $\dfrac{5}{6}$

5. $-\dfrac{3}{8}$

6. -12

7. $-2\dfrac{1}{4}$

8. D

Chapter 8

ADDING AND SUBTRACTING POSITIVE AND NEGATIVE FRACTIONS

ADDING POSITIVE AND NEGATIVE FRACTIONS WITH LIKE DENOMINATORS

To add fractions that have the same denominator, just add the numerators and keep the denominator.

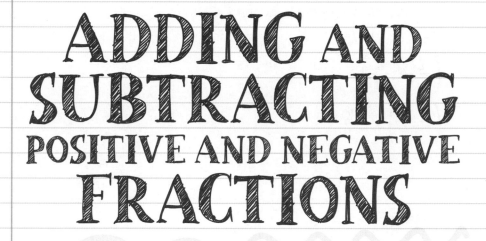

EXAMPLE: Simplify $\frac{3}{5} + \frac{4}{5}$.

$$= \frac{3+4}{5} = \frac{7}{5} = 1\frac{2}{5}$$

EXAMPLE: Simplify $\left(-\dfrac{2}{11}\right) + \left(-\dfrac{8}{11}\right)$.

$\left(\downarrow -\dfrac{2}{11}\right) + \left(\downarrow -\dfrac{8}{11}\right)$ Both fractions are negative, so the answer is negative.

$= -\left(\dfrac{2}{11} + \dfrac{8}{11}\right)$

$= -\left(\dfrac{2+8}{11}\right) = -\dfrac{10}{11}$

EXAMPLE: Simplify $\left(-\dfrac{7}{9}\right) + \dfrac{2}{9}$.

$\left(-\dfrac{7}{9}\right)$ and $\dfrac{2}{9}$ have different signs, so subtract the absolute value of $\left(-\dfrac{7}{9}\right)$ and the absolute value of $\dfrac{2}{9}$:

$\left|-\dfrac{7}{9}\right| - \left|\dfrac{2}{9}\right| = \dfrac{7}{9} - \dfrac{2}{9} = \dfrac{5}{9}$

$-\dfrac{7}{9}$ has the greater absolute value, so the answer is negative:

$-\dfrac{5}{9}$

SUBTRACTING POSITIVE AND NEGATIVE FRACTIONS WITH LIKE DENOMINATORS

To subtract negative fractions, rewrite the subtraction problem as an addition problem by using the additive inverse.

EXAMPLE: Simplify $\left(-\dfrac{5}{7}\right) - \left(-\dfrac{1}{7}\right)$.

$\left(-\dfrac{5}{7}\right) - \left(-\dfrac{1}{7}\right)$

$= \left(-\dfrac{5}{7}\right) + \left(\dfrac{1}{7}\right)$

Change into an addition problem. Use the additive inverse of $\dfrac{1}{7}$.

$\left|-\dfrac{5}{7}\right| - \left|\dfrac{1}{7}\right| = \dfrac{5}{7} - \dfrac{1}{7} = \dfrac{4}{7}$

Subtract the absolute values.

$-\dfrac{4}{7}$

This is the greater absolute value, so the answer is also negative.

ADDING AND SUBTRACTING POSITIVE AND NEGATIVE FRACTIONS WITH UNLIKE DENOMINATORS

To add or subtract fractions with different denominators, we can create equivalent fractions that have the same denominators. We can do that by finding the LEAST COMMON MULTIPLE (LCM) of the denominators.

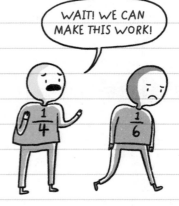

WAIT! WE CAN MAKE THIS WORK!

$\frac{1}{4}$ $\frac{1}{6}$

EXAMPLE Simplify $\frac{2}{5} + \frac{1}{4}$.

Step 1: Find the LCM of both denominators.

The multiples of **5** are: 5, 10, 15, **20**, 25, 30, 35, **40**, 45, . . .
The multiples of **4** are: 4, 8, 12, 16, **20**, 24, 28, 32, 36, **40**, 44, . . .

The **Least** Common Multiple of **5** and **4** is: 20.

Step 2: Rename the fractions as equivalent fractions.

Ask, 5 times what number equals 20? 4.

Multiply the numerator and denominator by 4 to change to an equivalent fraction.

$$\frac{2}{5} = \frac{2 \times 4}{5 \times 4} = \frac{8}{20}$$

4 times what number equals 20? 5.

Multiply the numerator and denominator by 5 to change to an equivalent fraction.

$$\frac{1 \times 5}{4 \times 5} = \frac{5}{20}$$

Step 3: Add or subtract the fractions, and simplify.

$$\frac{2}{5} + \frac{1}{4} = \frac{8}{20} + \frac{5}{20} = \frac{13}{20}$$

EXAMPLE: Simplify $\frac{1}{4} - \frac{5}{6}$.

Step 1: Find the LCM of both denominators.

The multiples of **4** are: 4, 8, **12**, 16, 20, **24**, 28, . . .
The multiples of **6** are: 6, **12**, 18, **24**, 30, . . .

The Least Common Multiple of 4 and 6 is: 12.

Step 2: Rename the fractions as equivalent fractions.

$$\frac{1 \times 3}{4 \times 3} = \frac{3}{12} \quad \text{and} \quad \frac{5 \times 2}{6 \times 2} = \frac{10}{12}$$

Step 3: Subtract the fractions, and simplify.

$$= \frac{3}{12} - \frac{10}{12}$$

Change the subtraction into addition. $\frac{10}{12}$ is the additive inverse of $-\frac{10}{12}$

$$= \frac{3}{12} + \left(-\frac{10}{12}\right)$$

$$\left|-\frac{10}{12}\right| - \left|\frac{3}{12}\right| = \frac{10}{12} - \frac{3}{12} = \frac{7}{12}$$

Subtract the absolute values.

$-\frac{10}{12}$ has the greater absolute value, so the answer is also negative:

$$-\frac{7}{12}$$

CHECK YOUR KNOWLEDGE

Calculate. Simplify each answer if possible.

1. $\dfrac{7}{10} + \dfrac{5}{10}$

2. $\dfrac{5}{12} - \dfrac{7}{12}$

3. $-\dfrac{6}{7} + \left(-\dfrac{4}{7}\right)$

4. $-\dfrac{5}{8} + \dfrac{2}{3}$

5. $-3 - \left(-\dfrac{5}{6}\right)$

6. $4\dfrac{1}{8} - 2\dfrac{5}{8}$

7. $1\dfrac{3}{5} - \left(-7\dfrac{4}{5}\right)$

8. $2\dfrac{1}{4} - \left(-3\dfrac{1}{6}\right)$

9. $-14\dfrac{1}{2} + \left(-2\dfrac{4}{5}\right)$

10. May Ling has $9\dfrac{1}{4}$ chocolate bars. She gives Ahmad $2\dfrac{3}{5}$ of her chocolate bars. How many chocolate bars does May Ling have left?

ANSWERS

57

CHECK YOUR ANSWERS

1. $1\frac{1}{5}$

2. $-\frac{1}{6}$

3. $-1\frac{3}{7}$

4. $\frac{1}{24}$

5. $-2\frac{1}{6}$

6. $1\frac{1}{2}$

7. $9\frac{2}{5}$

8. $5\frac{5}{12}$

9. $-17\frac{3}{10}$

10. May Ling has $6\frac{13}{20}$ chocolate bars left.

Chapter 9

ADDING AND SUBTRACTING DECIMALS

To add or subtract decimal numbers, you can rewrite the problem vertically. First, line up the decimal points to align the place values of the digits. Next, add or subtract the same way you add or subtract whole numbers. Last, write the decimal point in the sum or difference.

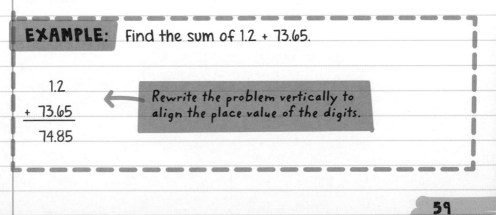

EXAMPLE: Find the sum of 1.2 + 73.65.

```
   1.2
+ 73.65
  74.85
```

Rewrite the problem vertically to align the place value of the digits.

EXAMPLE: Find the sum of 56.09 + 7.8.

```
  56.09
+  7.80
  63.89
```

← Rewrite the problem vertically to align the place value of the digits.

Think: 7.8 could be rewritten as 7.80.

Anytime you add a whole number and a decimal, include the decimal point to the right of the whole number.

EXAMPLE: Find the sum of 8 + 1.45.

Rewrite 8 as 8.00, so that there are the same number of digits after the decimal point as 1.45.

```
  8.00
+ 1.45
  9.45
```

ADDING DECIMALS WITH DIFFERENT SIGNS

To add decimal numbers with different signs, subtract the absolute value of the numbers. Then use the sign of the number with the greatest absolute value for the difference.

EXAMPLE: Find the sum of −9.81 + 3.27.

−9.81 and 3.27 have different signs. So, subtract their absolute values:

$|-9.81| - |3.27| = 9.81 - 3.27$

Rewrite the expression to align the place value of the digits.

$$
\begin{array}{r}
9.81 \\
-\ 3.27 \\
\hline
6.54
\end{array}
$$

−9.81 has the larger absolute value, so the answer is negative: −6.54

SUBTRACTING DECIMALS WITH DIFFERENT SIGNS

Align the decimal points of each number and then subtract.
Be sure to write the decimal point in the answer.

EXAMPLE: Calculate the difference of 8.01 – 5.4.

$$
\begin{array}{r}
8.01 \\
-\ 5.40 \\
\hline
2.61
\end{array}
$$

Rewrite the problem vertically to align the place value of the digits.

8.01 has the greater absolute value, so the answer is also positive: 2.61

EXAMPLE: Calculate the difference of –0.379 – 10.5.

= –0.379 – 10.5

= –0.379 + (–10.5)

Change the subtraction to an addition problem.
-10.5 is the additive inverse of 10.5.

Add the absolute values of both numbers:

|–0.379| + |–10.5| = 0.379 + 10.5

Both numbers are negative, so the answer is also negative:
–10.879

62

EXAMPLE: A scientist boils a liquid to 142.07°F. The scientist then puts the liquid in a freezer where the temperature of the liquid decreases by 268.3 degrees. What is the final temperature of the liquid?

The temperature of the liquid decreases, so subtract:
142.07 − 268.3

Arrange vertically and align decimal points:

```
 268.30
−142.07
 126.23
```

−268.3 has the greater absolute value. So, the answer is negative:
−126.23 degrees

The final temperature is −126.23°F.

CHECK YOUR KNOWLEDGE

For questions 1 through 9, simplify each expression.

1. 9.6 + (−1.5)

2. 7.1 + (−5.9)

3. −3.4 − 1.6

4. −7.3 − 3.9

5. 3.1 − (−0.4)

6. 0.15 − (−41.7)

7. −1.67 − (−5.9)

8. −5 + .07 + (−3.1)

9. −3.1 − (−8.67) + (−1.05)

10. Luis is asked to simplify the following expression: $-2.53 - (-1.26)$. His work has the following steps:

Step 1: $= -2.53 + (1.26)$

Step 2:

$$\begin{array}{r} 2.53 \\ +\ \ 1.26 \\ \hline 3.79 \end{array}$$

Step 3: -2.53 has the greater absolute value, so the answer is also negative: -3.79

However, Luis makes an error in his work.

On which step did Luis make an error? What should Luis have done?

CHECK YOUR ANSWERS

1. 8.1

2. 1.2

3. –5

4. –11.2

5. 3.5

6. 41.85

7. 4.23

8. –8.03

9. 4.52

10. Luis made an error in step 2. Because the numbers have different signs, Luis should have subtracted them, not added them.

Chapter 10

MULTIPLYING AND DIVIDING DECIMALS

MULTIPLYING DECIMALS

To multiply decimal numbers, you don't need to line up the decimals.

Steps for multiplying decimals:

1. Count the negative signs to find the sign of the product.

2. Multiply the numbers the same way you multiply whole numbers. In other words, ignore the decimal points!

3. Place the decimal point in your answer: The number of decimal places in the answer is the total number of decimal places in the two original factors.

EXAMPLE: Calculate the product of the following expression: 5.32 × 1.4

Step 1: Since there are no negative signs, the answer is positive.

Step 2: Multiply the numbers without the decimal point:

```
   532
×   14
  2128
 5320
 7448
```

Step 3: Determine where the decimal point goes in the answer.

Since 5.32 has 2 digits to the right of the decimal point, and 1.4 has 1 digit to the right of the decimal point, the total number of decimal places is 3.

So the product is: 7.448.

EXAMPLE: Calculate the product of the following expression: $3.120 \times (-0.5)$.

Step 1: Since there is one negative sign, the answer is negative.

Step 2: Multiply the numbers without the decimal point:

```
  3120
×    5
15600
```

Step 3: Determine where the decimal point goes in the answer.

The total number of decimal places is 4, so the product is -1.5600.

If there are zeros at the end, keep them while you multiply, but when you write the final answer remove the zeros:

-1.5600 has 4 decimal places,
but can be written as -1.56.

DIVIDING DECIMALS

To divide decimal numbers, turn them into whole numbers.

Steps for dividing decimals:

1. Count the negative signs to determine the sign of the quotient.

2. Multiply both the dividend and divisor by the same power of 10 (the number of times 10 is multiplied by itself) until they both become whole numbers.

3. Divide the two whole numbers to find the answer.

The **DIVIDEND** is the number that is being divided.
The **DIVISOR** is the number that "goes into" the dividend.
The answer to a division problem is called the **QUOTIENT**.

dividend ÷ divisor = quotient

OR

$$\text{divisor} \overline{)\text{dividend}}^{\text{quotient}}$$

EXAMPLE: Calculate the quotient of 2.8 ÷ 0.7.

Step 1: Since there are no negative signs, the answer is positive.

Step 2: Multiply both the dividend, 2.8, and the divisor, 0.7, by 10, so that they both become whole numbers.

2.8 × 10 = 28 and 0.7 × 10 = 7

2.8 ÷ 0.7 = 28 ÷ 7

Step 3: Divide the numbers: 28 ÷ 7 = 4

EXAMPLE: Calculate the quotient of (−6.912) ÷ 0.03.

Step 1: Since there is one negative sign, the answer is negative.

Step 2: Multiply both the dividend and the divisor by 1,000, so that they both become whole numbers: 6,912 and 30.

Step 3: Divide

= −(6912 ÷ 30)
= −230.4

EXAMPLE: Amina bikes 32.64 miles in 2.4 hours. If she keeps up the pace, how many miles does Amina travel each hour?

Step 1: Since there are no negative signs, the answer is positive.

Step 2: Multiply both the dividend and the divisor by 100, so that they both become whole numbers.

$32.64 \times 100 = 3264$ and $2.4 \times 100 = 240$

$32.64 \div 2.4 = 3264 \div 240$

Step 3: Divide

$3264 \div 240 = 13.6$

So, Amina travels on her bike 13.6 miles each hour.

CHECK YOUR KNOWLEDGE

For questions 1 through 8, simplify each expression.

1. $7 \times (-3.2)$

2. -8.3×1.02

3. $(-0.3) \times (-1.07)$

4. $(-37.8) \div 9$

5. $(-235.6) \div 0.04$

6. $(-32.04) \div (-0.6)$

7. $(-0.0168) \div 0.00007$

8. $-1.2 \times 0.8 \div (-0.03)$

9. A machine pumps 2.1 gallons of water every 1.6 minutes. How many gallons does the machine pump each minute?

10. Sandy jogs 19.7 miles in 4.5 hours. How many miles does she jog each hour? Round your answer to the nearest hundredth.

ANSWERS

CHECK YOUR ANSWERS

1. −22.4

2. −8.466

3. 0.321

4. −4.2

5. −5,890

6. 53.4

7. −240

8. 32

9. The machine pumps 1.3125 gallons each minute.

10. Sandy jogs 4.26 miles each hour.

Unit 3

Ratios,
Proportions,
and Percents

$15.75 25% OFF

1 CUP

Chapter 11

RATIO

A **RATIO** is a comparison of two or more quantities.
For example, you might use a ratio to compare the
number of green jelly beans
to the number of red jelly
beans. A ratio can be written
in various ways.

The ratio 5 green jelly beans to 4 red jelly beans can
be written:

5 to 4 or 5:4 or $\frac{5}{4}$

When comparing group a to group b we write the ratio as:

a to b or $a:b$ or $\frac{a}{b}$ | We can let a represent the first quantity and b represent the second quantity.

EXAMPLE: Thirteen students joined after-school clubs in September. Eight joined the drama club and five joined the chess club. What is the ratio of students who joined the drama club to students who joined the chess club?

8 to 5 or 8:5 or $\frac{8}{5}$

> Another way to say this is,
> "For every 5 students
> who joined the chess club,
> 8 students joined the drama club."

What is the ratio of students who joined the chess club to the total number of students who joined clubs?

5 to 13 or 5:13 or $\frac{5}{13}$ ← students who joined chess club

total number of students

Drama Club   Chess Club

SIMPLIFYING RATIOS

We can simplify ratios just like we simplify fractions.

EXAMPLE: Janelle makes a beaded key ring. She uses 12 beads total. Among the 12 beads are 3 purple beads and 6 green beads. What is the ratio of purple beads to green beads? What is the ratio of green beads to the total number of beads?

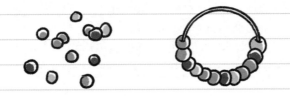

The ratio of purple beads to green beads written as a fraction is $\frac{3}{6}$. This can be simplified to $\frac{1}{2}$.

So for every 1 purple bead, there are 2 green beads.

The ratio of green beads to the total number of beads used is $\frac{6}{12}$. This can be simplified to $\frac{1}{2}$.

So, 1 out of every 2 beads used is green.

EQUIVALENT RATIOS

EQUIVALENT RATIOS have the same value. We can multiply or divide both a and b by any value (except zero), and the ratio a to b remains the same (equivalent).

For example, ratios that are equivalent to 3:5 include:

6:10	18:30	120:200
(3 × 2:5 × 2)	(3 × 6:5 × 6)	(3 × 40:5 × 40)

EXAMPLE: Find equivalent ratios for $\frac{18}{24}$.

$$\frac{18}{24} = \frac{18 \div 2}{24 \div 2} = \frac{9}{12}$$

$$\frac{18}{24} = \frac{18 \div 3}{24 \div 3} = \frac{6}{8}$$ } equivalent ratios

$$\frac{18}{24} = \frac{18 \div 6}{24 \div 6} = \frac{3}{4}$$

$\frac{18}{24}$ is equivalent to $\frac{9}{12}$, $\frac{6}{8}$, $\frac{3}{4}$, and many others.

A ratio is often used to make a scale drawing—a drawing that is similar to an actual object or place but bigger or smaller.

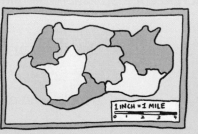

1 INCH = 1 MILE

A map's key shows the ratio of the distance on the map to the actual distance in the real world.

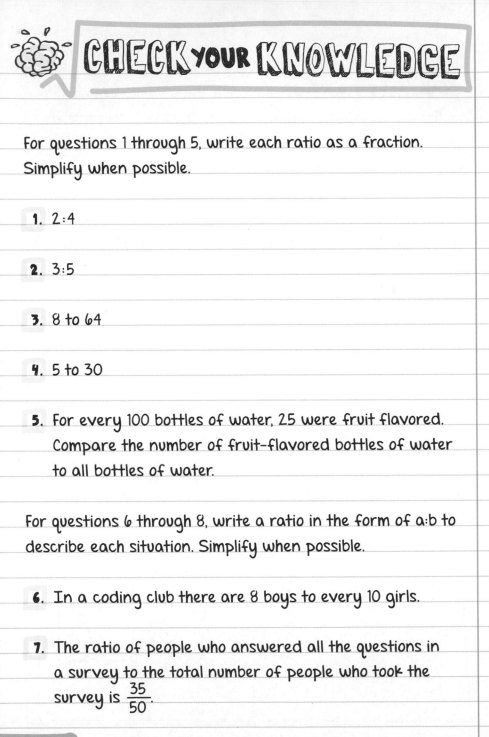

For questions 1 through 5, write each ratio as a fraction. Simplify when possible.

1. 2:4

2. 3:5

3. 8 to 64

4. 5 to 30

5. For every 100 bottles of water, 25 were fruit flavored. Compare the number of fruit-flavored bottles of water to all bottles of water.

For questions 6 through 8, write a ratio in the form of a:b to describe each situation. Simplify when possible.

6. In a coding club there are 8 boys to every 10 girls.

7. The ratio of people who answered all the questions in a survey to the total number of people who took the survey is $\frac{35}{50}$.

8. Mr. Jeffrey bought masks for the drama club's fundraiser. He bought 10 blue masks, 8 red masks, and 12 white masks. What was the ratio of white masks to total masks bought?

9. Write three ratios that are equivalent to 14:21.

10. Write three ratios that are equivalent to 1:5.

1. $\frac{1}{2}$

2. $\frac{3}{5}$

3. $\frac{1}{8}$

4. $\frac{1}{6}$

5. $\frac{1}{4}$

6. 8:10; simplified: 4:5

7. 35:50; simplified: 7:10

8. 12:30; simplified: 2:5

9. Sample answers: 1:1.5, 2:3, 28:42

10. Sample answers: 2:10, 3:15, 4:20

Chapter 12

UNIT RATE

A **RATE** is a special kind of ratio where the two amounts being compared have different units. For example you might use rate to compare 3 cups of water to 2 tablespoons of cornstarch. The units compared—cups and tablespoons—are different.

1 tablespoon

1 CUP

Rate: Units are different.

A **UNIT RATE** is a rate that has 1 as its denominator. To find a unit rate, set up a ratio as a fraction and then divide the numerator by the denominator.

Unit rate compares an amount to one unit.

EXAMPLE: Jackson swims $\frac{1}{2}$ mile every $\frac{1}{3}$ hour. What is the unit rate of Jackson's swim?

This means, "How many miles per hour did Jackson swim?"

$\frac{1}{2}$ mile : $\frac{1}{3}$ hour $= \dfrac{\frac{1}{2}}{\frac{1}{3}} = \frac{1}{2} \times \frac{3}{1} = \frac{3}{2} = \frac{1.5}{1}$

$= 1\frac{1}{2}$ miles per hour

Jackson swims at a rate of $1\frac{1}{2}$ miles per hour.

EXAMPLE: A car can travel 300 miles on 15 gallons of gasoline. What is the unit rate per gallon of gasoline?

divide

300 miles : 15 gallons $= \dfrac{300 \text{ miles}}{15 \text{ gallons}} = \frac{20}{1} = 20$ miles per gallon

The unit rate is 20 miles per gallon.

This means that the car can travel 20 miles on 1 gallon of gasoline.

UNIT PRICE

When the unit rate describes a price, it's called a **UNIT PRICE**. Unit price can be used to compare value between different quantities.

When calculating unit price, put the price in the numerator, and divide the denominator into the numerator.

EXAMPLE: Ana pays $2.70 for 3 bottles of apple juice. What is the unit price of each bottle?

$2.70:3 bottles or $\frac{\$2.70}{3} = \$0.90$

unit price

The unit price is $0.90 per bottle.

$2.70

EXAMPLE: A school supplier sells packages of 8 notebooks for $40 and 5 notebooks for $30. Alexa says that the package of 5 notebooks is the (better deal.) Is she correct? Explain.

lower price

$40:8 books or $\dfrac{40}{8}$ = $5

$30:5 books or $\dfrac{30}{5}$ = $6

unit price

Compare unit costs: $5 < $6

Alexa is incorrect. The better deal is 8 notebooks for $5 each.

CHECK YOUR KNOWLEDGE

For questions 1 through 8, find the unit rate or unit price.

1. Andrew pumped 66 gallons of gasoline in 11 minutes.

2. Eric swam 150 yards in 3 minutes.

3. The lunch team serves 24 meals every 4 minutes.

4. Andrea does 250 jumping jacks in 5 minutes.

5. It costs $3.20 to purchase 8 yards of lace.

6. An athlete ran 50 miles in 12 hours for an ultramarathon.

7. Abdul spends $44.40 for 12 gallons of gas.

8. 7 show tickets cost $42.70.

9. Which is the better deal: paying $42.67 for 7 show tickets or paying $63.18 for 9 show tickets?

10. Which is the better deal: 20 soccer balls for $70 or 50 soccer balls for $157?

ANSWERS

CHECK YOUR ANSWERS

1. 6 gallons per minute

2. 50 yards per minute

3. 6 meals per minute

4. 50 jumping jacks per minute

5. $.40 per yard of lace

6. $4\frac{1}{6}$ miles per hour

7. $3.70 per gallon

8. $6.10 per ticket

9. Unit costs: 7 tickets = $6.10 each, and 9 tickets = $7.02 each. The better deal is 7 tickets for $42.67.

10. Unit costs: 20 balls = $3.50 each, and 50 balls = $3.14 each. The better deal is 50 balls for $157.

Chapter 13

PROPORTION

PROPORTION is an equation that states that two ratios are equal.

For example, if someone divides a circle into 2 equal pieces and colors 1 piece, the ratio of pieces colored to total number of pieces is $\frac{1}{2}$.

The number $\frac{1}{2}$ is the same ratio if that person instead divided the circle into 4 equal pieces and colored 2 of the pieces.

$$\frac{1}{2} = \frac{2}{4}$$

When you write a proportion, you can use fractions or you can use colons.

$$\frac{1}{2} = \frac{2}{4} \quad \text{or} \quad 1:2 = 2:4$$

> Two ratios that form a proportion are called **EQUIVALENT FRACTIONS**.

You can check if two ratios form a proportion by using CROSS PRODUCTS or CROSS MULTIPLICATION. To find cross products, set the two ratios next to each other, then multiply diagonally. If both products are equal to each other, then the two ratios are equal and form a proportion.

$\frac{2}{3} \times \frac{8}{12}$

$2 \times 12 = 24$ $3 \times 8 = 24$

Since the cross products are equal, $\frac{2}{3} = \frac{8}{12}$. So, the ratio forms a proportion.

EXAMPLE: Are ratios $\frac{3}{4}$ and $\frac{4}{8}$ proportional?

$\frac{3}{4} \times \frac{4}{8}$

$3 \times 8 = 24$
$4 \times 4 = 16$
$24 \neq 16$

Since the cross products are not equal, $\frac{3}{4} \neq \frac{4}{8}$. So, the ratio does not form a proportion.

FINDING AN UNKNOWN QUANTITY

You can also use a proportion to find an unknown quantity.

For example, you are making lemonade, and the recipe says to use 4 cups of water for every lemon you squeeze. How many cups of water do you need if you have 3 lemons?

Step 1: Set up a ratio:

$$\frac{4 \text{ cups of water}}{1 \text{ lemon}}$$

Step 2: Set up a ratio for what you are trying to figure out. Let *x* represent the unknown quantity.

$$\frac{x \text{ cups}}{3 \text{ lemons}}$$

Step 3: Set up a proportion by setting the ratios equal to each other.

$$\frac{4 \text{ cups of water}}{1 \text{ lemon}} \times \frac{x \text{ cups of water}}{3 \text{ lemons}}$$

> The units in the numerators and denominators match.

91

Step 4: Use cross products to find the value of the unknown quantity.

$$\frac{4}{1} = \frac{x}{3}$$

$1 \cdot x = 4 \cdot 3$

$1 \cdot x = 12$ Divide both sides by 1 so you can get x alone.

$x = 12$ The unknown quantity is 12.

You need 12 cups of water for 3 lemons.

EXAMPLE: Solve: $\frac{3}{4} = \frac{x}{12}$.

$\frac{3}{4} \diagdown\!\!\!\!\diagup \frac{x}{12}$

$3 \cdot 12 = 4 \cdot x$ Cross-multiply.

$36 = 4x$ Divide both sides by 4 to isolate x on one side of the equal sign.

$x = 9$ The unknown quantity is 9.

The proportion is: $\frac{3}{4} = \frac{9}{12}$

CONSTANT OF PROPORTIONALITY

Sometimes a proportion stays the same, even in different scenarios. For example, James runs $\frac{1}{2}$ a mile, and then he drinks 1 cup of water. If James runs 1 mile, he needs 2 cups of water. The proportion stays the same. This is called the CONSTANT OF PROPORTIONALITY or the CONSTANT OF VARIATION and is closely related to unit rate (or unit price).

EXAMPLE: Nguyen swims laps at a pool. The table shows how much time he swims and how many laps he completes. How many minutes does Nguyen swim per lap?

Total minutes swimming	18	30
Total number of laps	3	5

Step 1: Set up a proportion.

$$\frac{18 \text{ minutes}}{3 \text{ laps}} = \frac{x \text{ minutes}}{1 \text{ lap}} \quad \text{or} \quad \frac{30 \text{ minutes}}{5 \text{ laps}} = \frac{x \text{ minutes}}{1 \text{ lap}}$$

Step 2: Cross-multiply to solve for x.

18 minutes = 3x or   30 minutes = 5x

$x = 6$ $x = 6$

Nguyen swims for 6 minutes per lap.

For questions 1 through 4, indicate whether each of the following ratios form a proportion. Explain using cross products.

1. $\dfrac{3}{4}$ and $\dfrac{6}{12}$

2. $\dfrac{4}{5}$ and $\dfrac{12}{20}$

3. $\dfrac{2}{3}$ and $\dfrac{4}{6}$

4. $\dfrac{1}{9}$ and $\dfrac{4}{36}$

For questions 5 through 8, solve for the unknown number.

5. $\dfrac{2}{8} = \dfrac{6}{x}$

6. $\dfrac{5}{20} = \dfrac{x}{25}$

7. $\dfrac{1}{x} = \dfrac{7}{35}$

8. $\dfrac{x}{5} = \dfrac{16}{40}$

9. It takes Greg 16 minutes to trim 6 rosebushes. At that rate, how many minutes will it take him to trim 30 rosebushes?

10. It snowed 4 inches in 15 hours. At this rate, about how much will it snow in 25 hours?

CHECK YOUR ANSWERS

1. No, because $\frac{3}{4} \diagup\!\!\!\!\diagdown \frac{6}{12}$

   $3 \times 12 = 36$
   $6 \times 4 = 24$
   $36 \neq 24$

2. No, because $\frac{4}{5} \diagup\!\!\!\!\diagdown \frac{12}{20}$

   $4 \times 20 = 80$
   $12 \times 5 = 60$
   $80 \neq 60$

3. Yes, because $\frac{2}{3} \diagup\!\!\!\!\diagdown \frac{4}{6}$

   $2 \times 6 = 12$
   $4 \times 3 = 12$
   $12 = 12$

4. Yes, because $\frac{1}{9} \diagup\!\!\!\!\diagdown \frac{4}{36}$

   $1 \times 36 = 36$
   $4 \times 9 = 36$
   $36 = 36$

5. $x = 24$

6. $x = 6.25$

7. $x = 5$

8. $x = 2$

9. 80 minutes

10. Approximately 6.7 inches

Chapter 14

PERCENT

PERCENT means "per hundred." A percent (%) is a ratio or comparison of a quantity to 100.

Think of the root "cent":
There are 100 cents in one dollar.

For example, 25% means 25 PER HUNDRED and can be written as $\frac{25}{100}$ or 0.25.

100 is the whole, and percent is part of the whole.

$$\frac{part}{whole} = \frac{x}{100} = x\%$$

x per hundred

Most percentages we encounter are less than 1, such as 25%. However, percentages can also be greater than 1, such as 125%.

There are 100 boxes in this grid and 25 are shaded. 25% of the boxes are shaded!

To convert a percent to a fraction:

Write the percent in the numerator and 100 as the denominator. Then reduce.

$7\% = \dfrac{7}{100}$ $75\% = \dfrac{75}{100} = \dfrac{3}{4}$

To convert a fraction to a percent:

Step 1: Divide the numerator by the denominator.

$\dfrac{12}{100} = 0.12$

Step 2: Multiply by 100. Write the % sign.

$0.12 \times 100 = 12\%$

When multiplying a decimal number by 100, move the decimal point two places to the right.

Another example: $\dfrac{1}{5} = \dfrac{20}{100} = 20\%$

This is a proportion.

To convert a percent to a decimal:

Remove the % sign and divide by 100.

For example, $45\% = \dfrac{45}{100} = 0.45 \quad 4.5\% = \dfrac{4.5}{100} = 0.045$

> When dividing a decimal number by 100,
> move the decimal point two places to the left.

EXAMPLE: Three out of every five games in Lin's video game collection are sport games. What percentage of the game collection is sports?

$\dfrac{3}{5} = 3 \div 5 = 0.6$ \qquad Move the decimal two places to the right and include a percent sign.

$0.6 = 60\%$

Sports make up 60% of Lin's video game collection.

CALCULATING PERCENT

To calculate a percent of a number, first convert the percentage to a fraction or decimal and then multiply.

To find 50% of 40:

$$\frac{5}{10} \cdot 40 = 20 \quad \text{or} \quad 0.5 \cdot 40 = 20$$

To find 10% of 65:

$$\frac{1}{10} \cdot 65 = 6.5 \quad \text{or} \quad 0.10 \cdot 65 = 6.5$$

EXAMPLE: Debra donated 15% of her babysitting earnings to charity. If Debra earned $95 babysitting, how much did she donate?

Find 15% of 95.

$$0.15 \cdot 95 = 14.25 \quad \text{or} \quad \frac{15}{100} \cdot 95 = \frac{3}{20} \cdot 95 = 14.25$$

Debra donated $14.25.

You can also use equations or proportions to find percent.

information given → $\dfrac{part}{whole} = \dfrac{percent}{100}$ ← what you need to find

For example, what percent of 20 is 5?

$$\dfrac{5}{20} = \dfrac{x}{100}$$

$5 \cdot 100 = 20x$

$500 = 20x$

$x = 25$

5 is 25% of 20.

EXAMPLE: There are 29 students in Evan's class. Nine students handed in their trip permission slips on time. Approximately what percentage of Evan's class handed their slips in on time?

Ask yourself: 9 is what percent of 29?

$$\dfrac{part}{whole} = \dfrac{percent}{100}$$

$$\dfrac{9}{29} = \dfrac{x}{100}$$

$9 \cdot 100 = 29x$

$900 = 29x$

$x =$ about 31 (31.03)

About 31% of students
returned their slips on time.

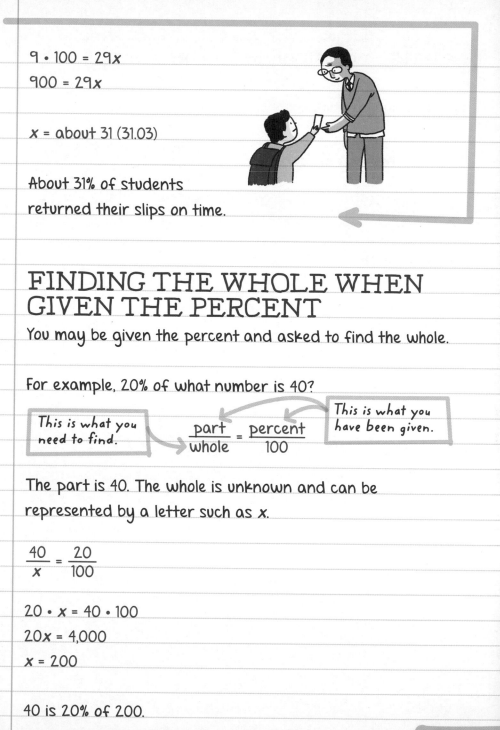

FINDING THE WHOLE WHEN GIVEN THE PERCENT

You may be given the percent and asked to find the whole.

For example, 20% of what number is 40?

This is what you need to find. → $\dfrac{\text{part}}{\text{whole}} = \dfrac{\text{percent}}{100}$ ← This is what you have been given.

The part is 40. The whole is unknown and can be
represented by a letter such as x.

$$\dfrac{40}{x} = \dfrac{20}{100}$$

$20 \cdot x = 40 \cdot 100$

$20x = 4,000$

$x = 200$

40 is 20% of 200.

130% of what number is 143?

Identify the part: 143

Identify the percent: 130%

> The percent is greater than 100, so the part must also be greater than the whole.

$$\frac{143}{x} = \frac{130}{100}$$

$143 \cdot 100 = 130x$

$14,300 = 130x$

$x = 110$

130% of 110 is 143.

1. Write 85% as a fraction.

2. Write 17% as a decimal.

3. What is $\frac{8}{20}$ written as a percent?

4. What is $\frac{3}{5}$ written as a percent?

5. What is 17% of 30?

6. What is 20% of 300?

7. 6 out of every 8 flavors in a juice pack are orange. What percentage of the juice pack is orange flavored?

8. What percent of 40 is 9?

9. 120% of what number is 90?

10. Jackson received requests for 150 tickets for his art show. The number of requests was 120% of the number of tickets he had. How many tickets did Jackson have?

CHECK YOUR ANSWERS

1. $\frac{85}{100}$

2. 0.17

3. 40%

4. 60%

5. 5.1

6. 60

7. 75%

8. 22.5%

9. 75

10. 125 tickets

Chapter 15

PERCENT APPLICATIONS

Percent is used in many different areas of our lives. We use it in grading, banking, shopping, paying taxes or commissions, and tipping.

CALCULATING SALES TAX

SALES TAX is the amount of tax added to the listed price of an item. It is often given as a percent.

The tax rate stays the same, even when the price changes. So the more something costs, the more sales tax you have to pay. This is proportional.

Most states charge sales tax to cover the costs of services to people. Sales tax rates vary from state to state.

For example, a 6% sales tax means that you pay an extra 6 cents for every 100 cents ($1) you spend. This can be written as a ratio (6:100) or a fraction ($\frac{3}{50}$).

EXAMPLE: The price of a hat is $3. The state's sales tax is 7%. How much in sales tax will someone pay on the hat?

Method 1: Multiply the cost of the hat by the percent to find the tax.

7% × $3

Step 1: Change 7% to a decimal.

7% = 0.07

Step 2: Multiply the decimal by the price.

0.07 × 3 = 0.21

The sales tax would be $0.21, or 21 cents.

Method 2: Set up a proportion and solve to find the tax.

Step 1: Change 7% to a fraction.

$$7\% = \frac{7}{100}$$

Step 2: Set the tax equal to the proportional ratio with the unknown quantity.

$$\frac{7}{100} = \frac{x}{3}$$

represents the same relationship

Step 3: Cross-multiply to solve.

$100x = 21$

$x = 0.21$

The sales tax for the hat will be $0.21, or 21 cents.

Method 3: Create an equation to find the answer.

Step 1: Ask: "What is 7% of $3?"

Step 2: Translate the question into a math equation.

$x = 0.07 \times 3$

$x = 0.21$

The sales tax for the hat would be $0.21, or 21 cents.

Finding the Original Price

If you know the final price and the tax percentage, you can find the original price of an item.

EXAMPLE: Julia bought new earbuds. The total cost of the earbuds is $43.99, including an 8% sales tax. What was the price of the earbuds without tax?

SOUND CITY

- - - - - - - - - - - - - - - -

ITEM PRICE	?
SALES TAX	8%
TOTAL	$43.99

- - - - - - - - - - - - - - - -

Thank you!
Please come again.

Step 1: Add the percent of the cost of the earbuds and the percent of the tax to get the total cost percent.

100% + 8% tax = 108%

Think: Julia paid the listed price, so the cost of the earbuds is 100% of the original price.

Step 2: Convert the total cost percent to a decimal.

108% = 1.08

Step 3: Solve for the original price.

43.99 = 1.08x   Divide both sides by 1.08 to isolate x on
x = 40.73   one side of the equation. (Round to the
                     nearest hundredth, or cent.)

The original price of the earbuds was $40.73.

CALCULATING DISCOUNTS

A **DISCOUNT** is an amount deducted from the original price of an item or service. If an item has been discounted, that means it is selling for a lower price than the original price.

Other words and phrases that mean you will save money (and that you subtract the discount from the original price) are: *savings*, *price reduction*, *markdown*, *sale*, and *clearance*.

Calculating a discount is like calculating tax, but because you are saving money you subtract it from the original price rather than add it to the original price.

EXAMPLE: A backpack costs $15.75. A sign in the store says "**ALL ITEMS 25% OFF.**" What is the discount on the backpack? What is the discounted price of the backpack?

Method 1: Determine the amount of the discount and subtract that quantity from the original price.

Step 1: Convert the percent discount to a decimal.

25% = 0.25

Step 2: Multiply the discount percentage converted to a decimal by the original amount to get the discount.

0.25 × $15.75 = $3.94   (Round to the nearest hundredth, or cent.)

Step 3: Subtract the discount from the original price.

$15.75 − $3.94 = $11.81

The discounted price of the backpack is $11.81.

Method 2: Create an equation to find the discounted price.

Step 1: Write a question.

What is 25% of $15.75?

Step 2: Translate the question into a mathematical equation.

$x = 0.25 \cdot \$15.75$
$x = \$3.94$

Discount = $3.94

Step 3: Subtract the discount from the original price.

$15.75 − 3.94 = $11.81

The discounted price of
the backpack is $11.81.

SWEET DEAL!

You can also find the original price if you know the final price and the discount.

Finding the Percent Discount

You can find the percent discount if you know the final price and the original price.

EXAMPLE: Todd pays $22 for a jacket that is on sale. The original price of the jacket was $65. What is the percent discount?

The discounted price is the unknown percent discount, x, multiplied by the original price.

$22 = x \cdot 65$

$22 = 65x$ Divide both sides by 65 to get x alone.

$x = 0.34$ This tells us that Todd paid 34% of 1 or 100% for the jacket.

$1 - 0.34 = 0.66$ Subtract the percent paid from 1 or 100% to find the percent discount.

The percent discount was 66% off the original price.

CALCULATING MARKUPS

Stores and manufacturers increase the price of their products to make a profit. These increases are called **MARKUPS**.

EXAMPLE: A video game costs $15 to manufacture. To make a profit, the TJY company marks the price up 25%. What is the markup amount? What is the company's selling price of the game?

Method 1: Determine the value of the markup.

Step 1: Convert the percent markup to a decimal.

25% = 0.25

Step 2: Multiply the percentage written as a decimal by the original cost. This is the markup.

0.25 x $15 = $3.75

Step 3: Add the markup price to the original cost.

$15 + $3.75

The company's selling price of the game is $18.75.

Create an equation to find the answer.

Step 1: Write a question.

What is 25% of $15?

Step 2: Translate the question into a math equation.

$x = 0.25 \cdot 15$

$x = 3.75$

Step 3: Add the markup price to the original cost.

$15 + $3.75

The company's selling price of the game is $18.75.

Finding the Original Cost

You can find the original cost if you know the final price and the markup.

EXAMPLE: A chocolatier marks up its store's chocolate by 70%. It charges $27.50 for a large, imported box of chocolates. What is the original cost of the chocolates?

Step 1: Add the percent of the original cost for the box of chocolates to the percent of the markup to determine the total cost percent.

100% + 70% = 170%

Think: A purchaser will pay the full original cost plus the store's markup, so the cost of the chocolate is actually 170% of the original cost.

Step 2: Convert the percent to a decimal.

170% = 1.7

Step 3: Solve for the original cost.

$27.50 = 1.7 • *x*

x = 16.18   (Round to the nearest hundredth, or cent.)

The original cost of the box of chocolates is $16.18.

CALCULATING GRATUITIES AND COMMISSIONS

A **GRATUITY** is a tip or a gift, usually in the form of money, that you give in return for a service. We usually talk about tips or gratuities in regard to servers at restaurants.

A **COMMISSION** is a fee paid for a person's service in helping to sell a product.

EXAMPLE: At the end of a meal, a server brings Armaan a bill for $45. Armaan wants to leave a 20% gratuity. How much is the tip in dollars? How much should Armaan leave in total?

20% = 0.20   Convert the gratuity from percent to a decimal.

$45 × 0.20 = $9   Multiply the bill by the gratuity. The tip is $9.

$45 + $9 = $54   Add the tip amount to the bill.

Armaan should leave $54.

EXAMPLE: Esinam works in a clothing store. She earns 15% commission on her total sales. At the end of her first week, her sales totaled $1,700. How much did Esinam earn in commission her first week?

15% = 0.15   Convert the commission from percent to a decimal.

$1,700 x 0.15 = $255   Multiply sales by commission.

Esinam earned $255 in commission her first week.

CHECK YOUR KNOWLEDGE

1. A software package costs $94. The sales tax rate is 7%. How much will the sales tax be?

2. A sweater costs $40. The sales tax rate is 4%. How much will the sales tax be?

3. A rug costs $450. The sales tax rate is $5\frac{1}{2}$%. How much will the sales tax be?

4. A couch displays a price tag of $400. There is a 15% discount on the price. What is the discount amount and the final price of the couch?

5. A laptop is on sale for 45% off the regular price. If the sale price is $299.75, what was the original price?

6. Al pays $25 for a shirt that is on sale. The original price was $40. What was the percent discount?

7. A store buys beach umbrellas for $40 each. To make a profit, the store owner marks up the price of the umbrellas 40%. What is the markup amount? What is the selling price of each umbrella?

8. A toy store retailer charges $26.88 for a board game. He marks up his goods by 25% before selling them. What was the cost of the board game before the markup?

9. Hannah's meal costs $52.25. She wants to leave a 10% tip. How much will her meal cost with tip?

10. Lesli and Kareem sell skateboards at different stores. Lesli earns 8% commission on all sales. Kareem earns 9.5% commission on all sales. Last week Lesli's sales were $5,450, while Kareem's sales were $4,500. Who earned more money in commission?

CHECK YOUR ANSWERS

1. $6.58

2. $1.60

3. $24.75

4. Discount: $60; final price: $340

5. $545

6. 37.5% discount

7. Markup: $16; new price $56

8. $21.50

9. $57.48

10. Lesli earned $436 in commission; Kareem earned $427.50 in commission. Lesli earned more.

Chapter 16

SIMPLE INTEREST

INTEREST is a fee that someone pays in order to borrow money. You **receive** interest from a bank if you put your money into an interest-bearing account. Depositing your money makes the bank stronger and allows it to lend money to other people. The bank pays you interest for that service.

You **pay** interest to a bank if you borrow money from it. Banks charge a fee so that you can use somebody else's money.

To determine the amount of money that must be paid back (if you are the BORROWER) or will be earned (if you are the LENDER), you need to know:

1. The PRINCIPAL: The amount of money that is being borrowed or loaned.

2. The INTEREST RATE: The percentage that will be paid for every year the money is borrowed or loaned.

3. TIME: The amount of time that money will be borrowed or loaned.

> If you are given a term of weeks, months, or days, write a fraction to calculate interest in terms of years.
>
> **Examples:** 8 months = $\dfrac{8}{12}$ years   80 days = $\dfrac{80}{365}$ years
>
> 12 weeks = $\dfrac{12}{52}$ years

Once you have determined the principal, interest rate, and time, you can use this SIMPLE INTEREST FORMULA:

> **Interest = principal × interest rate × time**
>
> or
>
> $I = P \cdot R \cdot T$

BALANCE is the total amount when you add the interest and beginning principal together.

Simple interest can also be thought of as a ratio.

3% interest = $\frac{3}{100}$. So for every $100 deposited, the bank will pay $3 each year. Then you multiply $3 by the number of years.

SIMPLE INTEREST VERSES COMPOUND INTEREST

Simple interest is the same amount of interest calculated on the principal every period. For example, Jason invests $1,000 and earns 2% simple interest per year. After 1 year, Jason would have $1,000 + $20 for a total of $1,020. After 2 years, Jason would have $1,000 + $20 (simple interest year 1) + $20 (simple interest year 2) for a total of $1,040.

Compound interest is interest calculated on the principal plus interest from the previous principal. For example, Jason invested $1,000 and earns 2% compound interest. After 1 year, Jason would earn $1,000 + $20 for a total of $1,020. After 2 years, Jason would have $1,000 (principal) + $20 (interest year 1) + $20.40 (interest calculated on the $1,020, the principal and interest from the previous period) for a total of $1,040.40.

EXAMPLE: Serena deposited $250 into her savings account. She earns a 3% interest rate. How much interest will Serena have earned at the end of 2 years?

Principal (P) = $250

Rate (R) = 3% = 0.03

Remember: You must convert the interest percentage to a decimal to multiply.

Time (T) = 2 years

Substitute the numbers into the formula and solve.

$I = P \cdot R \cdot T$

$I = (\$250)(0.03)(2)$

$I = \$15$

COOL

After 2 years, Serena would earn $15 in interest.

EXAMPLE: Marcos has $4,000. He invests it in an account that offers an (annual) ← *each year* interest rate of 4%. How long does Marcos need to leave his money in the bank in order to earn $600 in interest?

$$I = P \cdot R \cdot T$$

I = $600
P = $4,000
R = 4%
T = x

> You know what the interest will be, but you don't know the length of time. Use x to represent time and substitute all the other information you know.

$$600 = \$4,000 \, (0.04)x$$

$600 = 160x   Divide both sides by 160 to get the unknown time, x, on one side of the equation.

$x = 3.75$

Marcos will earn $600 in 3.75 years, or 3 years and 9 months.

NOPE. NOT TIME YET.

CHECK YOUR KNOWLEDGE

For questions 1 through 5, use the scenario below.

Mario deposited $1,500 into a savings account that pays 3.25% interest annually. He plans to leave the money in the bank for 5 years.

1. What is the principal?

2. What is the interest rate? (Write the interest rate as a decimal.)

3. What is the time period?

4. How much interest will Mario earn after 5 years?

5. What will Mario's balance be after 5 years?

6. How much interest is earned on $500 at 5% for 4 years?

7. Amanda takes out a loan for $1,200 from a bank that charges 5.4% interest per year. If Amanda borrows the money for 1.5 years, how much does she repay?

8. Milo borrows $5,000 from an institution that charges 8.5% interest per year. How much more will Milo have to pay in interest if he chooses to pay the loan in 3 years instead of 2 years?

9. Greg deposits $3,000 in a bank that offers an annual interest rate of 4%. How long does Greg need to leave his money in the bank in order to earn $600 in interest?

10. Tyler borrows $2,000 at 9.5% interest per year. How much interest will Tyler pay in 2 years? If Tyler pays back the loan in 2 years, what is the total amount he will pay?

ANSWERS

CHECK YOUR ANSWERS

1. The principal is $1,500.

2. The interest rate is 0.0325.

3. The time period is 5 years.

4. Mario will earn $243.75.

5. The balance will be $1,743.75.

6. The interest earned is $100.

7. Amanda will repay $1,297.20.

8. Milo will pay $425 more; 2 years' interest: $850; 3 years' interest: $1,275.

9. 5 years

10. The interest paid will be $380. Tyler will repay a total amount of $2,380.

Chapter 17

PERCENT RATE OF CHANGE

We use percent rate of change to show how much an amount has changed in relation to the original amount. Another way to think about it is:

When the original amount goes **UP**, calculate percent **INCREASE**.

When the original amount goes **DOWN**, calculate percent **DECREASE**.

To calculate the percent rate of change:

Step 1: Set up this ratio: $\dfrac{\text{change in quantity}}{\text{original quantity}}$

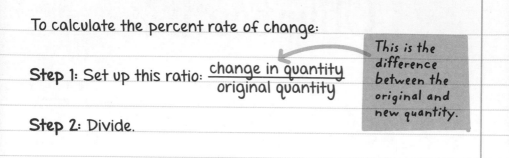

This is the difference between the original and new quantity.

Step 2: Divide.

Step 3: Move the decimal two spaces to the right and add your % symbol.

EXAMPLE: A store manager purchases T-shirts from a factory for $12 each and sells them to customers for $15 each. What is the percent increase in price?

change in quantity

$$\frac{15-12}{12} = \frac{3}{12}$$

original quantity

$= \dfrac{1}{4}$ ← Remember to reduce fractions.

$= 0.25 = 25\%$ increase

There is a 25% increase in price.

You can use the same methods to calculate percent decrease.

CHECK YOUR KNOWLEDGE

For questions 1 through 4, find the percent increase or decrease.

1. 6 to 18

2. $50 to $70

3. 0.08 to 0.03

4. 18 to 8

5. What is the percent increase or decrease on an item originally priced at $45 and newly priced at $63?

6. What is the percent increase or decrease on an item originally priced at $250 and newly priced at $100?

7. Mara answered 15 questions correctly on her first science quiz. On her second science quiz, she answered 12 questions correctly. What is the percent decrease from the first quiz to the second quiz?

8. A store purchases skateboards for $150 each. They then sell the skateboards for $275 each. What percent of change is this?

CHECK YOUR ANSWERS

1. 200% increase

2. 40% increase

3. 62.5% decrease

4. 55.6% decrease

5. 40% increase

6. 60% decrease

7. 20% decrease

8. 83.3% increase

Chapter 18

TABLES AND RATIOS

You can use tables to compare ratios and proportions.

For example, Ari runs laps around a track. The track coach records Ari's time.

Number of Laps	Total Minutes Run
3	9
6	18

What if Ari's coach wanted to determine how long it would take Ari to run 1 lap? If Ari's speed remains constant, the coach could find the unit rate by setting up a proportion:

$$\frac{1}{x} = \frac{3}{9}$$

— time it takes to run one lap

Another option is to set up this proportion: $\dfrac{1}{x} = \dfrac{6}{18}$

$6x = 18$

$x = 3$

The answer is 3 minutes per lap.

 We can use tables only if rates are PROPORTIONAL.

Otherwise there is no ratio or proportion on which to base our calculations.

EXAMPLE: Hiro and Ann run around a track. Their coach records their times below.

ANN	
Number of Laps	Total Minutes Run
1	?
3	12
7	28

HIRO	
Number of Laps	Total Minutes Run
1	?
2	10
4	20

If each runner's speed stays constant, how could their coach find out who runs faster? Their coach must complete the table and find out how much time it would take Ann to run 1 lap and how much time it would take Hiro to run 1 lap, and then compare the times.

The coach can find out the missing times using proportions.

Ann: $\dfrac{1}{x} = \dfrac{3}{12}$ $x = 4$

So, it takes Ann 4 minutes to run 1 lap.

Hiro: $\dfrac{1}{x} = \dfrac{2}{10}$ $x = 5$

So, it takes Hiro 5 minutes to run 1 lap.

Four minutes is a faster running time than five minutes. So, Ann runs faster than Hiro.

Val, Omar, Evan, and Keisha are planting bulbs. They record their times in the tables below. Assume that their rates are proportional and complete the tables.

1.

VAL	
Number of Bulbs	Minutes
1	?
3	6
6	12

2.

OMAR	
Number of Bulbs	Minutes
1	?
2	1
5	2.5

3.

EVAN	
Number of Bulbs	Minutes
1	?
?	8
8	16

4.

KEISHA	
Number of Bulbs	Minutes
1	?
?	3
5	7.5
?	9

5. Who planted 1 bulb in the least amount of time?

6. Who took the most amount of time to plant 1 bulb?

CHECK YOUR ANSWERS

1.

VAL	
Number of Bulbs	Minutes
1	2
3	6
6	12

2.

OMAR	
Number of Bulbs	Minutes
1	.5 or 30 sec
2	1
5	2.5

3.

EVAN	
Number of Bulbs	Minutes
1	2
4	8
8	16

4.

KEISHA	
Number of Bulbs	Minutes
1	1.5
2	3
5	7.5
6	9

5. Omar

6. Val and Evan

140

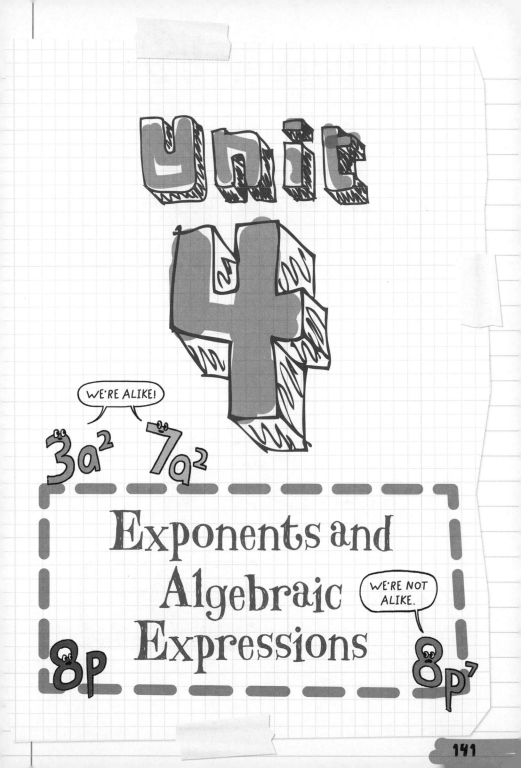

Unit

4

WE'RE ALIKE!

$3a^2$ $7a^2$

Exponents and
Algebraic
Expressions

WE'RE NOT
ALIKE.

$8p$ $8p^7$

Chapter 19

EXPONENTS

An **EXPONENT** is the number of times a base number is multiplied by itself.

An exponent is also known as the power of the base number.

$$4^3$$

exponent

base number

Therefore:

$$4^3 = 4 \times 4 \times 4 = 64$$

4^3 is read as "four to the third power."

Exponents have special properties:

- Any base without an exponent has an unwritten exponent of 1.

  In other words, any number raised to the first power is itself.

  For example, $7^1 = 7$

- Any base with an exponent 0 is equal to 1.

  For example, $\left(\dfrac{2}{3}\right)^0 = 1$

When simplifying negative numbers with exponents, ask yourself, "What is the base number?"

For example, simplify $(-2)^4$.

What is the base number?

The parenthesis is next to the exponent. This means that everything inside the parentheses is the base number.

The base number is –2.

Include the negative sign when multiplying the base number by itself.

$(-2)^4 = (-2) \times (-2) \times (-2) \times (-2) = 16$

Now, simplify: -2^4

Be careful! This is very different than $(-2)^4$

The number 2 is next to the exponent with no parenthesis between them. Only the 2 (and not the negative sign) is being raised to the fourth power:

The base number is **2**.

$-2^4 = -(2 \times 2 \times 2 \times 2) = -16$

NEGATIVE EXPONENTS

A **NEGATIVE EXPONENT** indicates the base needs to be rewritten in the denominator of a fraction. Negative exponents are calculated by using reciprocals.

A negative exponent in the numerator becomes a positive exponent when moved to the denominator.

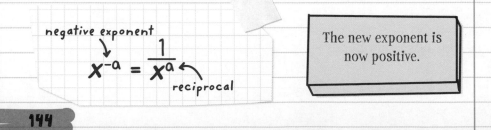

negative exponent

$$x^{-a} = \frac{1}{x^a}$$

reciprocal

The new exponent is now positive.

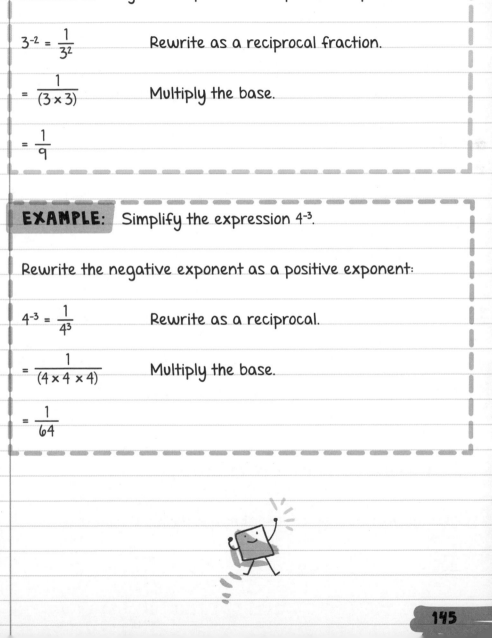

EXAMPLE: Simplify the expression 3^{-2}.

Rewrite the negative exponent as a positive exponent:

$3^{-2} = \dfrac{1}{3^2}$ Rewrite as a reciprocal fraction.

$= \dfrac{1}{(3 \times 3)}$ Multiply the base.

$= \dfrac{1}{9}$

EXAMPLE: Simplify the expression 4^{-3}.

Rewrite the negative exponent as a positive exponent:

$4^{-3} = \dfrac{1}{4^3}$ Rewrite as a reciprocal.

$= \dfrac{1}{(4 \times 4 \times 4)}$ Multiply the base.

$= \dfrac{1}{64}$

FRACTIONS WITH NEGATIVE EXPONENTS

A negative exponent in the numerator of a fraction becomes a positive exponent when we use its reciprocal.

It looks like this: $\left(\dfrac{x}{y}\right)^{-a} = \left(\dfrac{y}{x}\right)^a$

> The new exponent is now positive.

EXAMPLE: Simplify the expression $\left(\dfrac{3}{4}\right)^{-2}$.

Rewrite the negative exponent into a positive exponent:

$$\left(\dfrac{3}{4}\right)^{-2} = \left(\dfrac{4}{3}\right)^2 \longrightarrow = \dfrac{4}{3} \times \dfrac{4}{3} = \dfrac{16}{9}$$

A negative exponent in the denominator becomes a positive exponent when moved to the numerator.

It looks like this: $\dfrac{1}{x^{-a}} = x^a$ ← *this is the same as* $\dfrac{x^a}{1}$

EXAMPLE: Simplify the expression $\dfrac{1}{9^{-2}}$.

Rewrite the negative exponent into a positive exponent:

$$\dfrac{1}{9^{-2}} = 9^2 \longrightarrow = 9 \times 9 = 81$$

Simplify each of the following expressions.

1. 5^3

2. 2^5

3. $\left(-\dfrac{3}{8}\right)^0$

4. 3^{-4}

5. $(-2)^6$

6. -2^6

7. 2^{-6}

8. $\left(\dfrac{1}{6}\right)^{-3}$

9. $\left(\dfrac{2}{5}\right)^{-3}$

10. $\left(\dfrac{4}{3}\right)^{-3}$

CHECK YOUR ANSWERS

1. 125

2. 32

3. 1

4. $\dfrac{1}{81}$

5. 64

6. −64

7. $\dfrac{1}{64}$

8. 216

9. $\dfrac{4}{9}$

10. $\dfrac{-64}{27}$

Chapter 20

SCIENTIFIC NOTATION

We usually write numbers in STANDARD NOTATION, like 5,700,000 or 0.0000684.

SCIENTIFIC NOTATION is a shortened way of writing numbers by using powers of 10. We do this by expressing the number as a product of two other numbers.

- The first number in scientific notation is greater than or equal to 1, but less than 10.

- The second number in scientific notation is in exponential form and a power of 10.

For example, 5.7×10^6.

power of 10 that shows how many places to move the decimal point

the number with the decimal placed after the first digit

This is the same as 5,700,000.

To convert a Positive Number from Standard Form to Scientific Notation:

Count how many places you have to move the decimal point so that there is only a number between 1 and 10 that remains. The number of places that you move the decimal point is related to the exponent of 10.

If the standard form of a number is greater than 1, the exponent of 10 will be **POSITIVE**.

EXAMPLE: Convert 8,710,000 to scientific notation.

8,710,000   Move the decimal point six places to the
                   left to get a number between 1 and 10.
                   The number is: **8.71.**

8.71×10^6 The standard form (8,710,000) is greater
                   than 1. So the exponent of 10 is positive 6.

If the standard form number is less than 1, the exponent of 10 will be **NEGATIVE**.

EXAMPLE: Convert 0.000092384 to scientific notation.

0.000092384   Move the decimal point five places to the right to get a number between 1 and 10. The number is: **9.2384**.

9.2384×10^{-5} The standard form (0.000092384) is less than 1. So the exponent of 10 is negative **5**.

To Convert a Number from Scientific Notation to Standard Form:

If the exponent of the 10 is positive, move the decimal to the **RIGHT**.

EXAMPLE: Write 1.29×10^5 in standard form.

1.29×10^5 The exponent is positive, so move the decimal five places to the right and fill

129,000   in zeros to complete the place value of the number written in standard form.

If the exponent of the 10 is negative, move the decimal to the **LEFT**.

EXAMPLE: Convert 9.042×10^{-3} to standard form.

9.042×10^{-3} The exponent is negative, so move the
                           decimal three places to the left and fill

0.009042 in zeros to complete the place value of
                           the number written in standard form.

For questions 1 through 6, rewrite each of the numbers.

1. Write 307 in scientific notation.

2. Write 7,930,451 in scientific notation.

3. Write 0.0001092 in scientific notation.

4. Write 6.91×10^2 in standard form.

5. Write 1.2×10^{-6} in standard form.

6. Write 3.495×10^8 in standard form.

7. Arrange the following numbers from least to greatest:

4.006×10^{-3}, 2.7×10^9, 2.7×10^{-5}, 8.30×10^{-7}

8. A questionnaire asks people what their favorite ice cream flavor is. A total of 2.139×10^8 people choose chocolate, and a total of 7.82×10^6 choose strawberry. How many more people choose chocolate than strawberry? Write your answer using scientific notation.

ANSWERS ➤ 153

CHECK YOUR ANSWERS

1. 3.07×10^2

2. 7.930451×10^6

3. 1.092×10^{-4}

4. 691

5. 0.0000012

6. 349,500,000

7. 8.30×10^{-7}, 2.7×10^{-5}, 4.006×10^{-3}, 2.7×10^9

8. There are 2.0608×10^8 more people who choose chocolate than strawberry.

Chapter 21

EXPRESSIONS

An **EXPRESSION** is a mathematical phrase that contains numbers, variables, and operators (which are: +, −, ×, and ÷).

> letters or symbols representing a value

Examples: $3x + 9$ $-7y + \dfrac{1}{2}$ $1.3a^2 - 4ab$

$7a^2 - \dfrac{3}{5}ab + 6b^2$ $38m$ $7 - 13$

Expressions are made up of 1 or more **TERMS**. A term is a number by itself or the product of a number and a variable (or more than one variable). Each term below is separated by a plus or minus sign.

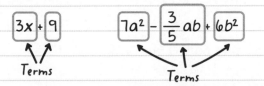

$3x + 9$
Terms

$7a^2 - \dfrac{3}{5}ab + 6b^2$
Terms

A **MONOMIAL** is an expression that has only 1 term.

For example, $38m$

A **BINOMIAL** is an expression that has 2 terms.

For example, $\boxed{-7y} + \boxed{\dfrac{1}{2}}$

Terms

A **TRINOMIAL** is an expression that has 3 terms.

For example, $\boxed{8a^2} - \boxed{\dfrac{3}{5}ab} + \boxed{6b^2}$

Terms

A **POLYNOMIAL** is an expression consisting of variables and coefficients. *POLY* means "many" and *NOMIAL* means "term."

Whenever a term has both a number and a letter (or letters), the numerical part is called the COEFFICIENT and the letter (or letters) is called the VARIABLE(S).

Sometimes, the variable can contain an EXPONENT.

$$7a^2 \qquad 1.79x^3y^2$$

Exponent → (pointing to the 2 in $7a^2$)

Coefficient (pointing to 7) Variable (pointing to a)

Exponents ↗↘ (pointing to the 3 and 2 in $1.79x^3y^2$)

Coefficient (pointing to 1.79) Variables (pointing to x and y)

The DEGREE of a monomial can be found by adding the sum of the exponents:

For example:

$7a^2$ has a degree of 2.

$1.79x^3y^2$ has a degree of 3 + 2 = 5.

$\frac{3}{5}a^4bc^2$ has a degree of 4 + 1 + 2 = 7.

> If a variable doesn't have a
> written exponent, the power is 1.

The degree of a polynomial is the largest exponent of that variable.

For example:

$5x + 1$ has a degree of 1.

$-x^2 + 2x - 5$ has a degree of 2.

A **CONSTANT** is a number that is fixed or does not vary in an expression (it stays "constant"). For example, in the expression $-7y + \frac{1}{2}$, the constant is $\frac{1}{2}$. All constants have a degree of 0.

STANDARD FORM OF AN EXPRESSION

When writing an expression, we often write the term with the greatest exponent first, and write the constant last. This is called writing an expression in STANDARD FORM or DESCENDING ORDER.

For example, to rewrite $3 + 7y^2$ into standard form, write $7y^2$ first because it has the greatest exponent, and then write the constant, 3:

$3 + 7y^2 \rightarrow 7y^2 + 3$

Rewrite $9x^2 - 4x + \dfrac{5}{2} + 10x^3$ into standard form.

Since $10x^3$ has the greatest exponent, it goes first.

$9x^2$ has the next greatest exponent, so it goes second.

$-4x$ has the next greatest exponent, so it goes third.

$\dfrac{5}{2}$ is the last term.

> Since $4x$ is being subtracted in the problem, make sure that it is also being subtracted in the rewritten form.

$$9x^2 - 4x + \frac{5}{2} + 10x^3 \rightarrow 10x^3 + 9x^2 - 4x + \frac{5}{2}$$

When there are multiple variables, use alphabetical order to determine the order of the variables.

EXAMPLE: Rewrite $7x^3y^5 - 8x^4y^2$ into standard form.

Since there are two variables x and y, first sort by the variable that comes first alphabetically, x.

Since $-8x^4y^2$ has the greatest exponent in terms of x, it goes first.

Since $7x^3y^5$ has the next greatest exponent in terms of x, it goes next.

$$7x^3y^5 - 8x^4y^2 \rightarrow -8x^4y^2 + 7x^3y^5$$

EXAMPLE: Rewrite $4a^3b^2c^5 + 7abc^2 - \frac{2}{9}a^4bc^8$ into standard form.

Since there are three variables, a, b, and c, first sort by the variable that comes first alphabetically, a.

$-\frac{2}{9}a^4bc^8$ has the greatest exponent in terms of a. Write it first.

$4a^3b^2c^5$ has the next greatest exponent in terms of a. Write it next.

Since $7abc^2$ has the next greatest exponent in terms of a, write it last.

$4a^3b^2c^5 + 7abc^2 - \frac{2}{9}a^4bc^8 \rightarrow -\frac{2}{9}a^4bc^8 + 4a^3b^2c^5 + 7abc^2$

CHECK YOUR KNOWLEDGE

For questions 1 through 3, label each expression as a monomial, binomial, trinomial, or none of these.

1. $6x^3 - 5y$

3. $8x^2y$

2. $9x^3 + 5x^2 - 4x + 7$

For questions 4 and 5, write all the coefficients and all the variables.

4. $9a^3 + 7ab^2 - 0.4b$

5. $3h^4 - 0.7k - 51mn$

For questions 6 through 8, rewrite the expression in descending order.

6. $5a^3 - 0.9a^4 + a^5 + 7$

8. $-9mn^2 + 7m^3n^6 + \dfrac{3}{4} - \dfrac{15}{11}m^2n^{10}$

7. $3.2x - 0.8x^3 + 5$

For questions 9 and 10, state the degree of each expression.

9. $4x^2\, y^3\, z^8$

10. $-\dfrac{3}{2}\, pqr^7$

ANSWERS

CHECK YOUR ANSWERS

1. binomial

2. none of these

3. monomial

4. coefficients: 9, 7, –0.4; variables: a, b, c

5. coefficients: –0.7, 51; variables: h, k, m, n

6. $a^5 - 0.9a^4 + 5a^3 + 7$

7. $-0.8x^3 + 3.2x + 5$

8. $7m^3n^6 - \dfrac{15}{11}m^2n^{10} - 9mn^2 + \dfrac{3}{4}$

9. degree: 13

10. degree: 9

Chapter 22

EVALUATING ALGEBRAIC EXPRESSIONS

EVALUATION is the process of simplifying an algebraic expression by first SUBSTITUTING (replacing) a variable with a number and then computing the value of the expression using the order of operations.

EXAMPLE: Evaluate $3x + 5$ when $x = 4$.

$3x + 5$

$= 3(4) + 5$

$= 12 + 5$

$= 17$

$x = 4$.
So substitute 4 for x.

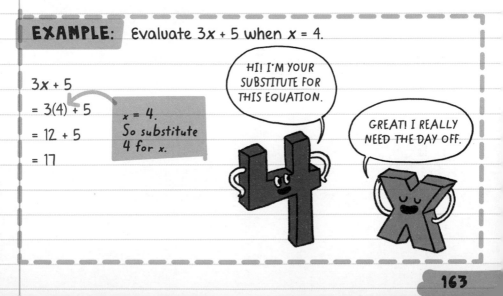

HI! I'M YOUR SUBSTITUTE FOR THIS EQUATION.

GREAT! I REALLY NEED THE DAY OFF.

EXAMPLE: Evaluate $5y^2 + 7y + 3$ when $y = -4$.

$= 5(-4)^2 + 7(-4) + 3$

$= 5(16) - 28 + 3$

$= 80 - 28 + 3$

$= 52 + 3$

$= 55$

Follow the same steps when there are two or more variables.

EXAMPLE: Evaluate $-6x + 7y$ when $x = 3$ and $y = -5$.

$= -6(3) + 7(-5)$ Substitute 3 for x and -5 for y.

$= -18 - 35$

$= -53$

EXAMPLE: Evaluate $\dfrac{6f - 4g}{5fg^2}$ when $f = 8$ and $g = 3$.

$= \dfrac{6(8) - 4(3)}{5(8)(3^2)}$

$= \dfrac{48 - 12}{5(8)(9)}$

$= \dfrac{36}{360}$

$= \dfrac{1}{10}$

When variables are in a numerator or denominator, first simplify the numerator, then simplify the denominator; then divide the numerator by the denominator.

EXAMPLE: The profit a ticket agent makes is represented by the expression $95x + 72y$, where x represents the number of adult tickets sold and y represents the number of child tickets sold. If 40 adult tickets are sold and 15 child tickets are sold, how much profit does the ticket agent make?

95 (40) + 72 (15)

= 3,800 + 1,080

= 4,880

The ticket agent makes $4,880 in profit.

For problems 1 through 8, evaluate each of the expressions.

1. Evaluate $2x - 9$ when $x = 4$.

2. Evaluate $5y - 3y$ when $y = -7$.

3. Evaluate $4a^3 + 57$ when $a = -2$.

4. Evaluate $8m^2 - 12m + 3$ when $m = 1$.

5. Evaluate $8a^2 - 6a$ when $a = \dfrac{1}{2}$.

6. Evaluate $9x - 4y$ when $x = 2$ and $y = 3$.

7. Evaluate $7p^2 - 6q$ when $p = -1$ and $q = 8$.

8. Evaluate $\dfrac{8x + y}{4 - xy^2}$ when $x = -2$ and $y = 2$.

9. The amount of pet food that Robin buys is represented by the expression $8c + 5d$, where c represents the pounds of cat food and d represents the pounds of dog food. If Robin buys 21 pounds of cat food and 13 pounds of dog food, how many total pounds of pet food does she buy?

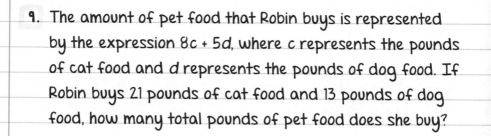

CHECK YOUR ANSWERS

1. −1

2. −14

3. 25

4. −1

5. −1

6. 6

7. −41

8. $-\dfrac{7}{6}$

9. Robin buys 233 pounds of pet food.

Chapter 23

COMBINING LIKE TERMS

LIKE TERMS are terms that have the same variable and the same exponent. Like terms can have different coefficients, as long as they share the same variable and the same exponent.

We COLLECT LIKE TERMS (also referred to as **COMBINING LIKE TERMS**) to simplify an expression.

In other words, we rewrite the expression so that it contains fewer numbers, variables, and operations. Basically, we are simplifying to make the expression simpler to use.

Example: Tomás has 4 marbles in his bag. Let *m* represent each marble.

We could express the number of marbles as *m* + *m* + *m* + *m*, but it is much *simpler* to write 4 • *m*, or 4*m*.

Notice that to combine terms with the same variable, we added a coefficient.

Example: Tomás has 5 marbles in his green bag, 1 marble in his red bag, and 3 marbles in his yellow bag. Let *m* represent each marble.

We could express all of his bags of marbles as 5*m* + *m* + 3*m*, but it is much simpler to write 9*m*.

EXAMPLE: Simplify by combining like terms: 7*x* – 2*x* + 4*x*.

= 7*x* – 2*x* + 4*x*   When there is a minus sign in front of any term, we have to subtract.

= 5*x* + 4*x*

= 9*x*

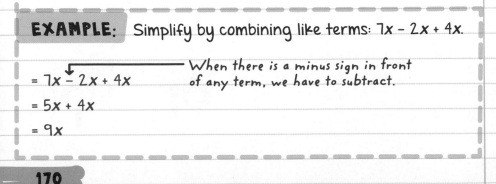

If two terms do **NOT** have the same variable, they **CANNOT** be combined.

EXAMPLE: Simplify $7a - 8b + 13c + 5a + b - 2$.

$= 7a - 8b + 13c + 5a + b - 2$ Combine $7a$ and $5a \rightarrow 12a$
Combine $-8b$ and $b \rightarrow -7b$

$= 12a - 7b + 13c - 2$ $13c$ and -2 do not combine
with any other term

Note: $3xy$ can combine with $10yx$. That is because the Commutative Property of Multiplication states that xy is equivalent to yx.

When simplifying algebraic expressions or equations, put all variables in alphabetical order and all terms in descending order. That means the the term with the greatest exponent goes first, and the constant goes last.

Write $8a - 4a^2 + 9c - 6 + 10d^2 - 3b^2 - 4.7c^5$ in descending order.

$8a - 4a^2 - 3b^2 + 9c - 4.7c^5 + 10d^2 - 6$ First, sort in alphabetical order.

$= -4a^2 + 8a - 3b^2 - 4.7c^5 + 9c + 10d^2 - 6$ Then, sort in descending order.

Sometimes, we may need to apply the Distributive Property first and then collect like terms.

$$a(b + c) = a \cdot b + a \cdot c$$

EXAMPLE: Simplify $2 + 11x - 3(x - 5) + 7x + \frac{1}{4}x$.

$2 + 11x - 3(x - 5) + 7x + \frac{1}{4}x$ First, apply the Distributive Property to distribute the –3.

$= 2 + 11x - 3x + 15 + 7x + \frac{1}{4}x$ Next, combine like terms.

$= 17 + \frac{61}{4}x$ $11x - 3x + 7x + \frac{1}{4}x = 15 + \frac{1}{4}x = \frac{61}{4}x$

$= \frac{61}{4}x + 17$ Arrange in descending order.

In questions 1 through 8, simplify each expression. Write your answer in descending order.

1. $9x + 2x$

2. $12m + 3m - m$

3. $3p - 5q + 4q - 1$

4. $3a - 4b + 5c + 6c + 7b - 8a$

5. $3x^2 - 8x + 1 + 7x - 10x^2$

6. $9m + 3n^2 - 5m + 7n + \dfrac{3}{2}n$

7. $-6.1ab + 3c + 5.4ba$

8. $8y - 3(x - 2y) + 15$

9. The number of miles that Roberto bikes on Monday can be represented by the expression $4a - 3b - 5$. The number of miles that he bikes on Tuesday can be represented by the expression $9b + 12$. What is the total number of miles that Roberto biked?

CHECK YOUR ANSWERS

1. $11x$

2. $14m$

3. $3p - q - 1$

4. $-5a + 3b + 11c$

5. $-7x^2 - x + 1$

6. $4m + 3n^2 + \dfrac{17}{2}n$

7. $-0.7ab + 3c$

8. $-3x + 14y + 15$

9. The total miles that Roberto biked was $4a + 6b + 7$.

Unit 5

Linear Equations and Inequalities

Chapter 24

INTRODUCTION TO EQUATIONS

An **EQUATION** is a mathematical sentence with an equal sign. There are expressions on the left and right sides of the equal sign.

Expression $\longrightarrow$ $\boxed{7x + 8y}$ = $\boxed{5a - b + 6}$ $\longleftarrow$ Expression

To solve an equation, we find the value of the variable that makes the equation true. This value is called the **SOLUTION**.

EXAMPLE: Is $x = -3$ a solution for $4x = -12$?

$4(-3) \overset{?}{=} -12$ $\longleftarrow$ Substitute -3 for x.

$-12 \overset{?}{=} -12$

Both sides of the equation are equivalent, so the solution $x = -3$ makes the equation true.

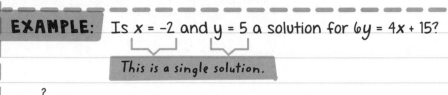

EXAMPLE: Is $x = -2$ and $y = 5$ a solution for $6y = 4x + 15$?

This is a single solution.

$6(5) \overset{?}{=} 4(-2) + 15$

$30 \overset{?}{=} 7$

Both sides of the equation are <u>NOT</u> equivalent, so $x = -2$ and $y = 5$ is <u>NOT</u> a solution of the equation.

INDEPENDENT AND DEPENDENT VARIABLES

There are two types of variables that can appear in an equation:

- INDEPENDENT VARIABLE: The variable you are substituting for.

- DEPENDENT VARIABLE: The variable that you solve for.

Remember: The dependent variable **DEPENDS** on the independent variable.

The *independent variable* is also referred to as the *input* and the *dependent variable* as the *output*.

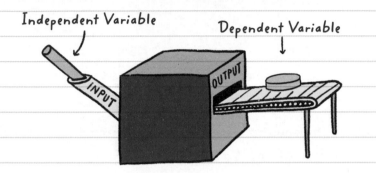

Independent Variable

Dependent Variable

Example: For the equation $y = 7x + 9$, find the independent variable and the dependent variable.

Since we solve for y by substituting values into x, the variable x is the **independent** variable and the variable y is the **dependent** variable.

EXAMPLE: Solve for y in the equation $y = 4x + 10$ when $x = -1$.

$y = 4(-1) + 10$ Substitute -1 for x.

$y = 6$

> x is the independent variable and y is the dependent variable.

EXAMPLE: Solve for n in the equation $n = \dfrac{r-9}{3} - 4r$ when $r = 6$.

$$n = \frac{(6) - 9}{3} - 4(6)$$

$$= \frac{-3}{3} - 24$$

$$n = -25$$

CHECK YOUR ANSWER

If you're unsure of your solution for any equation, you can check your answer by substituting your solution into the original equation.

$$n = \frac{r-9}{3} - 4r$$

$$(-25) \overset{?}{=} \frac{(6)-9}{3} - 4(6) \qquad \text{Substitute 6 for } r \text{ and } -25 \text{ for } n.$$

$$-25 \overset{?}{=} -1 - 24$$

$$-25 \overset{?}{=} -25 \checkmark \qquad \text{The answer is correct!}$$

LINEAR EQUATIONS

A **LINEAR EQUATION** is an equation in which the highest exponent of the variable(s) is 1.

A linear equation when graphed will appear as a straight line.

> A linear equation is also called a *first-degree equation*.

These are linear equations: $4a + 6 = 9a$ $y = 3x + 7$

These are <u>NOT</u> linear equations:

The highest exponent is 2, not 1.

There is no equal sign, so this is not an equation.

$3m^{②} + 7m - 6 = 0$ $9c + 7d - 4$

EXAMPLE: John picks any random number. Susan adds 3 to John's number.

Write a linear equation that represents this situation.

Let x represent John's number. Let y represent Susan's number.

Since Susan adds 3 to John's number, y is determined by adding x and 3: $y = x + 3$.

EXAMPLE: A bike store charges guests a $20 rental fee to rent a bike and $5 per hour for every hour that someone rides the bike. Write a linear equation that represents how much the bike store charges to rent and ride a bike.

Let x represent the number of hours the guest rides the bike. Let y represent the total cost that the guest pays.

The guest pays $5 per hour for x hours that they ride the bike: $5 \cdot x = 5x$ dollars.

The total price is obtained by adding the cost of the rental fee, $20, and $5x$:

So, $y = 5x + 20$

EXAMPLE: The sum of two numbers is 25. Write a linear equation that represents this situation.

Let x represent the first number and y represent the second number.

Since the sum is obtained by adding: $x + y = 25$.

EXAMPLE: Sami has some blue boxes that weigh 3 pounds each and some purple boxes that weigh 8 pounds each. Write a linear equation that represents the total weight of the boxes.

Let b represent the number of blue boxes and p represent the number of purple boxes.

Let t represent the total weight.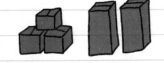

Each blue box weighs 3 pounds.
So, the total weight of the blue boxes is written as $3b$.

Each purple box weighs 8 pounds. So, the total weight of the purple boxes is: $8p$.

The total weight of the boxes is obtained by adding:
$t = 3b + 8p$.

For questions 1 through 5, solve each equation.

1. $y = 3 + x$ when $x = -5$

2. $y = 4x - \dfrac{1}{2}$ when $x = 3$

3. $a = \dfrac{b-3}{5} + 7b$ when $b = -2$

4. $w = (9 + z)^3$ when $z = -11$

5. $m = 3n^2 - n - 7$ when $n = -1$

6. The number of pineapples in a box is 8 less than the number of mangoes. Let p represent the number of pineapples. Write a linear equation that represents this situation.

7. Betty is 12 years older than twice John's age. Let b represent Betty's age and j represent John's age. Write a linear equation that represents this situation.

CHECK YOUR ANSWERS

1. $y = -2$

2. $y = \dfrac{23}{2}$ or $11\dfrac{1}{2}$

3. $a = -15$

4. $w = -8$

5. $m = -3$

6. $p = m - 8$

7. $b = 2j + 12$

Chapter

SOLVING ONE-VARIABLE EQUATIONS

In an equation, when we are not given a number to substitute for a variable, we must "solve" for that variable.

> Solving an equation is like asking, "What value makes this equation true?"

I LIKE TO BE ALONE.

When solving for a variable, we must ISOLATE THE VARIABLE to one side of the equal sign of the equation, so that it is "alone."

EXAMPLE: Solve for x: $x + 2 = 6$

To isolate the variable:

Think of an equation as a scale, with the equal sign as the middle.

You must keep the scale balanced at all times:

Whatever you do to one side of the scale, you must do to the other side of the scale.

Ask, "What is happening to this variable?"

In $x + 2 = 6$, 2 is being added to the variable on the left side.

To get the variable alone (to isolate it) use INVERSE OPERATIONS.

What is the inverse of adding 2? It is subtracting 2.

> **Inverse** means "opposites."

So we must subtract 2 from **BOTH** sides of the equation!

$x + 2 = 6$

$x + 2 - 2 = 6 - 2$ to keep the scale balanced

$x = 4$

$(4) + 2 \overset{?}{=} 6$ Substitute 4 for x.

$6 \overset{?}{=} 6$ ✓   The equation is true, so the answer is correct.

Some of the operations and their inverse operations:

OPERATION	INVERSE OPERATION
Addition ⟶	Subtraction
Subtraction ⟶	Addition
Multiplication ⟶	Division
Division ⟶	Multiplication
Squaring (exponent of 2) ⟶	Square root ($\sqrt{}$)
Cubing (exponent of 3) ⟶	Cube root ($\sqrt[3]{}$)

EXAMPLE: Solve for x: $x - 7 = 12$

$x - 7 = 12$ What is happening to the x?
                        7 is being subtracted from x.
$x - 7 + 7 = 12 + 7$ The inverse of subtracting 7 is adding 7.
$x = 19$

$(19) - 7 \overset{?}{=} 12$ Substitute 19 for x.

$12 \overset{?}{=} 12$ ✓   The answer is correct.

EXAMPLE: Solve for t: $-6t = 138$

$-6t = 138$ What is happening to the t?
t is being multiplied by -6.

$\dfrac{-6t}{-6} = \dfrac{138}{-6}$ The inverse of multiplying by -6 is dividing by -6.

$t = -23$

CHECK YOUR ANSWER

$-6(-23) \overset{?}{=} 138$

$138 \overset{?}{=} 138$ ✓

Sometimes we may need to use inverse operations more than once.

EXAMPLE: Solve for x: $3x + 13 = 7$

$3x + 13 = 7$

$3x + \boxed{13} - \boxed{13} = 7 - 13$

The inverse of addition is subtraction.

$3x = -6$

$\dfrac{\boxed{3}x}{\boxed{3}} = \dfrac{-6}{3}$

The inverse of multiplication is division.

$x = -2$

Sometimes we may need to use the Distributive Property as well as inverse operations.

EXAMPLE: Solve for m: $4(m - 3) = 20$

$4(m - 3) = 20$

$4m - 12 = 20$

Distribute the 4 across the terms in the parentheses.

$4m - \boxed{12} + \boxed{12} = 20 + 12$

The inverse of subtraction is addition.

$4m = 32$

$\dfrac{\boxed{4}m}{\boxed{4}} = \dfrac{32}{4}$

The inverse of multiplication is division.

Another way to solve would be to divide by 4 first!

$m = 8$

189

Sometimes we may need to combine like terms. Then use inverse operations.

EXAMPLE: Solve for p: $9p - 5p = 52$

$9p - 5p = 52$ $9p$ and $5p$ are like terms, so we can combine them first.

$4p = 52$

$\dfrac{4p}{4} = \dfrac{52}{4}$

$p = 13$

EXAMPLE: Solve for x: $-4(2x - 1) - 3x = 6x - 5$

$-4(2x - 1) - 3x = 6x - 5$ First, use the Distributive Property.

$-8x + 4 - 3x = 6x - 5$ Combine like terms on each side of the equal sign.

$-11x + 4 = 6x - 5$

$-11x - 6x + 4 - 4 = 6x - 6x - 5 - 4$ Use inverse operations.

$-17x = -9$

$$\frac{\boxed{-17}x}{\boxed{-17}} = \frac{-9}{-17}$$

$$x = \frac{9}{17}$$

EXAMPLE: Eddie needs to pay $690 in rent for his ski shop today. He rents skis to customers for $40 a day. How many customers does Eddie need to rent skis to so that he can pay his rent and have $150 left over?

Let s represent the number of skis that Eddie rents out.

Since Eddie needs to pay $690 in rent, use subtraction to create an equation:

$$40s - 690 = 150$$

$$40s - 690 + 690 = 150 + 690$$

$$40s = 840$$

$$\frac{\boxed{40}s}{\boxed{40}} = \frac{840}{40}$$

Eddie's SKI SHOP

$$s = 21$$

Eddie needs to rent skis to 21 customers.

CHECK YOUR KNOWLEDGE

For questions 1 through 9, solve each equation.

1. $6x + 25 = 7$

2. $-2y - 3 = -29$

3. $a - 3a + 8a = 54$

4. $5m - 2 = 12m - 16$

5. $3x - 5 = x + 2 - 10 - 7x$

6. $2(x - 3) = 18$

7. $-3(n + 5) = -26 + 2$

8. $2p - 13 = 5p - (1p - 7)$

9. $-4(x - 3) = 3(x + 2)$

10. Patty sells pies to customers at a price of $16 per pie. Patty starts the day with $90 in her cash register. How many pies does Patty need to sell so that she has $538 in the cash register?

CHECK YOUR ANSWERS

1. $x = -3$

2. $y = 13$

3. $a = 9$

4. $m = 2$

5. $x = -\dfrac{1}{3}$

6. $x = 12$

7. $n = 3$

8. $p = -10$

9. $x = \dfrac{6}{7}$

10. Patty must sell 28 pies.

Chapter 26

SOLVING ONE-VARIABLE INEQUALITIES

WRITING INEQUALITIES

While an equation is a mathematical sentence that contains an equal sign, an INEQUALITY is a mathematical sentence that contains a sign that indicates that the values on each side make a nonequal comparison.

An inequality compares two expressions and uses the symbols $>$, $<$, $\geq$, or $\leq$.

Examples: $x < 2$ $x > 2y + 7$

$$a + 7b \geq 3c - 4d \qquad 7x^2 - 5 \leq \frac{1}{2}x + y$$

SYMBOL	MEANING
<	is less than
>	is greater than
≤	is less than or equal to
≥	is greater than or equal to

GRAPHING INEQUALITIES

In addition to writing inequalities using symbols, we can GRAPH INEQUALITIES on a number line. There are various ways to graph inequalities.

1. If the sentence uses a < or > sign, we use an OPEN CIRCLE to indicate that the number is *not* included.

Example: Graph $x > 3$.

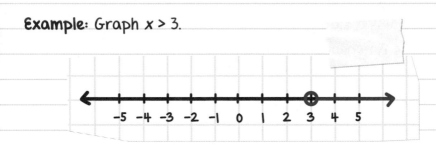

The number represented by x is *greater than* 3, so 3 is NOT included in the possible solutions.

2. If the sentence uses a ≤ or ≥ sign, we use a CLOSED CIRCLE to indicate that the number *is* included. This shows that the solutions could equal the number itself.

Example: Graph $x \leq -2$.

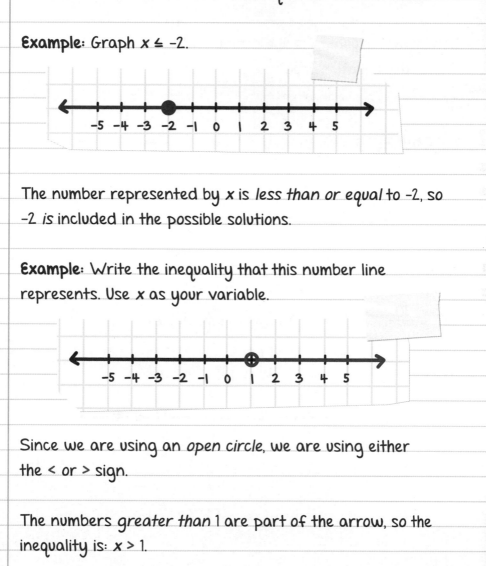

The number represented by x is *less than or equal* to -2, so -2 *is* included in the possible solutions.

Example: Write the inequality that this number line represents. Use x as your variable.

Since we are using an *open circle*, we are using either the < or > sign.

The numbers *greater than* 1 are part of the arrow, so the inequality is: $x > 1$.

SOLVING INEQUALITIES

To solve inequalities, follow the same steps as solving an equation.

Solving an inequality is like asking, "Which set of values makes this equation true?"

EXAMPLE: Solve $2x - 1 \leq 9$ and graph the answer on a number line.

$2x - 1 + 1 \leq 9 + 1$ Add 1 to both sides.

$2x \leq 10$

$\dfrac{2x}{2} \leq \dfrac{10}{2}$ Divide both sides by 2.

$x \leq 5$

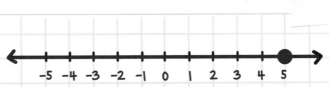

Anytime you **MULTIPLY** or **DIVIDE** by a negative number, you must reverse the direction of the inequality sign.

However, you do not need to reverse the direction of the inequality sign when you are ADDING or SUBTRACTING by a negative number. We reverse the comparison symbol because the negative number changes the comparison.

EXAMPLE: Solve for x: $-3x \le 12$

$-3x \le 12$

$$\dfrac{\boxed{-3}x}{\boxed{-3}} \ge \dfrac{12}{-3}$$

— symbol reversed

$x \ge -4$

CHECK YOUR ANSWER

Check the answer by picking any number that is greater than or equal to -4.

Test $x = -4$:   Test $x = 0$:

$-3(-4) \overset{?}{\le} 12$ $-3(0) \overset{?}{\le} 12$

$12 \overset{?}{\le} 12$ ✓ $0 \overset{?}{\le} 12$ ✓   Both answers are correct.

Inequality symbols can translate into many different phrases.

- < "less than," "fewer than"

- > "greater than," "more than"

- ≤ "less than or equal to," "at most," "no more than"

- ≥ "greater than or equal to," "at least," "no less than"

EXAMPLE: Kristina's toy store receives crates of dolls. Each crate contains 12 dolls. Kristina's store already has 26 dolls. How many boxes of dolls does Kristina have to order so that her store has at least 89 dolls?

(Write your answer to the nearest whole number.)

Let x represent the number of boxes that Kristina has to order.

Since her store needs to have at least 89 dolls, we will use the ≥ symbol:

$26 + 12x \geq 89$

$12x \geq 63$

$x \geq 5.25$

Since Kristina cannot order part of a box,
she must order at least 6 boxes.

> The answer to any inequality is an infinite set of numbers.
>
> The answer $x \geq -4$ means **ANY** number greater than
> (which can go on infinitely) or equal to -4.

1. Graph the inequality $x \leq 1$ on a number line.

2. Graph the inequality $y > -2$ on a number line.

3. Write the inequality that this number line represents, using x as your variable.

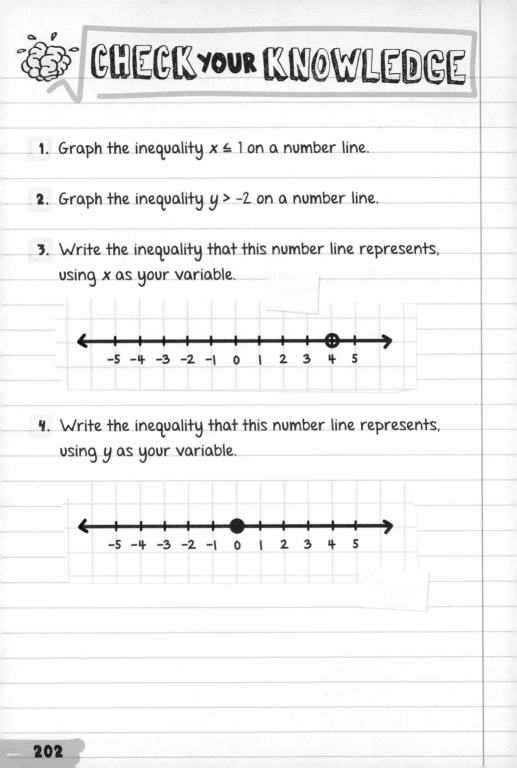

4. Write the inequality that this number line represents, using y as your variable.

For questions 5 through 9, solve and graph the inequality on a number line.

5. $4x < -12$

6. $-7x \leq -7$

7. $4x + 3 \geq -5$

8. $10x + 15 > 6x - 5$

9. $-9x + 16 \geq -5x + 28$

10. Padma sells tickets to customers for \$8 a ticket. Padma has already made \$22 in sales so far. How many tickets does Padma need to sell so that she makes at most \$300?

CHECK YOUR ANSWERS

1.

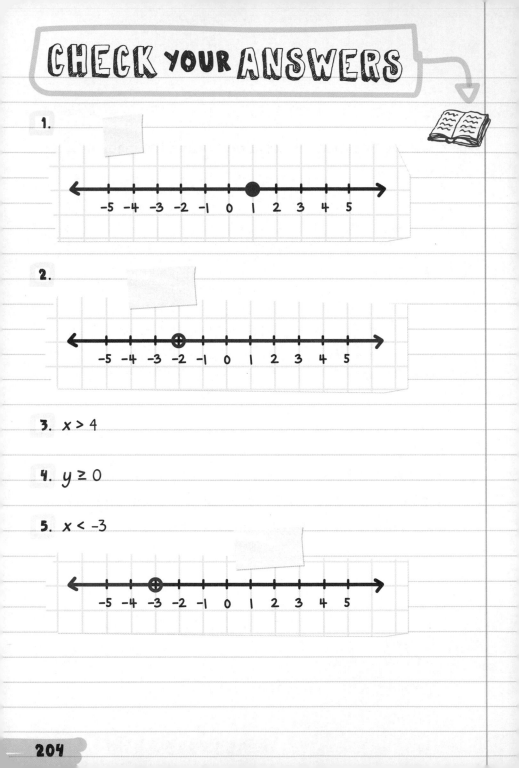

A number line from -5 to 5 with a filled dot at 1.

2.

A number line from -5 to 5 with an open dot at -2.

3. $x > 4$

4. $y \geq 0$

5. $x < -3$

A number line from -5 to 5 with an open dot at -3.

6. $x \geq 1$

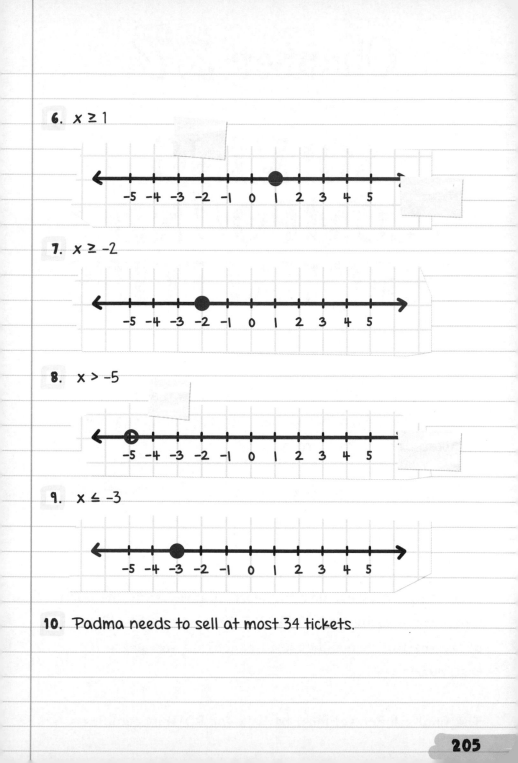

7. $x \geq -2$

8. $x > -5$

9. $x \leq -3$

10. Padma needs to sell at most 34 tickets.

Chapter 27

SOLVING COMPOUND INEQUALITIES

A COMPOUND INEQUALITY is a statement that consists of at least two distinct inequalities that are joined together by the word **and** or the word **or**.

Examples: $x < -1$ or $x \geq 3$

$x \geq 3$ and $x \leq 4$

INTERSECTION (and)

In a compound inequality the word *and* refers to the point where the inequalities INTERSECT. In other words, if we graph the two inequalities, we are looking for where they *overlap*.

The final solution set must be true for BOTH inequalities.

EXAMPLE: Using number lines, solve and graph:
$x \geq -1$ and $x \leq 4$.

Step 1: Graph each inequality on a separate number line.

$x \geq -1$:

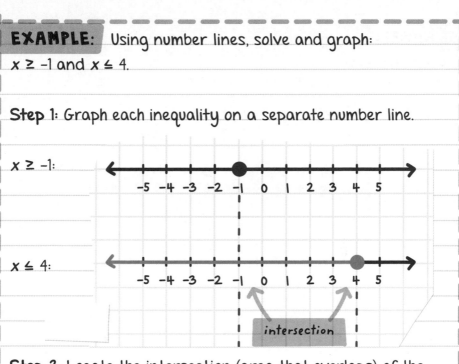

$x \leq 4$:

intersection

Step 2: Locate the intersection (area that overlaps) of the two graphs.

Based on the two graphs above, the intersection is:

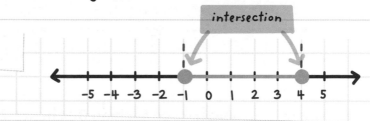

intersection

This means that any number between or including −1 and 4 satisfies BOTH inequalities.

We can write this solution set as $-1 \leq x \leq 4$.

EXAMPLE: Using number lines, solve and graph
$x > 0$ and $x \geq -3$.

Step 1: Graph each inequality on a separate number line.

$x > 0$:

$x \geq -3$:

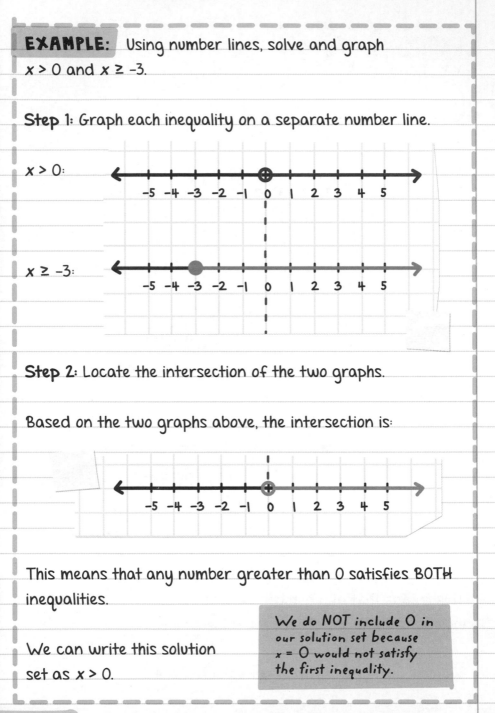

Step 2: Locate the intersection of the two graphs.

Based on the two graphs above, the intersection is:

This means that any number greater than 0 satisfies BOTH inequalities.

We can write this solution set as $x > 0$.

We do NOT include 0 in our solution set because $x = 0$ would not satisfy the first inequality.

EXAMPLE: Using number lines, solve and graph
$x > 2$ and $x < -4$.

Step 1: Graph each inequality on a separate number line.

$x > 2$:

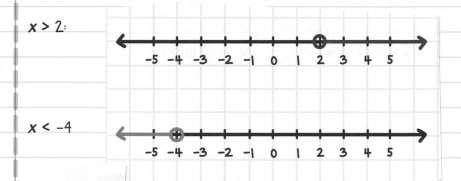

$x < -4$

Step 2: Locate the intersection of the two graphs.

Based on the two graphs above, there is no overlap.

Therefore, the solution is
no solution.

> There is no solution because
> there is no answer that is
> true for BOTH inequalities.

UNION (or)

The word *or* means that you are looking at the UNION of the inequalities.

If we graph the two inequalities, we are looking at what happens when they are put together. The final solution must be true for AT LEAST ONE of the inequalities.

EXAMPLE: Using number lines, solve and graph
$x < -2$ and $x \leq -1$.

Step 1: Graph each inequality on a separate number line.

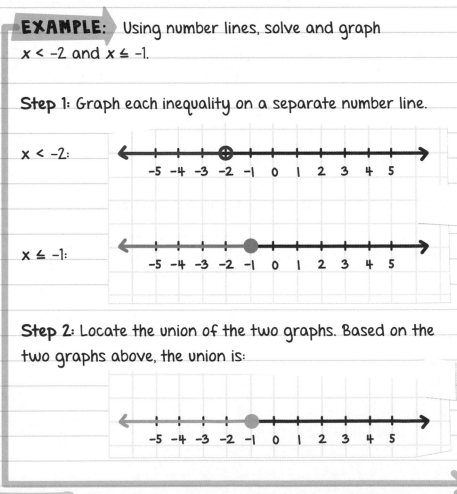

x < -2:

x ≤ -1:

Step 2: Locate the union of the two graphs. Based on the two graphs above, the union is:

This means that any number less than or equal to –1 satisfies AT LEAST ONE of the inequalities.

We can write this solution set as: $x \le -1$.

> We include -1 in our final solution because $x = -1$ satisfies at least one of the inequalities.

EXAMPLE: Using number lines, solve and graph $x > 0$ or $x < 2$.

Graph the two inequalities separately.

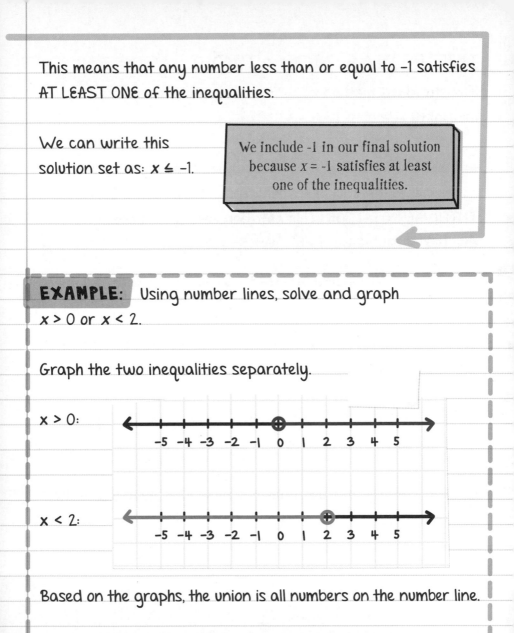

$x > 0$:

$x < 2$:

Based on the graphs, the union is all numbers on the number line.

Therefore, the solution set is: **all real numbers**.

We include all real numbers because every number satisfies at least one of the inequalities.

INTERVAL NOTATION

The standard method of writing inequalities is using inequality symbols.

Another method of writing inequalities is using brackets or parentheses instead of inequality symbols. This is called INTERVAL NOTATION. This notation tells and represents the INTERVAL of the final solution set.

the numbers between two numbers in a set

When using interval notation, do not write the variable in the answer.

1. Parentheses, ( ), are used when a number is NOT included in the solution set.

2. Brackets, [ ], are used when a number is included in the solution set.

(1, 5) represents all the numbers between 1 and 5, where 1 and 5 are NOT included.

Another way to write (1, 5): $1 < x < 5$.

[-3, 2] represents all the numbers between -3 and 2, where -3 and 2 ARE included.

Another way to write [-3, 2] is: $-3 \le x \le 2$.

$[-7, -\frac{1}{2})$ represents all the numbers between -7 and $-\frac{1}{2}$, where -7 IS included but $-\frac{1}{2}$ IS NOT included.

Another way to write $[-7, -\frac{1}{2})$ is: $-7 \le x < -\frac{1}{2}$.

EXAMPLE: Represent $2 \le x < 4$ in interval notation.

Step 1: Graph the inequality on a number line.

The inequality $2 \le x < 4$ represents all the values of x that are **greater than or equal to 2** ($2 \le x$ is the same as $x \ge 2$) AND **less than 4**.

Graphing the inequality $2 \le x < 4$ on a number line:

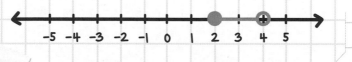

213

Step 2: Use parentheses and/or brackets to write the solution set in interval notation.

Since the solution includes the number 2, use a bracket with 2.

Since the solution does NOT include the number 4, use a parenthesis with 4.

Therefore, the inequality written in interval notation is [2, 4).

EXAMPLE: Represent $x \geq -3$ in interval notation.

Step 1: Graph the inequality on a number line.

The inequality $x \geq -3$ represents all the values of x that are greater than or equal to -3.

Graphing the inequality $x \geq -3$ on a number line:

$x \geq -3$:

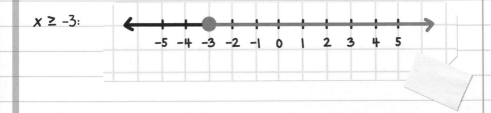

Step 2: Use parentheses and/or brackets to write the answer in interval notation.

Since the solution includes the number –3, use a bracket with –3.

We are including every number that is greater than or equal to –3, so it includes every number through infinity.

> Infinity is represented by the symbol ∞ and represents that the possible solutions get greater and greater and never end.

Use a parenthesis with infinity.

Therefore, the solution set represented in interval notation is [–3, ∞).

If your solution is: all real numbers, you can write it in interval notation as (–∞, ∞).

If the solution set to a compound inequality is no solution, use the symbol Ø in interval notation, which is the number 0 with a line through it.

For questions 1 through 3, use interval notation to represent the shaded region.

1.

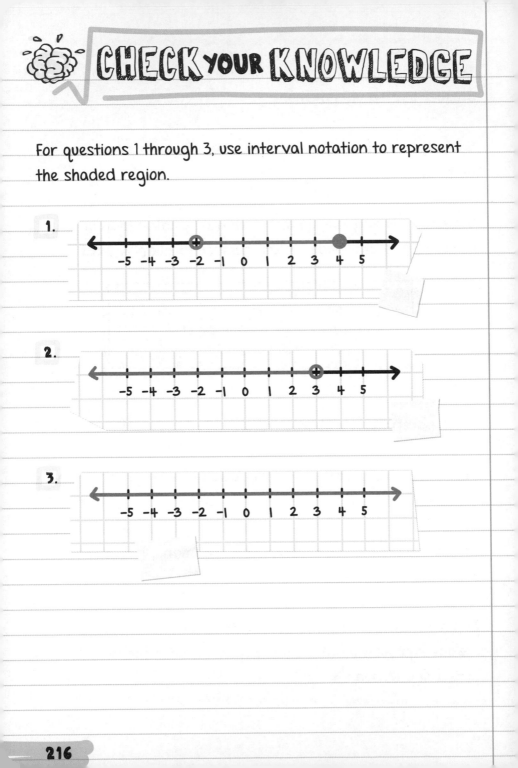

$$
\begin{array}{ccccccccccc}
& -5 & -4 & -3 & -2 & -1 & 0 & 1 & 2 & 3 & 4 & 5
\end{array}
$$

2.

$$
\begin{array}{ccccccccccc}
& -5 & -4 & -3 & -2 & -1 & 0 & 1 & 2 & 3 & 4 & 5
\end{array}
$$

3.

$$
\begin{array}{ccccccccccc}
& -5 & -4 & -3 & -2 & -1 & 0 & 1 & 2 & 3 & 4 & 5
\end{array}
$$

For questions 4 through 10, use a number line to solve and graph each compound inequality. Then write your solution set in interval notation.

4. $x < -1$ and $x \geq -5$

5. $x < 10$ or $x \leq 4$

6. $x \geq 2$ and $x < 8$

7. $x \geq -7$ or $x < 2$

8. $x \leq 1$ and $x \leq -6$

9. $x \geq 3$ and $x < -1$

10. $x > -9$ or $x < 4$

CHECK YOUR ANSWERS

1. (–2, 4]

2. (–∞, 3)

3. (–∞, ∞)

4. [–5, –1)

5. (–∞, 10)

6. [2, 8)

7. (–∞, ∞)

8. (–∞, –6]

9. ∅

10. (–∞, ∞)

Chapter 28

REWRITING FORMULAS

We can use formulas and equations to find all kinds of desired solutions. We can rewrite a formula or equation to solve for an unknown outcome or variable.

You can use inverse operations to rewrite formulas and equations.

EXAMPLE: Solve the equation $a + 8b = c$ for a.

$a + 8b$ = Represent	What is happening to the a? $8b$ is being added to a.
$a + 8b - 8b = c - 8b$	The inverse of adding $8b$ is subtracting $8b$.

$a = c - 8b$ (or $a = -8b + c$ if we write the right-hand side in alphabetical order)

EXAMPLE: Solve the equation $y = mx + b$ for x.

$y - b = mx + b - b$

$y - b = mx$

$\dfrac{y-b}{m} = \pm \boxed{\dfrac{+ mx}{- m}}$

$\dfrac{y-b}{m} = x$

$x = \dfrac{y-b}{m}$

EXAMPLE: Solve the equation $x^2 - 9 = c^2 - 5$ for x.

$x^2 - 9 + 9 = c^2 - 5 + 9$

$x^2 = c^2 + 4$ The inverse operation of squaring is square root.

$\sqrt{x^2} \pm \sqrt{c^2 + 4}$

$x = \sqrt{c^2 + 4}$

If the variable is in the denominator, multiply everything by the LCM.

EXAMPLE: Solve the equation $\dfrac{2}{x} = \dfrac{5}{3}$ for x.

Since x and 3 are in the denominators of the fractions, we can multiply all fractions by the LCM of x and 3, which is: $3x$.

$$\dfrac{2}{x} \cdot 3x = \dfrac{5}{3} \cdot 3x$$

$$6 = 5x$$

$$\dfrac{6}{5} = x \text{ or } x = \dfrac{6}{5}$$

EXAMPLE: Solve the equation $\dfrac{1}{p} + \dfrac{1}{q} = \dfrac{1}{f}$ for f.

Since f, p, and q are in the denominators, we can multiply all fractions by the LCM of p, q, and f, which is: pqf.

$$\dfrac{1}{p} \cdot pqf + \dfrac{1}{q} \cdot pqf = \dfrac{1}{f} \cdot pqf$$

$$\dfrac{1}{p} \cdot pqf + \dfrac{1}{q} \cdot pqf = \dfrac{1}{f} \cdot pqf$$

$qf + pf = pq$ Use factoring to isolate f.

$f(q + p) = pq$

$f = \dfrac{pq}{q + p}$

CHECK YOUR KNOWLEDGE

Solve each equation for the indicated variable.

1. $PV = nRT$ for V

2. $P = 2L + 2W$ for W

3. $A = P(1 + r)^t$ for P

4. $C = \dfrac{1}{2} h(a + b)$ for h

5. $C = \dfrac{1}{2} h(a + b)$ for a

6. $D = \dfrac{1}{2} at^2$ for a

7. $D = \dfrac{1}{2} at^2$ for t

8. $C = \dfrac{5}{9}(F - 32)$ for F

9. $2as = v^2 - t^2$ for v

10. $2as = v^2 - t^2$ for t

ANSWERS

1. $V = \dfrac{nRT}{P}$

2. $W = \dfrac{P-2L}{2}$ or $W = \dfrac{1}{2}P - L$

3. $P = \dfrac{A}{(1+r)^t}$

4. $h = \dfrac{2C}{a+b}$

5. $a = \dfrac{2C}{h} - b$ or $a = \dfrac{2C-bh}{h}$

6. $a = \dfrac{2D}{t^2}$

7. $t = \sqrt{\dfrac{2D}{a}}$

8. $F = \dfrac{9}{5}C + 32$ or $F = \dfrac{9C+160}{5}$

9. $v = \sqrt{2as + t^2}$

10. $t = \sqrt{v^2 - 2as}$

Chapter 29

SOLVING SYSTEMS OF LINEAR EQUATIONS BY SUBSTITUTION

We can take two linear equations and study them together. For example:

$$\begin{cases} ax + by = c \\ dx + ey = f \end{cases}$$

This pairing of equations is known as simultaneous linear equations or a SYSTEM OF LINEAR EQUATIONS (also known as a linear system).

Examples: $\begin{cases} 3x + 2y = 7 \\ 8x - 4y = -5 \end{cases}$ $\begin{cases} 3a - 9b = \dfrac{1}{2} \\ 7a - 8b = 4 \end{cases}$

SOLUTIONS OF A SYSTEM OF LINEAR EQUATIONS

A solution makes the system of linear equations true when both sides of each of the two equations are the same.

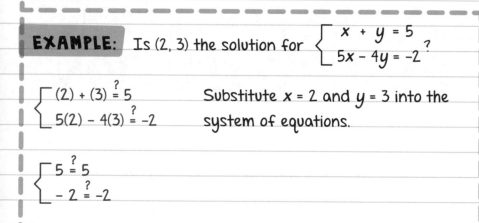

EXAMPLE: Is (2, 3) the solution for $\begin{cases} x + y = 5 \\ 5x - 4y = -2 \end{cases}$?

$$\begin{cases} (2) + (3) \overset{?}{=} 5 \\ 5(2) - 4(3) \overset{?}{=} -2 \end{cases}$$

Substitute $x = 2$ and $y = 3$ into the system of equations.

$$\begin{cases} 5 \overset{?}{=} 5 \\ -2 \overset{?}{=} -2 \end{cases}$$

Both sides of each of the two equations are the same, so the solution (2, 3) makes the system true.

THE SUBSTITUTION METHOD

To find the solution of a system of linear equations, we can solve the equations by using one of several strategies. The SUBSTITUTION METHOD is one strategy. The goal is to find the values of the variables that make both equations true.

Linear systems can be solved by SUBSTITUTING one equation into the other by following these steps:

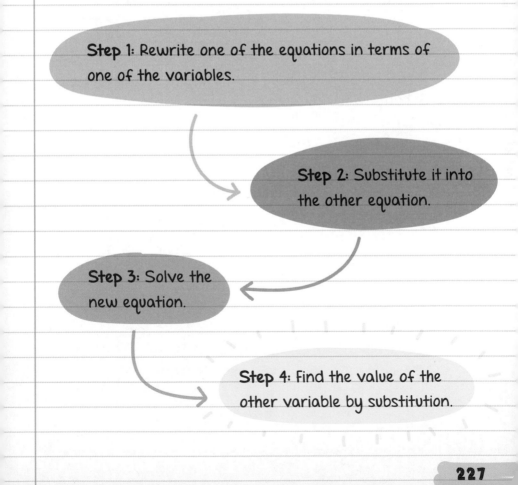

Step 1: Rewrite one of the equations in terms of one of the variables.

Step 2: Substitute it into the other equation.

Step 3: Solve the new equation.

Step 4: Find the value of the other variable by substitution.

EXAMPLE: Use the substitution method to solve the

following system: $\begin{cases} 5x + y = 11 \quad \boxed{1} \\ 2x - 3y = 1 \quad \boxed{2} \end{cases}$ ← It's helpful to number the equations to avoid confusion.

Step 1: Rewrite equation $\boxed{1}$ in terms of x. ←

$\boxed{1}$ $5x + y = 11$

$\boxed{5x} - \boxed{5x} + y = 11 - 5x$

$y = 11 - 5x$

> Look at the two equations and decide which variable in which equation is the easiest to rewrite.
>
> In this problem, it is simpler to rewrite equation $\boxed{1}$ in terms of x.

Step 2: Substitute the rewritten equation $\boxed{1}$ into equation $\boxed{2}$:

$\boxed{2}$ $2x - 3y = 1$

$2x - 3(11 - 5x) = 1$

Step 3: Solve the new equation.

$2x - 33 + 15x = 1$

$17x = 34$

$x = 2$

Step 4: Find the value of y by substitution.

Substitute $x = 2$ into equation ☐1 :

$$5(2) + y = 11$$

Since the solution makes both equations true, you can substitute this into either equation.

$$10 + y = 11$$

$$y = 1$$

Therefore, the solution to the system of equations is $(x, y) = (2, 1)$.

You can check your answer by substituting the values of the variables into both of the original equations.

EXAMPLE: Use the substitution method to solve the following system:
$$\begin{cases} -2x + 3y = 13 & ☐1 \\ x + 7y = 2 & ☐2 \end{cases}$$

Step 1: Rewrite equation ☐2 in terms of x.

☐2 $\quad x + 7y = 2$

In this problem, it is easiest to rewrite equation ☐2 in terms of x.

$$x = 2 - 7y$$

Step 2: Substitute the rewritten equation `2` into equation `1` :

`1` $-2x + 3y = 13$

   $-2(2 - 7y) + 3y = 13$

Step 3: Solve the new equation.

   $-4 + 14y + 3y = 13$

   $17y = 17$

   $y = 1$

Step 4: Find the value of x by substitution.

Substitute $y = 1$ into equation `2` :

   $x + 7(1) = 2$

   Since the solution makes both equations true, you can substitute this into either equation.

   $x + 7 = 2$

   $x = -5$

Therefore, the solution is: $(x, y) = (-5, 1)$.

Always look at the linear system first and think about which equation and which variable are simpler to isolate.

It's usually simpler to solve for the variable that has the smallest coefficient.

EXAMPLE: Use the substitution method to solve the following system: $\begin{cases} 3x - 2y = 2 & \boxed{1} \\ -5x + 4y = -6 & \boxed{2} \end{cases}$

Step 1: Rewrite equation $\boxed{1}$ in terms of x.

$\boxed{1}$ $\quad 3x - 2y = 2$

In this problem, y in equation $\boxed{1}$ has the smallest coefficient.

$-2y = 2 - 3x$

$\dfrac{\boxed{-2y}}{\boxed{-2}} = \dfrac{2 - 3x}{-2}$

$y = -\dfrac{2 - 3x}{2}$

Step 2: Substitute the rewritten equation $\boxed{1}$ into equation $\boxed{2}$:

$\boxed{2}$ $\quad -5x + 4y = -6$

$-5x + 4\left(-\dfrac{2 - 3x}{2}\right) = -6$

Step 3: Solve the new equation.

$$-5x - 2(2 - 3x) = -6$$

Don't forget to carefully distribute the negative sign.

$$-5x - 4 + 6x = -6$$

$$x = -2$$

Step 4: Find the value of y by substitution.

Substitute $x = -2$ into equation $\boxed{1}$:

$$3(-2) - 2y = 2$$

Since the solution makes both equations true, you can substitute this into either equation.

$$-6 - 2y = 2$$

$$y = -4$$

Therefore, the solution is $(x, y) = (-2, -4)$.

EXAMPLE: Adult tickets to a carnival cost $8 and child tickets cost $3. A family made up of adults and children paid $50 for 10 tickets. How many adults and how many children are in the family?

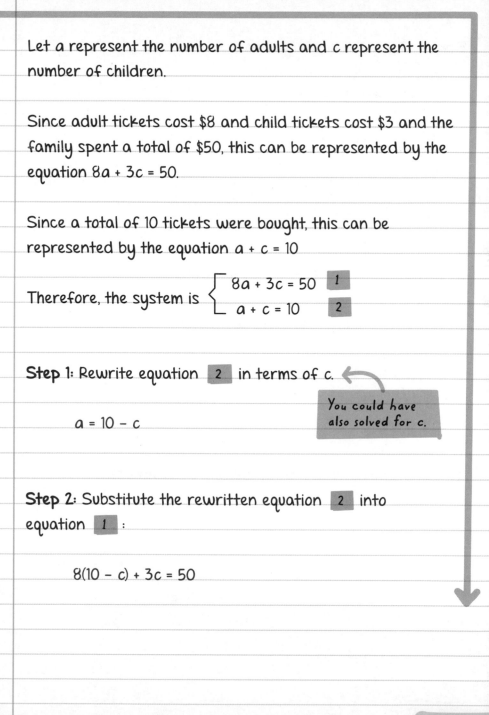

Let a represent the number of adults and c represent the number of children.

Since adult tickets cost $8 and child tickets cost $3 and the family spent a total of $50, this can be represented by the equation $8a + 3c = 50$.

Since a total of 10 tickets were bought, this can be represented by the equation $a + c = 10$

Therefore, the system is
$$\begin{cases} 8a + 3c = 50 \quad \boxed{1} \\ a + c = 10 \quad \boxed{2} \end{cases}$$

Step 1: Rewrite equation $\boxed{2}$ in terms of c. ←

$$a = 10 - c$$

You could have also solved for c.

Step 2: Substitute the rewritten equation $\boxed{2}$ into equation $\boxed{1}$:

$$8(10 - c) + 3c = 50$$

Step 3: Solve the new equation.

$$80 - 8c + 3c = 50$$

$$-5c = -30$$

$$c = 6$$

Step 4: Find the value of a by substitution.

Substitute $c = 6$ into equation ⬚2 :

$$a + (6) = 10$$

$$a = 4$$

Therefore, the solution to the system of equations is (4, 6), which tells us there are 4 adults and 6 children in this family.

CHECK YOUR KNOWLEDGE

Solve each of the linear systems using the substitution method.

1. $\begin{cases} 3x + y = 5 \\ 2x + 3y = 8 \end{cases}$

2. $\begin{cases} x + 2y = 5 \\ 4x + 5y = 8 \end{cases}$

3. $\begin{cases} 3x - y = -4 \\ 5x + 9y = -28 \end{cases}$

4. $\begin{cases} 8x - 3y = -5 \\ -2x + 5y = 14 \end{cases}$

5. $\begin{cases} 3x - 8y = -1 \\ 5x + 4y = -6 \end{cases}$

6. The total cost of purchasing 8 notebooks and 9 binders is $60. The total cost of purchasing 6 notebooks and 5 binders is $38. How much does each notebook cost? How much does each binder cost?

CHECK YOUR ANSWERS

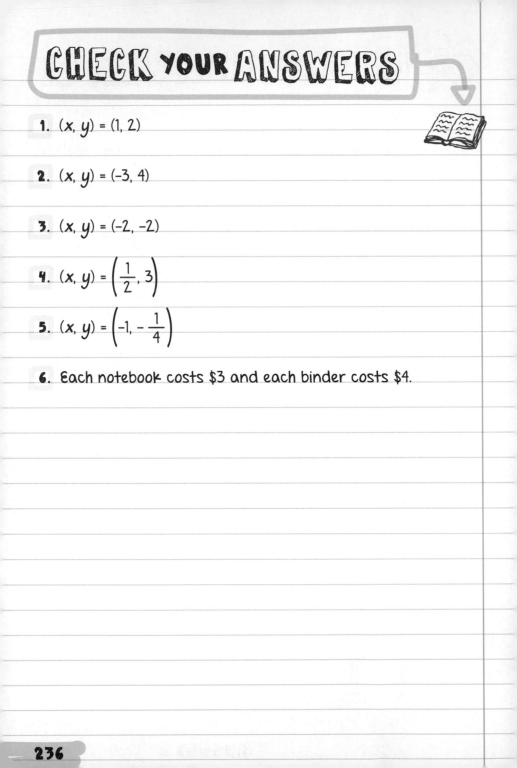

1. $(x, y) = (1, 2)$

2. $(x, y) = (-3, 4)$

3. $(x, y) = (-2, -2)$

4. $(x, y) = \left(\dfrac{1}{2}, 3\right)$

5. $(x, y) = \left(-1, -\dfrac{1}{4}\right)$

6. Each notebook costs \$3 and each binder costs \$4.

Chapter 30

SOLVING SYSTEMS OF LINEAR EQUATIONS BY ELIMINATION

One of the methods used to solve a system of linear equations is substitution. There is another method for solving systems of linear equations called ELIMINATION. When we eliminate something, we remove it.

THE ELIMINATION METHOD

Linear systems can be solved by eliminating one variable from all the equations by adding opposite values.

The elimination method follows these steps:

Note: Make sure both equations are set in standard form before beginning.

Step 1: Choose a variable to eliminate from both equations.

Step 2: Multiply ALL the terms of one equation by a constant, and then multiply ALL the terms of the other equation by another constant, so that when they are added together, a variable will be eliminated. Sometimes you only have to multiply one equation by a constant.

Step 3: Add the two equations and solve.

Step 4: Use substitution to find the value of the other variable.

Once the solution is found, it should be substituted into both equations to confirm that it is the correct solution.

EXAMPLE: Use the elimination method to solve the

following system: $\begin{cases} 2x + y = 5 & \boxed{1} \\ 3x - 2y = -3 & \boxed{2} \end{cases}$

Step 1: Choose to eliminate y.

Step 2: Multiply equation $\boxed{1}$ by 2, so that when the two equations are added together, y will be eliminated.

> y is easier to eliminate because you only have to multiply one of the equations by a constant.
>
> If you chose to eliminate x, you would have to multiply both equations by constants.

Equation $\boxed{1}$ × 2: $4x + 2y = 10$

Step 3: Add the two equations.

Adding the two equations $\left\{ \begin{array}{l} 4x + 2y = 10 \\ 3x - 2y = -3 \end{array} \right.$:

$$(4x + 3x) + (\boxed{2y} + \boxed{-2y}) = (10 + (-3))$$

$$7x = 7$$

$$x = 1$$

Step 4: Use substitution to solve for y:

Substitute $x = 1$ into equation $\boxed{1}$:

$$2(1) + y = 5$$

Since the solution makes both equations true, you can substitute $x = 1$ into either equation.

$$2 + y = 5$$

$$y = 3$$

Therefore, the solution to the system of equations is:
$(x, y) = (1, 3)$.

EXAMPLE: Use the elimination method to solve the

following system: $\begin{cases} 5x + 4y = 7 & \boxed{1} \\ 3x + y = 7 & \boxed{2} \end{cases}$

Step 1: Choose to eliminate y.

Step 2: Multiply equation $\boxed{2}$ by -4, so that when the two equations are added together, y will be eliminated.

Equation $\boxed{2}$ x (-4): $-12x + -4y = -28$

Step 3: Add the two equations.

Adding the two equations $\begin{cases} 5x + 4y = 7 \\ -12x - 4y = -28 \end{cases}$:

$$(5x + -12x) + (\boxed{4y} + \boxed{-4y}) = (7 + -28)$$

$$-7x = -21$$

$$x = 3$$

Step 4: Use substitution to solve for y:

Substitute $x = 3$ into equation $\boxed{2}$:

$$3(3) + y = 7$$

> This method is also called the
> **ADDITION METHOD** because we're
> adding one equation to the other.

$$9 + y = 7$$

$$y = -2$$

Therefore, the answer is: $(x, y) = (3, -2)$

> A system of equations can also have **infinite solutions**,
> for example, $(4x - 2y = 1$ and $-12x + 6y = -3)$,
> where there is an infinite number of coordinates that would be
> solutions to both equations.
>
> or **no solutions**, for example, $(5x + 3y = 7$ and $-10x - 6y = -20)$
> where there are no coordinates that would be
> solutions to both equations.

Multiplying Both Variables by a Constant

Instead of multiplying only one equation by a constant, sometimes we need to multiply both equations by constants.

To find out what constants to pick, first find the least common multiple (LCM) of the x-values (or the y-values) and multiply each equation accordingly.

EXAMPLE: Use the elimination method to solve the

following system: $\begin{cases} 2x + 5y = 3 & \boxed{1} \\ 3x + 4y = 1 & \boxed{2} \end{cases}$

Step 1: Choose to eliminate x.

Step 2: Multiply equation $\boxed{1}$ by 3 and multiply equation $\boxed{2}$ by –2, so that when the two equations are added together, x will be eliminated.

> x is easier to eliminate because the LCM of the x-values is $6x$, whereas the LCM of the y-values is $20y$.

Equation $\boxed{1}$ × 3: $6x + 15y = 9$

Equation $\boxed{2}$ × (–2): $-6x - 8y = -2$

Step 3: Add the two equations.

Adding the two equations $\begin{cases} 6x + 15y = 9 \\ -6x - 8y = -2 \end{cases}$:

$(\boxed{6x} - \boxed{6x}) + (15y - 8y) = 9 - 2$

$7y = 7$

$y = 1$

Step 4: Use substitution to solve for x:

Substitute $y = 1$ into equation $\boxed{2}$:

> Since the solution makes both equations true, you can substitute this into either equation.

$$3x + 4(1) = 1$$

$$3x + 4 = 1$$

$$x = -1$$

Therefore, the solution is $(x, y) = (-1, 1)$

EXAMPLE: Use the elimination method to solve the

following system: $\begin{cases} 8x + 6y = -4 \quad \boxed{1} \\ 10x + 9y = -11 \quad \boxed{2} \end{cases}$

Step 1: Choose to eliminate y.

Step 2: Multiply equation $\boxed{1}$ by 3 and multiply equation $\boxed{2}$ by -2, so that when the two equations are added together, y will be eliminated.

> y is simpler to eliminate because the LCM of the y-values is $18y$, whereas the LCM of the x-values is $40x$.

Equation $\boxed{1}$ × 3: $24x + 18y = -12$

Equation 2 x (–2): –20x – 18y = 22

Step 3: Add the two equations.

Adding the two equations $\begin{cases} 24x + 18y = -12 \\ -20x - 18y = 22 \end{cases}$:

$(24x + -20x) + (\boxed{18y} + \boxed{-18y}) = (-12 + 22)$

$4x = 10$

$x = \dfrac{5}{2}$

Step 4: Use substitution to solve for y:

Substitute $x = \dfrac{5}{2}$ into equation 1 :

$8\left(\dfrac{5}{2}\right) + 6y = -4$

$20 + 6y = -4$

$6y = -24$

$y = -4$

Therefore, the answer is: $(x, y) = \left(\dfrac{5}{2}, -4\right)$

Use the elimination method to solve each of the following systems of equations.

1. $\begin{cases} x - 2y = 1 \\ 4x - 7y = 5 \end{cases}$

2. $\begin{cases} 2x + y = 8 \\ -3x - 4y = -7 \end{cases}$

3. $\begin{cases} 6x + 2y = 24 \\ 4x - 5y = 16 \end{cases}$

4. $\begin{cases} 5x + 4y = -13 \\ 3x - 2y = 23 \end{cases}$

5. $\begin{cases} 8x + 3y = 14 \\ 6x - y = -9 \end{cases}$

6. $\begin{cases} 2x + y = \dfrac{11}{4} \\ x + 8y = -\dfrac{1}{2} \end{cases}$

CHECK YOUR ANSWERS

1. $(x, y) = (3, 1)$

2. $(x, y) = (5, -2)$

3. $(x, y) = (4, 0)$

4. $(x, y) = (3, -7)$

5. $(x, y) = \left(-\dfrac{1}{2}, 6\right)$

6. $(x, y) = \left(\dfrac{3}{2}, -\dfrac{1}{4}\right)$

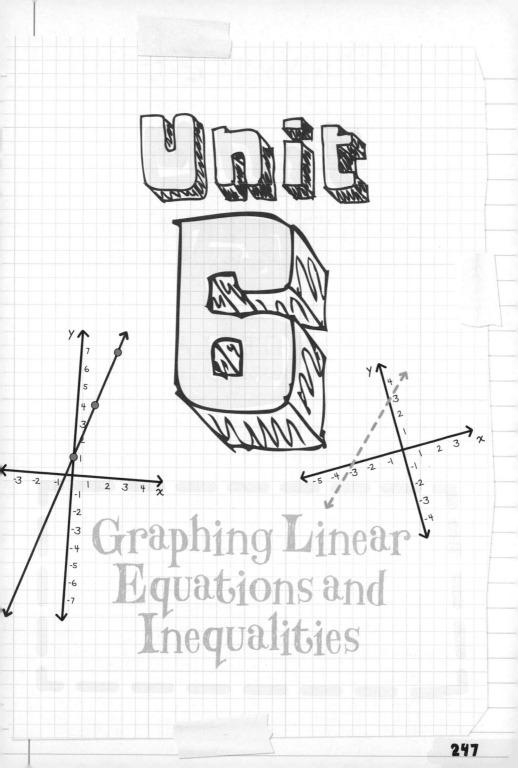

Unit 6

Graphing Linear Equations and Inequalities

Chapter 31

POINTS AND LINES

THE COORDINATE PLANE

A COORDINATE PLANE is a flat surface formed by the intersection of two lines or AXES. The horizontal line is called the X-AXIS, and the vertical line is called the Y-AXIS. The x- and y-axes intersect (cross) at the ORIGIN.

An ORDERED PAIR gives the coordinates (exact location) of a POINT. The x-coordinate always comes first, then the y-coordinate (x, y).

The x- and y-coordinates are separated by a comma and surrounded by parentheses.

For example, the x-coordinate of the origin is 0, and the y-coordinate of the origin is also 0. So, the ordered pair of the origin is (0, 0).

When plotting an ordered pair, start at the origin.

Then:

For the x-coordinate:
   If the x-coordinate is POSITIVE, move RIGHT from the origin.

   If the x-coordinate is NEGATIVE, move LEFT from the origin.

   If the x-coordinate is ZERO, STAY at the origin.

For the y-coordinate:
   If the y-coordinate is POSITIVE, move UP from the location.

   If the y-coordinate is NEGATIVE, move DOWN from the location.

   If the y-coordinate is ZERO, STAY at the location.

Plot the point (3, 4).

For the x-coordinate: start at the origin and move 3 units to the right on the x-axis.

For the y-coordinate: Move 4 units up on the y-axis.

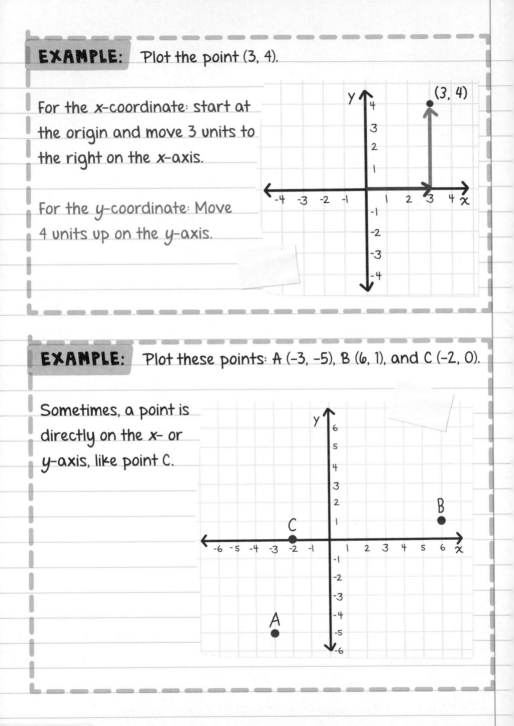

EXAMPLE: Plot these points: A (–3, –5), B (6, 1), and C (–2, 0).

Sometimes, a point is directly on the x- or y-axis, like point C.

The coordinate plane is divided into four QUADRANTS.

QUADRANT II
All x-values are
negative ($x < 0$),
and all y-values
are positive ($y > 0$).
($-x$, $+y$)

QUADRANT I
All x-values are
positive ($x > 0$),
and all y-values
are positive ($y > 0$).
($+x$, $+y$)

QUADRANT III
All x-values are
negative ($x < 0$),
and all y-values
are negative ($y < 0$).
($-x$, $-y$)

QUADRANT IV
All x-values are
positive ($x > 0$),
and all y-values are
negative ($y < 0$).
($+x$, $-y$)

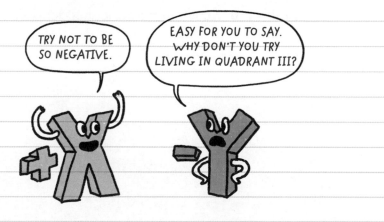

TRY NOT TO BE SO NEGATIVE.

EASY FOR YOU TO SAY. WHY DON'T YOU TRY LIVING IN QUADRANT III?

DOMAIN AND RANGE

A **RELATION** is a set of ordered pairs.

In a relation, the set of all the x-coordinates is called the **DOMAIN** and the set of all the y-coordinates is called the **RANGE**.

Whenever we write a set, we always use BRACES { }:

> Sometimes people call these curly brackets.

List the values of the domain and range in numerical order.

For example, name the domain and range for the relation: {(-5, 1), (-2, 0), (1, -1), (4, -2), (7, -3)}.

DOMAIN: list all the x-values in numerical order: {-5, -2, 1, 4, 7}

RANGE: list all the y-values in numerical order: {-3, -2, -1, 0, 1}

CHECK YOUR KNOWLEDGE

1. In which quadrant is (–3, –7) located?

2. In which quadrant is (1, –2) located?

3. In which quadrant is (8, 4) located?

For questions 4 and 5 use the coordinate grid below.

4. What are the coordinates of point A?

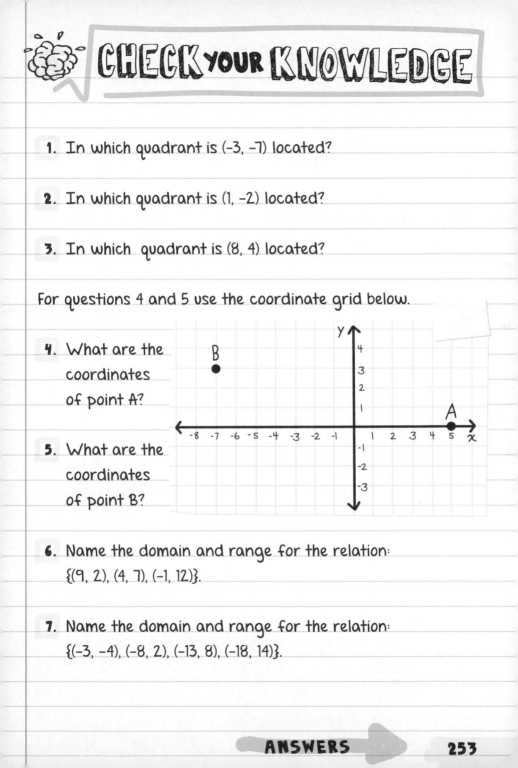

5. What are the coordinates of point B?

6. Name the domain and range for the relation: {(9, 2), (4, 7), (–1, 12)}.

7. Name the domain and range for the relation: {(–3, –4), (–8, 2), (–13, 8), (–18, 14)}.

ANSWERS

CHECK YOUR ANSWERS

1. quadrant III

2. quadrant IV

3. quadrant I

4. (5, 0)

5. (–7, 3)

6. domain {–1, 4, 9}; range {2, 7, 12}

7. domain {–18, –13, –8, –3}; range {–4, 2, 8, 14}

Chapter 32

GRAPHING A LINE FROM A TABLE OF VALUES

A line can be created by connecting multiple ordered pairs, or coordinates plotted on a coordinate plane. A line continues forever in both directions, and we indicate this by drawing arrows at each end.

A **TABLE OF VALUES** is a list of values that form a relation. When the coordinates are plotted on a coordinate plane and connected, they form a line.

x	y	
-2	-3	← forms the coordinates (-2, -3)
0	1	
2	5	

The relation formed by this table of values: {(-2, -3), (0, 1), (2, 5)}.

Graph the line formed by the table of values.

x	y
0	1
1	4
2	7

Step 1: Use the values in the table to write the coordinates of each point.

{(0, 1), (1, 4), and (2, 7)}

Step 2: Plot each point on a coordinate plane.

Step 3: Use a ruler or straightedge to draw a line that connects all the points.

EXAMPLE: Graph the line formed by the table of values.

x	y
–4	3
–2	3
4	3
6	3

Step 1: Use the values in the table to write the coordinates of each point.

{(–4, 3), (–2, 3), (4, 3), and (6, 3)}

Step 2: Plot each point on a coordinate plane.

Step 3: Draw a line that connects all the points.

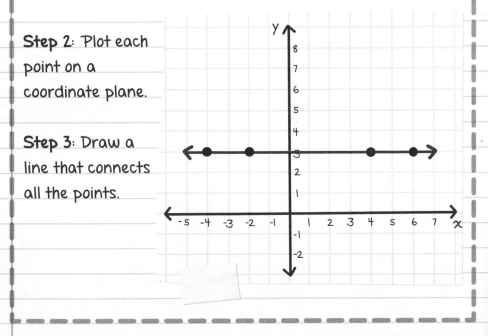

CHECK YOUR KNOWLEDGE

For questions 1 through 4, graph the line formed by each table.

1.

x	y
0	2
1	5
2	8

2.

x	y
2	4
4	-1
6	-6

3.

x	y
-2	-3
-2	2
-2	8

4.

x	y
−6	5
−3	1
0	−3
3	−7

5. Plot each of the points on a coordinate plane. Do the points form a line?

x	y
−5	−4
−3	−1
−1	2
1	5
3	6

1.

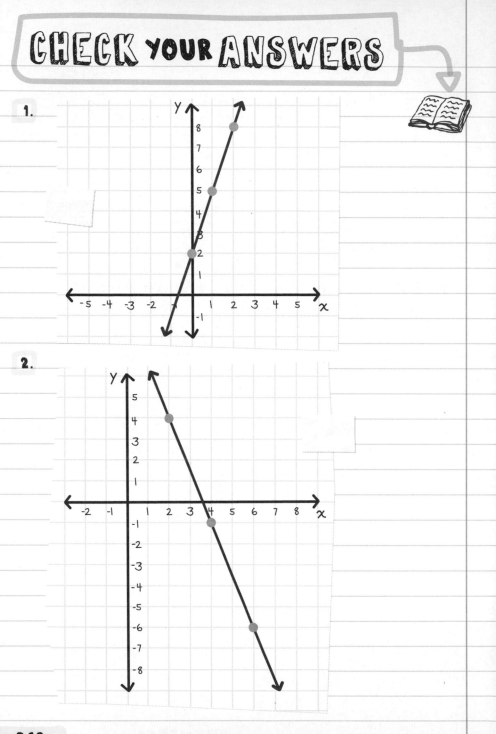

2.

3.

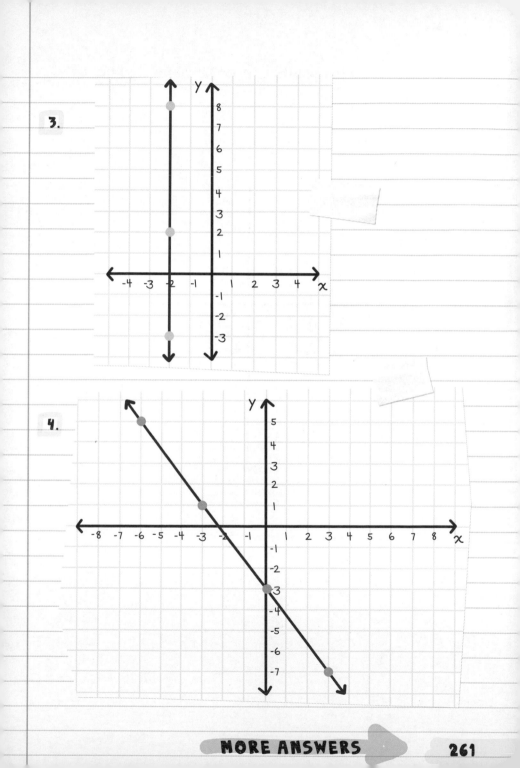

4.

5. No, because all the points cannot be connected by a straight line.

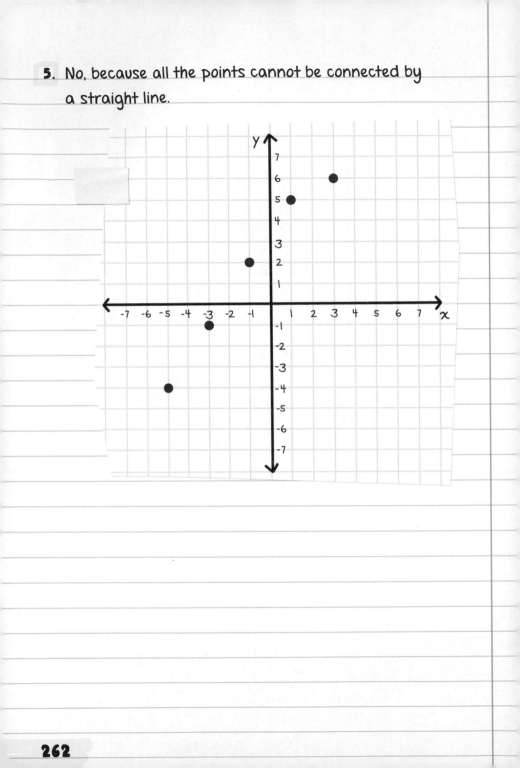

Chapter 33

SLOPE

SLOPE is generally referred to as the *steepness* of a line. More specifically, slope is a number that is a ratio describing the tilt of a line. Slope is calculated by finding the ratio of the vertical change (*rise*) to the horizontal change (*run*).

$\updownarrow$ RISE is how much a line goes up or down.

$$\text{SLOPE} = \frac{\text{RISE}}{\text{RUN}}$$

$\leftrightarrow$ RUN is how much a line moves left or right.

For example, a line has a slope of $\frac{2}{3}$. Since the formula for slope $= \frac{\text{rise}}{\text{run}}$, this means that the rise is 2 and the run is 3.

Since the rise is represented by a positive number, it means that the line is "rising vertically" or "going up."

Since the run is represented by a positive number, it means that the line is "running horizontally" or "going to the right."

If we start at the point (–5, –5) and plot a line with a slope of $\frac{2}{3}$, we get the graph below.

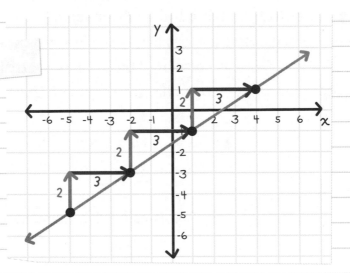

A slope of $\frac{2}{3}$ means that every time the line rises 2, it also runs 3.

Since the slope is a ratio, it can be expressed as various ratios of numbers.

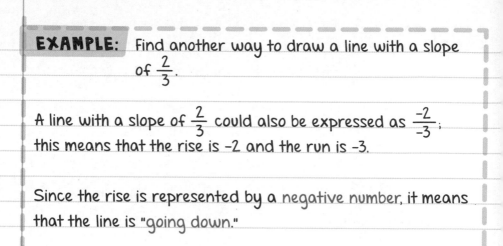

EXAMPLE: Find another way to draw a line with a slope of $\frac{2}{3}$.

A line with a slope of $\frac{2}{3}$ could also be expressed as $\frac{-2}{-3}$; this means that the rise is -2 and the run is -3.

Since the rise is represented by a negative number, it means that the line is "going down."

Since the run is represented by a negative number, it means that the line is "going left."

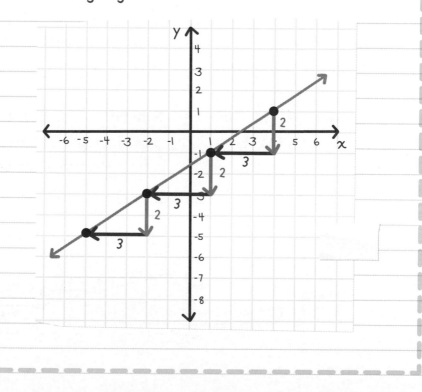

EXAMPLE: Find two ways to draw a line with a slope of $-\frac{1}{4}$ that passes through the coordinate (-2, -1).

The slope could be expressed as $\frac{-1}{4}$.

OR

The slope could be expressed as $\frac{1}{-4}$.

This means that the rise is -1 and the run is 4.

This means that the rise is 1 and the run is -4.

A negative number means that the line is "going down."

A positive number means that the line is "going up."

A positive number means that the line is "going right."

A negative number means that the line is "going left."

Starting at (-2, -1) we can plot other points that are on the same line by "rising -1" and "running 4":

Starting at (-2, -1) we can plot other points that are on the same line by "rising 1" and "running -4":

There are four types of slope:

1. A line that has a POSITIVE SLOPE rises from left to right.

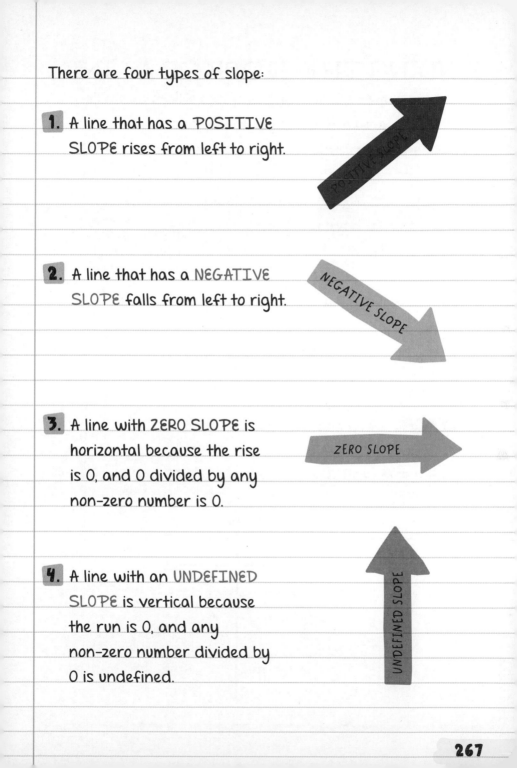

POSITIVE SLOPE

2. A line that has a NEGATIVE SLOPE falls from left to right.

NEGATIVE SLOPE

3. A line with ZERO SLOPE is horizontal because the rise is 0, and 0 divided by any non-zero number is 0.

ZERO SLOPE

4. A line with an UNDEFINED SLOPE is vertical because the run is 0, and any non-zero number divided by 0 is undefined.

UNDEFINED SLOPE

FINDING THE SLOPE OF A LINE

To find the slope of a line, pick any two points on the line. Starting at the point farthest to the left, draw a right triangle (one right angle that measures exactly 90°) that connects the two points and uses the line as the hypotenuse. How many units did you go up or down? That is your rise. How many units did you go left or right? That is your run.

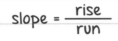

the longest side of a right triangle

Find the slope by using the slope formula:

$$\text{slope} = \frac{\text{rise}}{\text{run}}$$

EXAMPLE: Determine the slope of the line.

From point A to point B, the line has a rise of 3 and a run of 6.

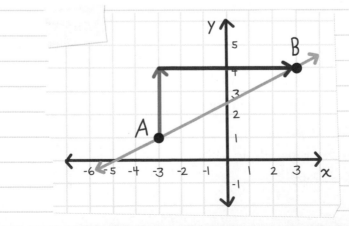

Therefore, the slope is: $\dfrac{\text{rise}}{\text{run}} = \dfrac{3}{6} = \dfrac{1}{2}$

(A slope of $\dfrac{1}{2}$ means that every time the line rises 1, it also runs 2.)

EXAMPLE: Determine the slope of the line that connects the points A (1, 2) and B (3, 1).

Step 1: Plot the two points on a coordinate plane and draw the line that connects the points.

Step 2: Starting with the point that is farthest to the left, draw a right triangle and calculate the rise and run.

Point A is farthest to the left.

From point A to point B, the line has a rise of -1 and a run of 2.

Step 3: Use the rise and run to calculate the slope.

Slope is: $\dfrac{\text{rise}}{\text{run}} = \dfrac{-1}{2} = -\dfrac{1}{2}$.

The slope is $-\dfrac{1}{2}$ everywhere on the line.
Anytime you rise -1 and run 2, you'll be back on the line.

There is a formula for slope that you can use when you know two points on a line. The two points are represented as (x_1, y_1) and (x_2, y_2). The notation $_1$ tells us it is the first x and y coordinate.

This is read as "y sub 1."

This is read as "x sub 1."

$$\text{slope} = \frac{\text{the change in } y}{\text{the change in } x}$$

or

$$m = \frac{y_2 - y_1}{x_2 - x_1}$$

This variable means slope.

EXAMPLE: Find the slope of the line that goes through the points (2, 5) and (3, 9).

Step 1: Find the values of x_1, y_1, x_2, and y_2.

The points are (2, 5) and (3, 9), so $(x_1, y_1) = (2, 5)$ and $(x_2, y_2) = (3, 9)$.

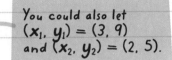

You could also let $(x_1, y_1) = (3, 9)$ and $(x_2, y_2) = (2, 5)$.

Step 2: Substitute the values into the slope formula:

$$m = \frac{y_2 - y_1}{x_2 - x_1}$$

$$= \frac{9 - 5}{3 - 2} = \frac{4}{1} = 4$$

This answer appears correct because a line that RISES from left to right has a POSITIVE slope.

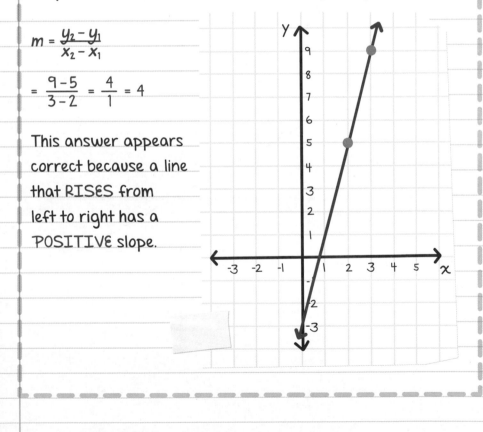

EXAMPLE: Determine the slope of the line that goes through the points (–5, 3) and (4, –2).

Step 1: Find the values of x_1, y_1, x_2, and y_2.

Since the points are (–5, 3) and (4, –2), (x_1, y_1) = (–5, 3) and (x_2, y_2) = (4, –2).

Step 2: Substitute the values into the slope formula:

$$m = \frac{y_2 - y_1}{x_2 - x_1}$$

$$= \frac{-2 - 3}{4 - (-5)} = \frac{-5}{9} = -\frac{5}{9}$$

This answer appears correct because a line that FALLS from left to right has a NEGATIVE slope

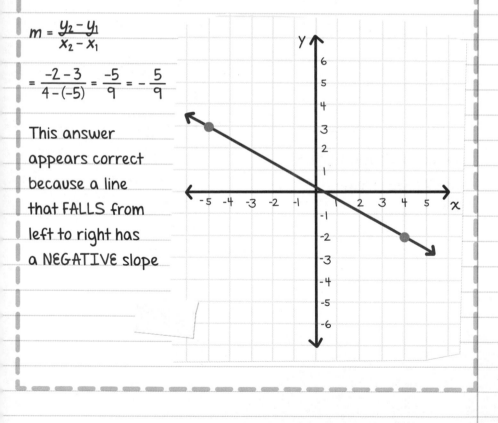

For questions 1 through 3 label the slope as positive, negative, zero, or undefined.

1.

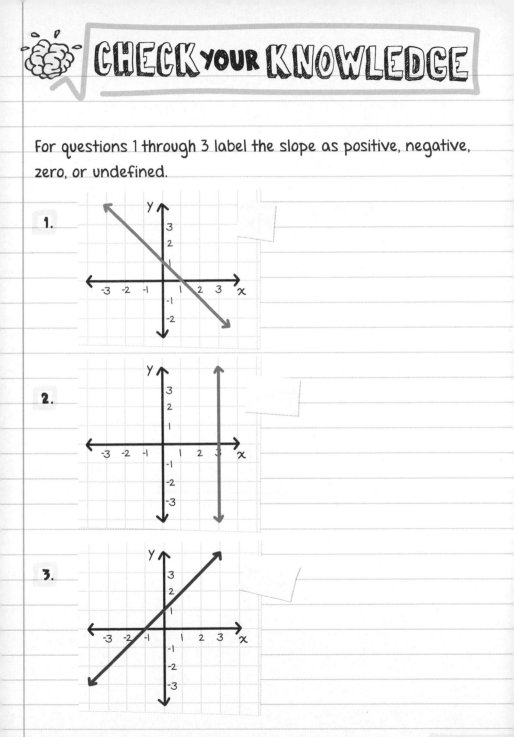

2.

3.

4. Find the slope of the line.

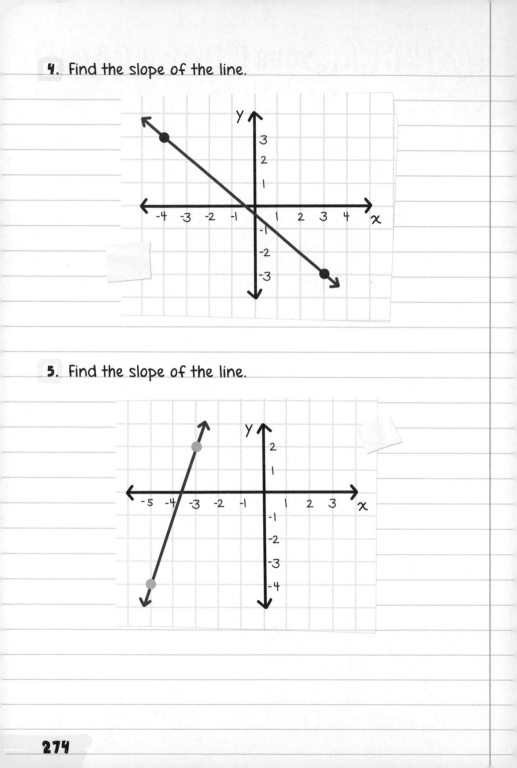

5. Find the slope of the line.

6. Use a slope triangle to find the slope of the line below.

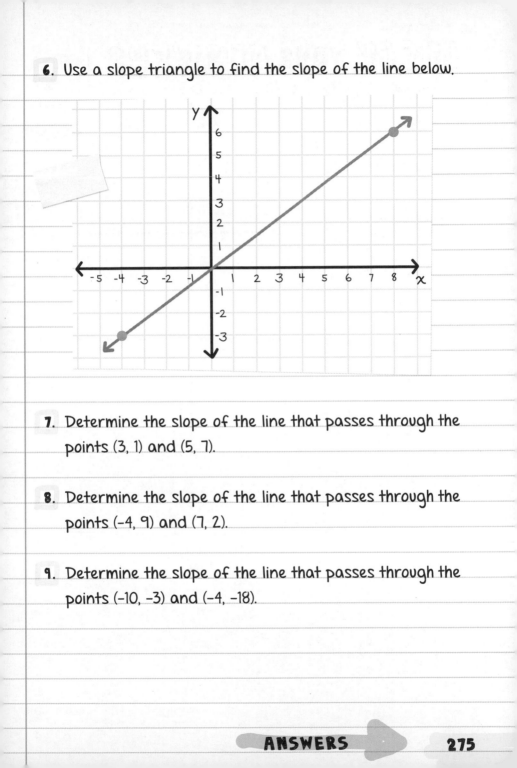

7. Determine the slope of the line that passes through the points (3, 1) and (5, 7).

8. Determine the slope of the line that passes through the points (−4, 9) and (7, 2).

9. Determine the slope of the line that passes through the points (−10, −3) and (−4, −18).

ANSWERS

1. negative

2. undefined

3. positive

4. slope = $-\dfrac{6}{7}$

5. slope = $\dfrac{6}{2}$ = 3

6. slope = $\dfrac{9}{12}$ = $\dfrac{3}{4}$

7. $m = \dfrac{7-1}{5-3} = \dfrac{6}{2} = 3$

8. $m = \dfrac{2-9}{7-(-4)} = \dfrac{-7}{11} = -\dfrac{7}{11}$

9. $m = \dfrac{-18-(-3)}{-4-(-10)} = \dfrac{-15}{6} = -\dfrac{5}{2}$

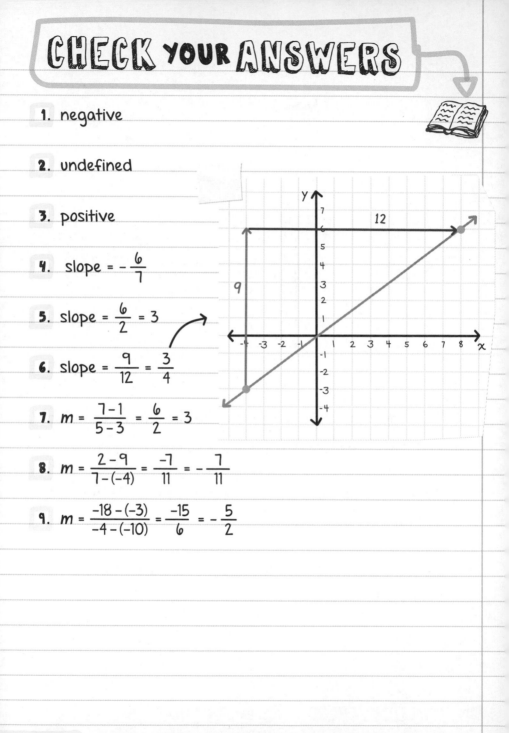

Chapter 34

SLOPE-INTERCEPT FORM

x- AND y-INTERCEPTS

An **INTERCEPT** is a point where a graph crosses either the x-axis or the y-axis.

The y-intercept is where a graph intersects the y-axis.

Since it crosses the y-axis, the x-value there is always 0.

The x-intercept is where a graph intersects the x-axis.

Since it crosses the x-axis, the y-value there is always 0.

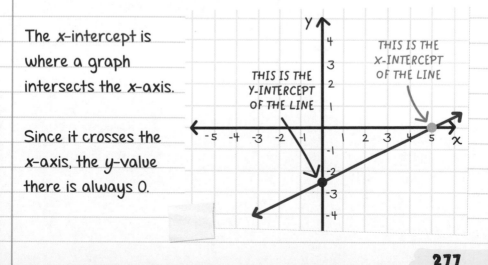

THIS IS THE X-INTERCEPT OF THE LINE

THIS IS THE Y-INTERCEPT OF THE LINE

An intercept can be expressed either as a single number or a coordinate.

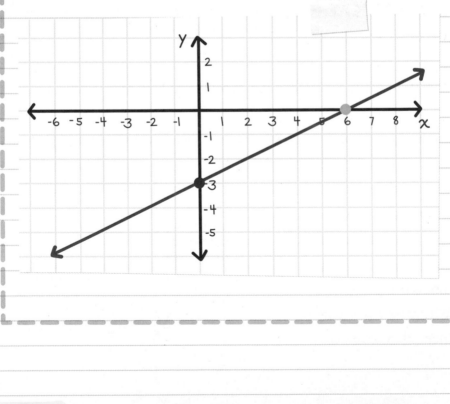

WRITING EQUATIONS IN SLOPE-INTERCEPT FORM

The equation of a line can be written in many ways. One of the ways is the SLOPE-INTERCEPT FORM:

slope

y-intercept

$$y = mx + b$$

For example, if a line has a slope of 7 and a y-intercept of –4, the equation can be written in slope-intercept form as:

$y = mx + b$

$y = 7x + (–4)$

$y = 7x – 4$ ← slope-intercept form

Graph the line that has a slope of $\frac{3}{2}$ and has a y-intercept of –1. Then find the equation of the line and write it in slope-intercept form.

Step 1: Plot the y-intercept.

Since the line has a y-intercept of –1, the coordinates of the y-intercept are: (0, –1).

Step 2: Use the RISE and RUN of the slope to find the location of the next point.

The formula of slope is $m = \dfrac{rise}{run}$.

This means that rise = 3 and run = 2.

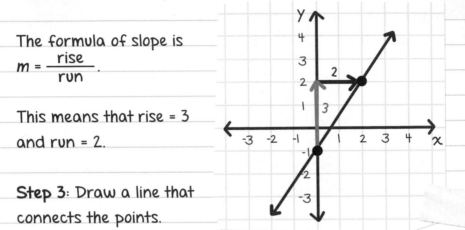

Step 3: Draw a line that connects the points.

Step 4: Use the value of the y-intercept and the slope to write the equation of the line.

Since the formula of the slope-intercept form is $y = mx + b$, the equation is $y = \dfrac{3}{2}x - 1$.

EXAMPLE: Graph the line $y = 3x - 4$.

Step 1: Identify the slope and the y-intercept.

Since the line is in slope-intercept form, the slope, m, is 3 or $\dfrac{3}{1}$ and the y-intercept, b, is –4.

Step 2: Plot the y-intercept.

Since the line has a y-intercept of –4, the coordinates of the y-intercept are (0, –4).

Step 3: Use the rise and run of the slope to find the location of the next point.

The formula for slope is
$$m = \frac{\text{rise}}{\text{run}}.$$

Rise = 3 and run = 1.

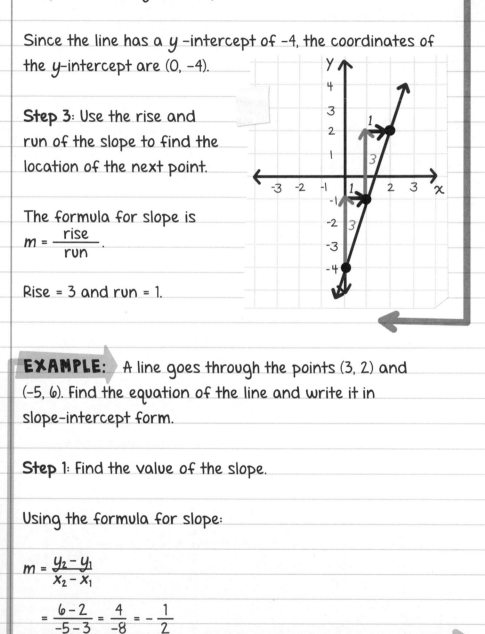

EXAMPLE: A line goes through the points (3, 2) and (–5, 6). Find the equation of the line and write it in slope-intercept form.

Step 1: Find the value of the slope.

Using the formula for slope:

$$m = \frac{y_2 - y_1}{x_2 - x_1}$$

$$= \frac{6 - 2}{-5 - 3} = \frac{4}{-8} = -\frac{1}{2}$$

Step 2: Substitute this slope value into the slope-intercept form.

Slope-intercept form: $y = mx + b$

$$y = \left(-\frac{1}{2}\right)x + b \text{ or } y = -\frac{1}{2}x + b$$

Step 3: Find the value of the y-intercept by substituting one of the points into the equation.

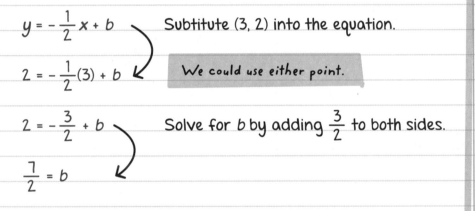

$y = -\frac{1}{2}x + b$ ⟩ Subtitute (3, 2) into the equation.

$2 = -\frac{1}{2}(3) + b$ ↙ We could use either point.

$2 = -\frac{3}{2} + b$ ⟩ Solve for b by adding $\frac{3}{2}$ to both sides.

$\frac{7}{2} = b$ ↙

Step 4: Use the value of the slope and the y-intercept to write the equation of the line.

Since the value of the slope is $m = -\frac{1}{2}$ and the value of the y-intercept is $b = \frac{7}{2}$, the equation is: $y = -\frac{1}{2}x + \frac{7}{2}$. ⟸

EXAMPLE: Find the coordinates of the x-intercept and the y-intercept of $y = \frac{2}{3}x - \frac{8}{3}$.

Step 1: Find the y-intercept.

Since the equation is in slope-intercept form, the y-intercept is $b = -\frac{8}{3}$.

Therefore, the coordinates of the y-intercept are $\left(0, -\frac{8}{3}\right)$.

Step 2: Find the x-intercept.

Since the x-intercept is where the line intersects the x-axis, the y-value is 0.

$y = \frac{2}{3}x - \frac{8}{3}$ ⟩ Substitute 0 for y.

$0 = \frac{2}{3}x - \frac{8}{3}$

$\frac{8}{3} = \frac{2}{3}x$

$4 = x$ or $x = 4$

Therefore, the coordinates of the x-intercept are (4, 0).

1. What is the slope and y-intercept of $y = 2x - 9$?

2. What is the slope and y-intercept of $y = \frac{7}{3}x + \frac{11}{8}$?

3. Draw a line that has a slope of 4 and a y-intercept of –3.

4. Draw a line that has a slope of $-\frac{3}{4}$ and a y-intercept of 2.

5. Draw a line that has a slope of $\frac{1}{2}$ and a y-intercept of $-\frac{3}{2}$.

6. A line passes through the points (3, 3) and (1, 10). Find the equation of the line and write it in slope-intercept form.

7. A line passes through the points (7, –8) and (–1, –5). Find the equation of the line and write it in slope-intercept form.

8. A line passes through the points $\left(\frac{1}{2}, -6\right)$ and $(1, -9)$. Find the equation of the line and write it in slope-intercept form.

9. Find the x-intercept and y-intercept of $y = \frac{1}{5}x - \frac{3}{5}$.

10. Find the x-intercept and y-intercept of $y = -2x - 3$.

CHECK YOUR ANSWERS

1. Slope = 2, y-intercept = -9 or (0, -9)

2. Slope = $\frac{7}{3}$, y-intercept = $\frac{11}{8}$ or $\left(0, \frac{11}{8}\right)$

3.

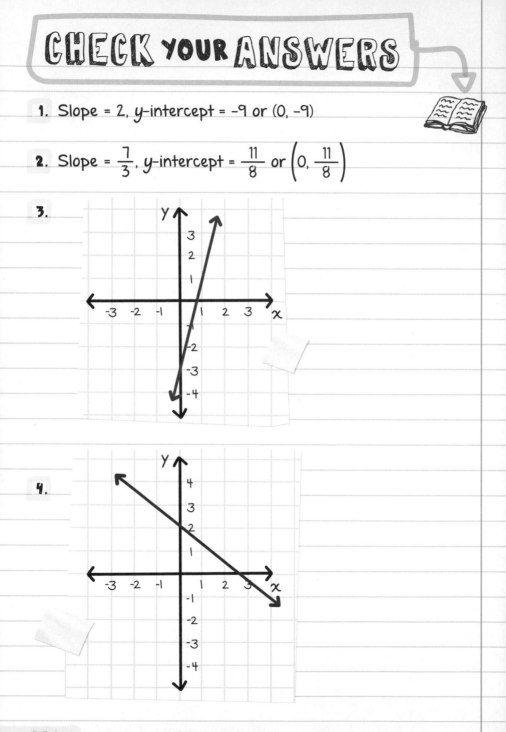

4.

5.

6. $y = -4x + 14$

7. $y = -\dfrac{3}{8}x - \dfrac{43}{8}$

8. $y = -6x - 3$

9. x-intercept = 3 or (3, 0)

y-intercept = $-\dfrac{3}{5}$ or $\left(0, -\dfrac{3}{5}\right)$

10. x-intercept = $-\dfrac{3}{2}$ or $\left(-\dfrac{3}{2}, 0\right)$

y-intercept = -3 or (0, -3)

A QUICK REMINDER:

$$y = mx + b$$

m is the slope

b is the y-intercept

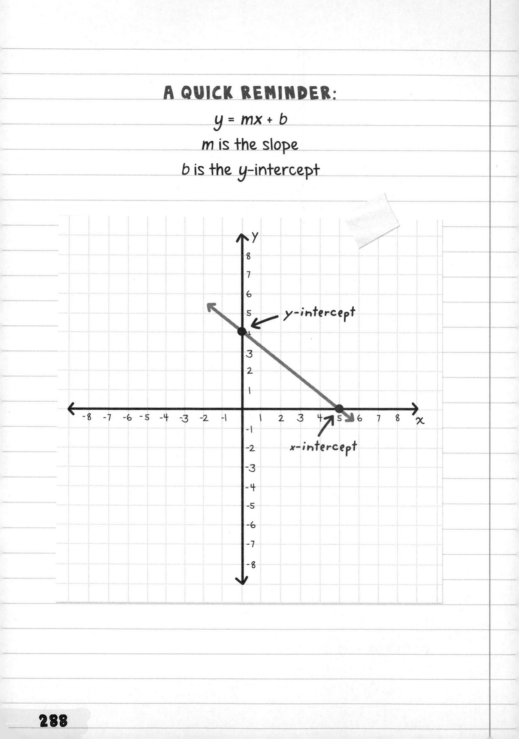

Chapter 35

POINT-SLOPE FORM

Another way to write the equation of a line is the POINT-SLOPE FORM, which uses the coordinates of a point (not just the y-intercept) and the slope of a line. Point-slope form is useful for finding a point on the line when you know the slope and one other point.

WHAT'S THE DIFFERENCE BETWEEN POINT-SLOPE AND SLOPE-INTERCEPT?

Point-slope form and slope-intercept form are both ways of expressing the equation of a straight line.

Point-slope form emphasizes the **slope** and ANY **point** on the line.

Slope-intercept form shows the **slope** and the **y-intercept** of a line.

Formula for the point-slope form:

$$y - y_1 = \overset{\text{slope}}{\underset{\downarrow}{m}}(x - x_1)$$

the coordinates of a point
that the line passes through

(x_1, y_1) is the known
point. m is the slope of
the line. (x, y) is any
other point on the line.

EXAMPLE: The equation of a line in point-slope form is
$y - 3 = 2(x - 7)$. Find the slope of the line and the coordinates
of a point that the line passes through.

The formula of the point-slope form is $y - y_1 = m(x - x_1)$;
this means that the slope, m, is 2, and the coordinates of
a point that it passes through are $(x_1, y_1) = (7, 3)$.

EXAMPLE: Graph the line that has a slope of 2 and passes through the point (–1, 4).

Step 1: Plot the given point.

Plot (–1, 4) on the coordinate plane.

Step 2: Use slope to plot another point.

Since the slope is $m = 2 = \frac{2}{1}$, this means that the rise = 2 and the run = 1.

Plot a second point that is located up 2 and right 1 from the first point.

Step 3: Draw a line that connects the points.

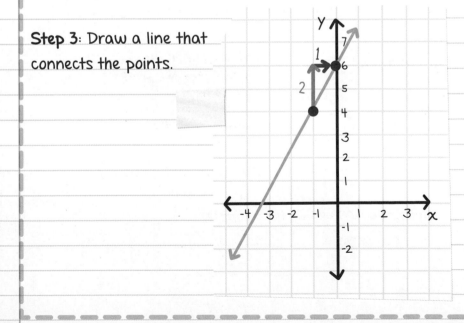

EXAMPLE: A line passes through the points (3, –5) and (7, 1). Find the equation of the line and write it in point-slope form.

Step 1: Identify which formula should be used.

Since we are given the coordinates of two points, we can calculate the slope of the line.

$$m = \frac{y_2 - y_1}{x_2 - x_1} = \frac{1 - (-5)}{7 - 3} = \frac{6}{4} = \frac{3}{2}$$

Step 2: Substitute the given information.

The slope is $m = \frac{3}{2}$ and one of the points is (3, –5).

We can substitute these values into the point-slope form:

$y - y_1 = m(x - x_1)$

$y - (-5) = \frac{3}{2}(x - 3)$

$y + 5 = \frac{3}{2}(x - 3)$

We could also have substituted the point (7, 1) in Step 2. In that case, the answer would be
$y - 1 = \frac{3}{2}(x - 7)$.

Therefore, the answer is: $y + 5 = \frac{3}{2}(x - 3)$.

EXAMPLE: A line has a slope of –2 and passes through the point (1, 6). Find the equation of the line and write it in slope-intercept form.

Step 1: Identify which formula should be used.

Since we are given the value of the slope and the coordinates of a point that it passes through, we should use point-slope form: $y - y_1 = m(x - x_1)$.

Step 2: Substitute the given information.

$y - y_1 = m(x - x_1)$

$y - 6 = -2(x - 1)$

Step 3: Rewrite the equation into slope-intercept form.

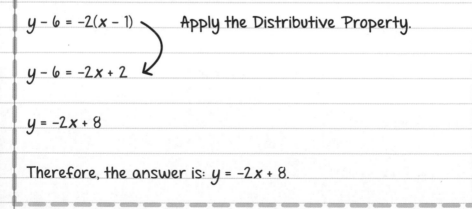

$y - 6 = -2(x - 1)$ Apply the Distributive Property.

$y - 6 = -2x + 2$

$y = -2x + 8$

Therefore, the answer is: $y = -2x + 8$.

STANDARD FORM

We can also write the equation of a line in STANDARD FORM:

$$Ax + By = C$$

In this form, A, B, and C are constants, and A is positive.

EXAMPLE: A line has a slope of $\frac{1}{3}$ and passes through the point (–12, 7).

Find the equation of the line and write it in standard form.

Step 1: Identify which formula should be used.

Since we are given the value of the slope and the coordinates of a point that it passes through, we should use point-slope form: $y - y_1 = m(x - x_1)$.

Step 2: Substitute the given information.

$y - y_1 = m(x - x_1)$

$y - 7 = \frac{1}{3}(x - (-12))$

Step 3: Rewrite the equation in standard form.

$$y - 7 = \frac{1}{3}x + 4$$

$$y - 7 = \frac{1}{3}(x + 12)$$

$$y - 7 = \frac{1}{3}x + 4$$

$$-\frac{1}{3}x + y = 11$$

This is A

This is B

This is C

Therefore, the answer is: $\frac{1}{3}x + -y = -11$.

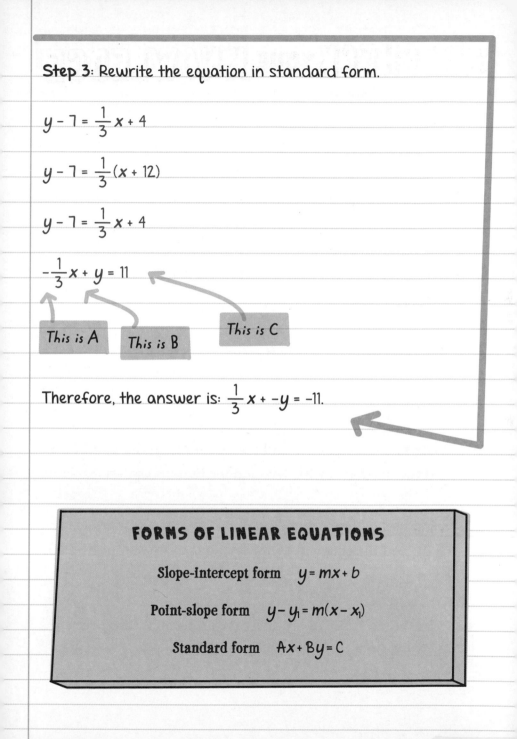

FORMS OF LINEAR EQUATIONS

Slope-intercept form $y = mx + b$

Point-slope form $y - y_1 = m(x - x_1)$

Standard form $Ax + By = C$

1. The equation of a line is $y - 1 = 5(x - 3)$. Find the slope of the line and the coordinates of a point that the line passes through.

2. The equation of a line is $y + 1 = -2(x - 9)$. Find the slope of the line and the coordinates of a point that the line passes through.

3. The equation of a line is $y = 5(x - \frac{4}{3})$. Find the slope of the line and the coordinates of a point that the line passes through.

4. A line has a slope of 4 and passes through the point (9, 5). Find the equation of the line and write it in point-slope form.

5. A line has a slope of $-\frac{7}{6}$ and passes through the point (3, 0). Find the equation of the line and write it in point-slope form.

6. A line has a slope of –3 and passes through the point (2, 5). Find the equation of the line and write it in slope-intercept form.

7. A line has a slope of $\frac{1}{2}$ and passes through the point (-6, 7). Find the equation of the line and write it in slope-intercept form.

8. A line has a slope of 2 and passes through the point (10, 3). Find the equation of the line and write it in standard form.

9. A line has a slope of 6 and passes through the point $(-\frac{3}{4}, 1)$. Find the equation of the line and write it in standard form.

10. A line has a slope of $-\frac{5}{4}$ and passes through the point (8, -6). Find the equation of the line and write it in standard form.

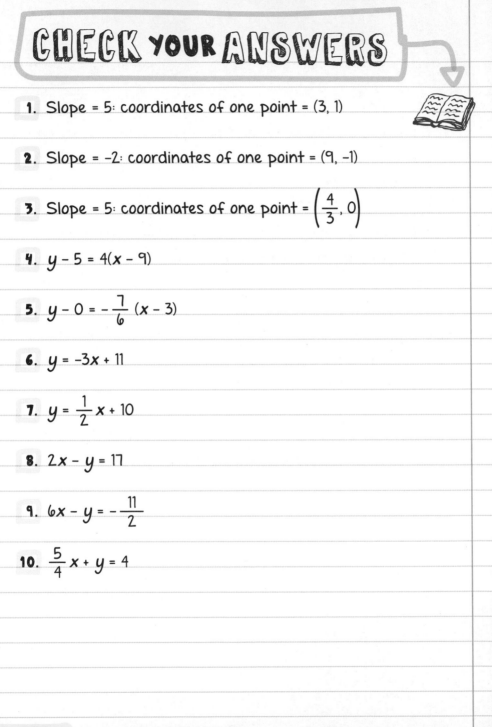

1. Slope = 5; coordinates of one point = (3, 1)

2. Slope = –2; coordinates of one point = (9, –1)

3. Slope = 5; coordinates of one point = $\left(\dfrac{4}{3}, 0\right)$

4. $y - 5 = 4(x - 9)$

5. $y - 0 = -\dfrac{7}{6}(x - 3)$

6. $y = -3x + 11$

7. $y = \dfrac{1}{2}x + 10$

8. $2x - y = 17$

9. $6x - y = -\dfrac{11}{2}$

10. $\dfrac{5}{4}x + y = 4$

Chapter 36

SOLVING SYSTEMS OF LINEAR EQUATIONS BY GRAPHING

When given a pair of linear equations, we can graph each linear equation on the same coordinate plane, and then find the point that both lines have in common. This intersection point is the solution to the system.

> The ordered pair that is the solution to both equations.

EXAMPLE: Graph the system of linear equations to find the solution.

$$\begin{cases} x + y = 5 & \boxed{1} \\ 2x - y = 4 & \boxed{2} \end{cases}$$

Step 1: Rewrite each of the equations into slope-intercept form ($y = mx + b$). This will make graphing simpler.

Rewrite 1 into slope-intercept form:

$x + y = 5$
$y = -x + 5$

Rewrite 2 into slope-intercept form:

$2x - y = 4$
$-y = -2x + 4$
$y = 2x - 4$

Step 2: Graph each of the equations on the same coordinate plane by using the slope and y-intercept of each line.

Step 3: Locate the point of intersection.

The two lines intersect at (3, 2).

So the solution to the system is (3, 2).

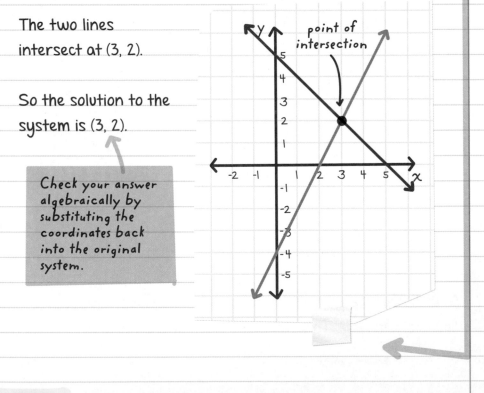

Check your answer algebraically by substituting the coordinates back into the original system.

EXAMPLE: Graph the system of linear equations to determine the solution.

$$\begin{cases} 2x + y = -2 & \boxed{1} \\ 4x + 2y = 6 & \boxed{2} \end{cases}$$

Step 1: Rewrite each of the equations in slope-intercept form $(y = mx + b)$.

Rewrite $\boxed{1}$ into slope-intercept form:

$2x + y = -2$
$y = -2x - 2$

Rewrite $\boxed{2}$ into slope-intercept form:

$4x + 2y = 6$
$2y = -4x + 6$
$y = -2x + 3$

Step 2: Graph each of the equations on the same coordinate plane by using the slope and y-intercept of each line.

Step 3: Locate the point of intersection.

There are NO intersection points. So there is **NO SOLUTION** to the system.

⬆ same slope, different y-intercepts

EXAMPLE: Graph the system of linear equations to find the solution.

$$\begin{cases} 4x - 2y = 6 \quad \boxed{1} \\ 2x - y = 3 \quad \boxed{2} \end{cases}$$

Step 1: Rewrite each equation in slope-intercept form.

$\boxed{1}$ $4x - 2y = 6$

    $-2y = -4x + 6$

    $y = 2x - 3$

$\boxed{2}$ $2x - y = 3$

    $-y = -2x + 3$

    $y = 2x - 3$

Step 2: Graph the equations on the same coordinate plane.

Step 3: Locate the point of intersection.

The graphs represent the same line, so the equations are EQUIVALENT.

There are an infinite number of solutions because there are an infinite number of points where the lines overlap.

SAME SLOPE and the SAME y-intercepts = INFINITE solutions

302

Graph each of the following systems of linear equations to determine the solution.

1. $\begin{cases} x + y = 5 \\ 3x + y = 7 \end{cases}$

2. $\begin{cases} 6x + 3y = -9 \\ -4x - 2y = 6 \end{cases}$

3. $\begin{cases} 2x - 4y = 10 \\ 3x + 4y = 15 \end{cases}$

4. $\begin{cases} 3x - 2y = -10 \\ -5x + 4y = 14 \end{cases}$

5. $\begin{cases} 5x - 3y = -14 \\ 3x + y = 0 \end{cases}$

6. $\begin{cases} 3x - 6y = 12 \\ x = 2y \end{cases}$

CHECK YOUR ANSWERS

1. Solution: (1, 4)

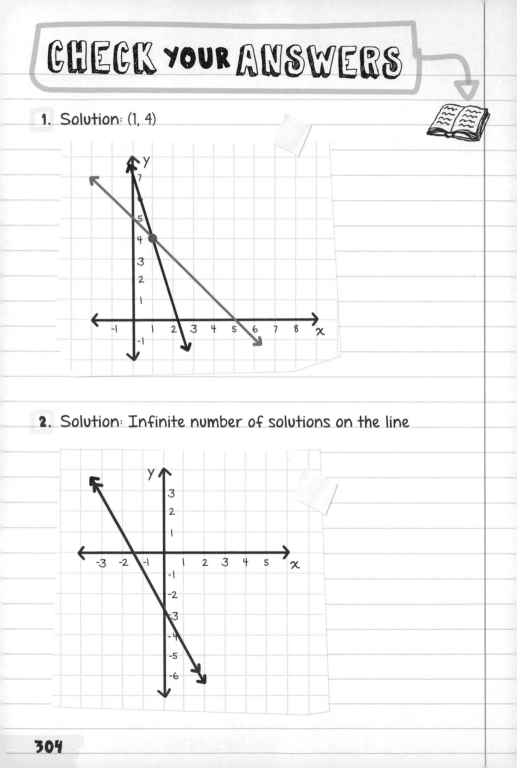

2. Solution: Infinite number of solutions on the line

3. Solution: (5, 0)

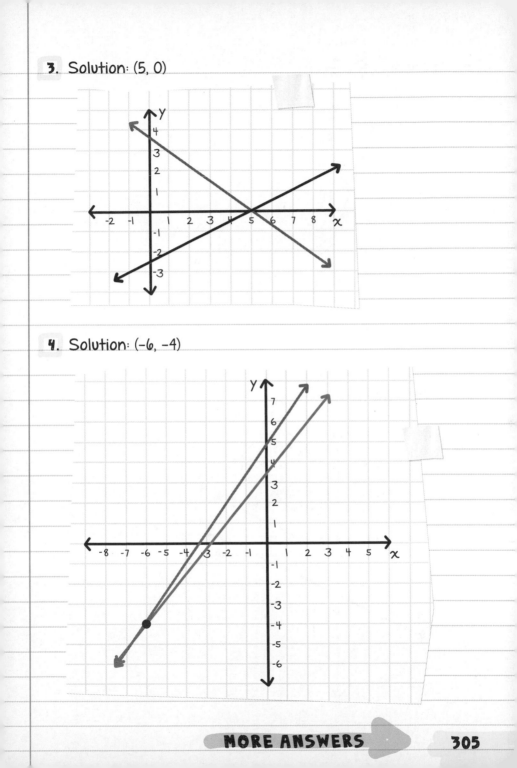

4. Solution: (−6, −4)

5. Solution: $\left(-\dfrac{5}{7}, \dfrac{16}{7}\right)$

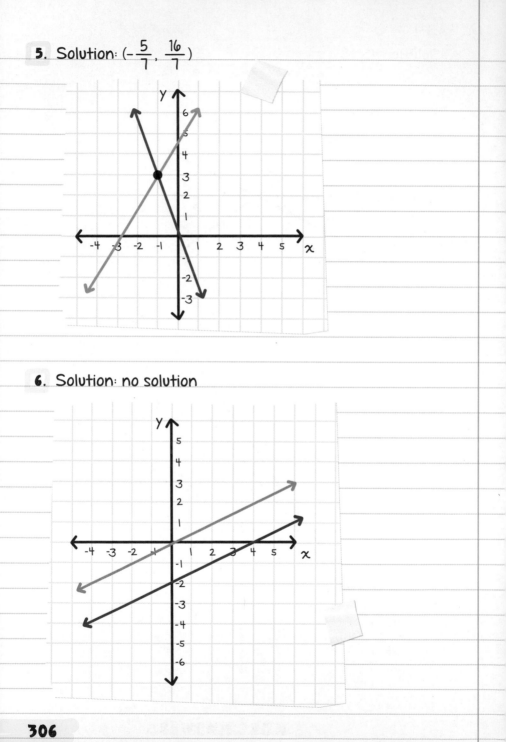

6. Solution: no solution

Chapter 37

GRAPHING LINEAR INEQUALITIES

When we solved one-variable inequalities, we graphed our answer on a number line, and we used an open circle when we *didn't* include a number in our solution, or we used a closed circle when we *did* include a number in our solution.

To solve linear inequalities with two variables, we can use what we know about graphing linear equations with two variables. Graphing linear inequalities with two variables means that the solution should be graphed on a coordinate plane.

EXAMPLE: Graph the inequality $y < x + 3$.

Step 1: Temporarily change the inequality to an equation and graph the equation.

Change the inequality to an equation.

$y < x + 3$
$y = x + 3$

Graph the equation $y = x + 3$. Check that your graph is accurate by using a test point.

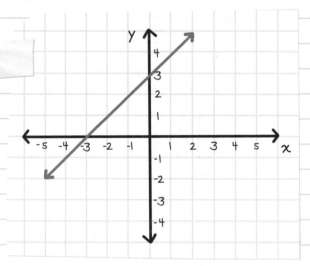

Step 2: Determine whether the line should be solid or dashed:

- If the inequality contains a < or > sign, the line should be dashed.

- If the inequality contains a ≤ or ≥ sign, the line should be solid.

Since the inequality $y < x + 3$ has a < sign, the line should be dashed.

> The dashed line is like the open circle on a linear equation graph on a number line. It means that the location is not included in the solution.

Step 3: Shade the correct region that makes the inequality true, by testing any point.

The line separates the graph into 2 sections.

Test (0, 0) to see if it is a solution to the given inequality.

> We can choose any point, but (0, 0) usually makes our calculations simpler and less likely to contain an error. If the point (0,0) lies on your line, you must choose a different point.

- If (0, 0) is a solution, shade the entire region that contains (0, 0).

- If (0, 0) is *not* a solution, shade the other region that does not contain (0, 0).

(0) $\overset{?}{<}$ (0) + 3

0 $\overset{?}{<}$ 3 ✓

Since the inequality is true, we shade the region that contains (0, 0).

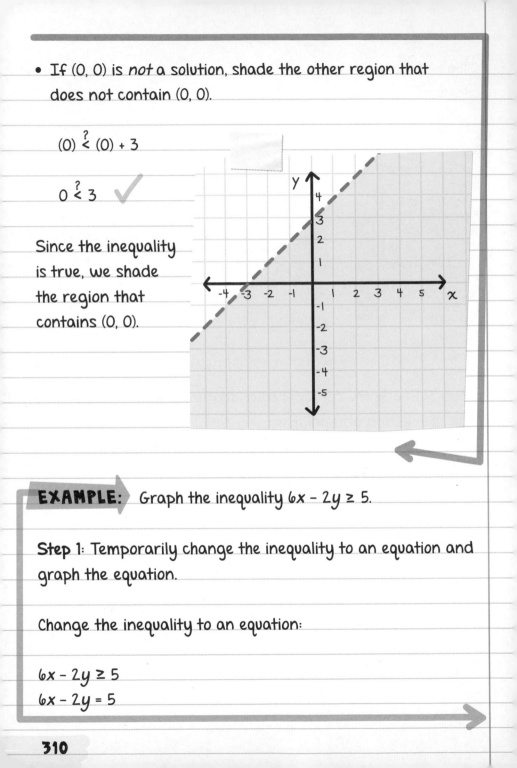

EXAMPLE: Graph the inequality $6x - 2y \geq 5$.

Step 1: Temporarily change the inequality to an equation and graph the equation.

Change the inequality to an equation:

$6x - 2y \geq 5$
$6x - 2y = 5$

Graph the equation $6x - 2y = 5$. Check that your graph is accurate by using a test point.

$6x - 2y = 5$

$-2y = -6x + 5$

$y = 3x - \dfrac{5}{2}$

Step 2: Determine whether the line should be solid or dashed:

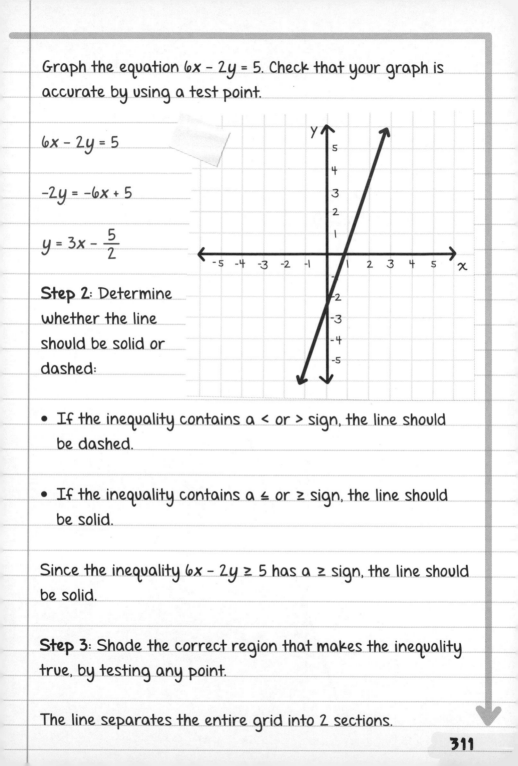

- If the inequality contains a < or > sign, the line should be dashed.

- If the inequality contains a ≤ or ≥ sign, the line should be solid.

Since the inequality $6x - 2y ≥ 5$ has a ≥ sign, the line should be solid.

Step 3: Shade the correct region that makes the inequality true, by testing any point.

The line separates the entire grid into 2 sections.

Test (0, 0) to see if it is a solution to the given inequality.

- If (0, 0) is a solution, shade the entire region that contains (0, 0).

- If (0, 0) is not a solution, shade the other region that does *not* contain (0, 0).

$6(0) - 2(0) \overset{?}{\geq} 5$

$0 \overset{?}{\geq} 5$ ✗

Since the inequality is *not* true, we shade the region that does *not* contain (0, 0).

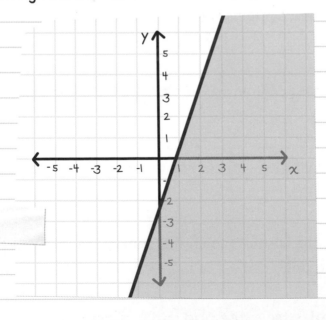

Graph the linear inequalities.

1. $y > 4 - x$

2. $x - y \geq -5$

3. $x - y \leq 6$

4. $4x + 3y > 12$

5. $y > -5$

6. $3x - 2y \geq -6$

CHECK YOUR ANSWERS

1.

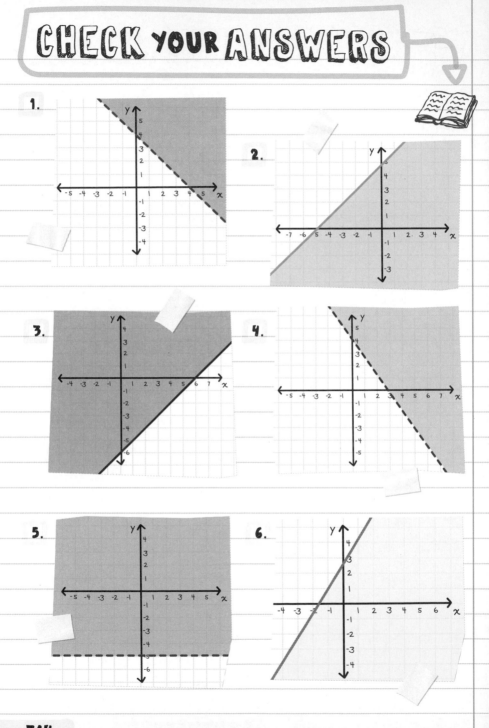

2.

3.

4.

5.

6.

Chapter 38

SOLVING SYSTEMS OF LINEAR INEQUALITIES BY GRAPHING

We solve systems of linear inequalities using the same approach as solving systems of linear equations.

EXAMPLE: Graph the system of linear inequalities to find the solution.

$$\begin{cases} x + y < 2 & \boxed{1} \\ 2x - y > 10 & \boxed{2} \end{cases}$$

Step 1: Temporarily change each inequality into an equation in slope-intercept form and graph the equation.

Change $\boxed{1}$ into an equation: Change $\boxed{2}$ into an equation:
$x + y = 2$ $2x - y = 10$

Rewrite in slope-intercept form:

$x + y = 2$
$y = -x + 2$

Rewrite in slope-intercept form:

$2x - y = 10$
$-y = -2x + 10$
$y = 2x - 10$

The two lines intersect at (4, -2).

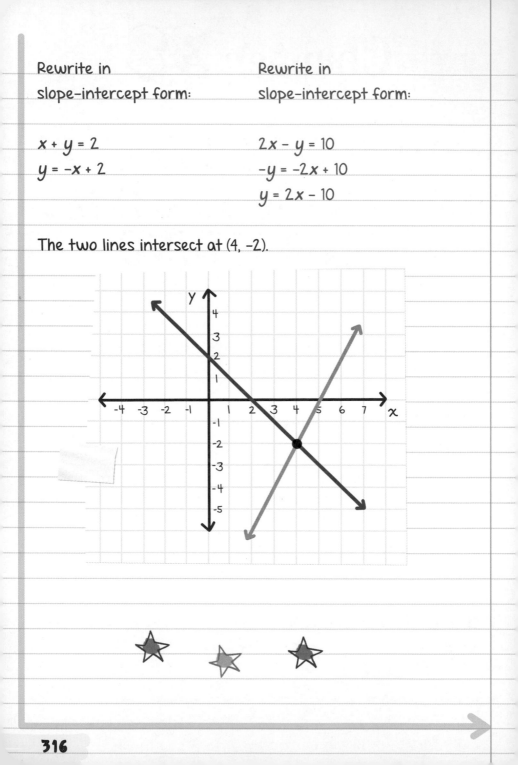

Step 2: Determine whether the lines should be solid or dashed.

Since the inequality $x + y < 2$ has a < sign, the line should be dashed.

Since the inequality $2x - y > 10$ has a > sign, the line should be dashed.

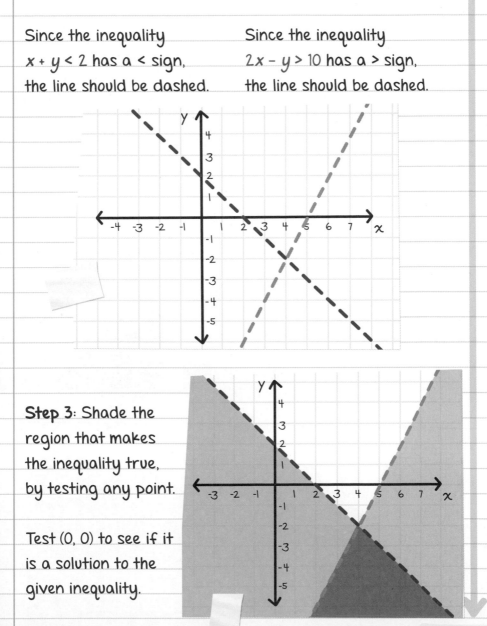

Step 3: Shade the region that makes the inequality true, by testing any point.

Test (0, 0) to see if it is a solution to the given inequality.

$(0) + (0) \overset{?}{<} 2$ $2(0) - (0) \overset{?}{>} 10$

$0 \overset{?}{<} 2$ ✓ $0 \overset{?}{>} 10$ ✗

Since the inequality is true, shade the region that contains (0, 0).

Since the inequality is *not* true, shade the region that does *not* contain (0, 0).

Since the final solution must satisfy BOTH inequalities, the solution must be the region that is shaded by BOTH colors.

EXAMPLE: Graph the system of linear inequalities to find the solution.

$$\begin{cases} x + y > -5 & \boxed{1} \\ -x + y \leq 1 & \boxed{2} \end{cases}$$

Step 1: Temporarily change each inequality into an equation in slope-intercept form and graph the equation.

Change ① into an equation:
$3x + y = -5$

Change ② into an equation:
$-x + y = -1$

Rewrite in slope-intercept form:

Rewrite in slope-intercept form:

$3x + y = -5$

$-x + y = -1$

$y = -3x - 5$

$y = x - 1$

The two lines intersect at (–1, –2).

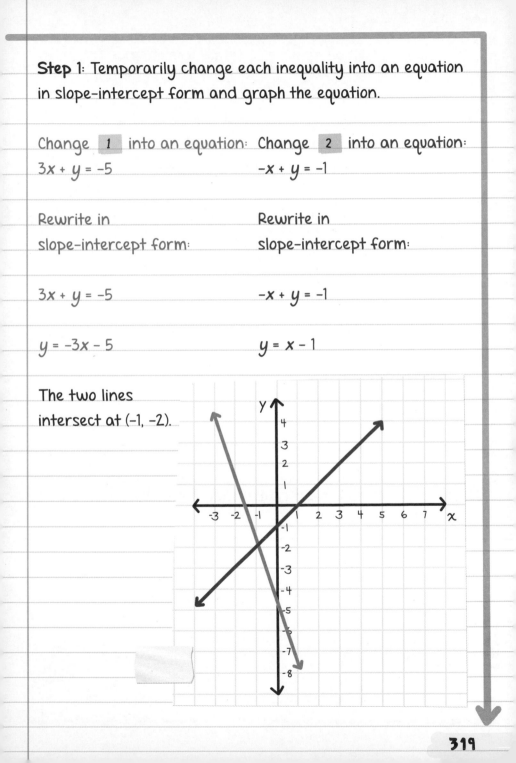

Step 2: Determine whether the line should be solid or dashed.

Since the inequality $3x + y > -5$ has a $>$ sign, this line should be dashed.

Since the inequality $-x + y \leq -1$ has a $\leq$ sign, this line should be solid.

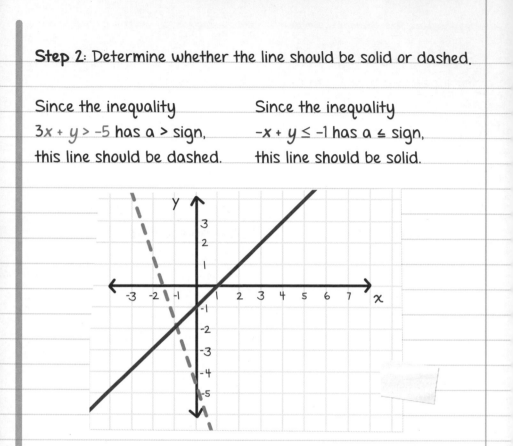

Step 3: Shade the correct region that makes the inequality true, by testing any point.

Test $(0, 0)$ to see if it is a solution to the given inequality.

$3(0) + (0) \overset{?}{>} -5$

$-(0) + (0) \overset{?}{\leq} -1$

$0 \overset{?}{>} -5$ ✓

$0 \overset{?}{\leq} -1$ ✗

Since the inequality is true, shade the region that contains (0, 0).

Since the inequality is *not* true, shade the region that does *not* contain (0, 0).

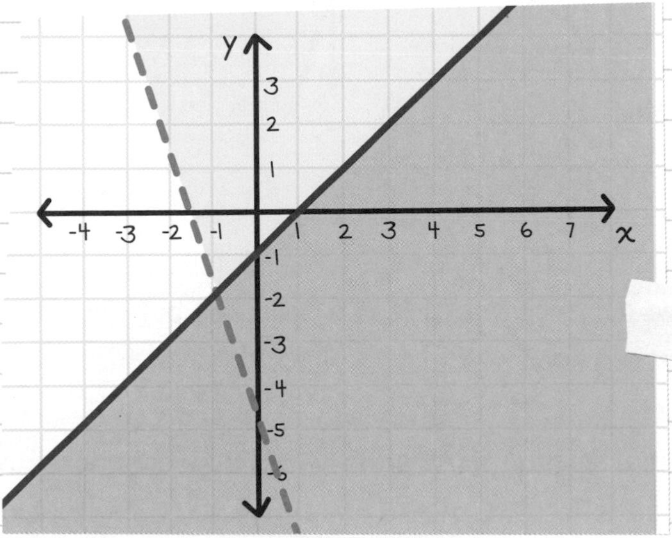

Since the final solution must satisfy BOTH inequalities, the solution must be the region that is shaded by BOTH colors.

What about the intersection point (-1, -2)?

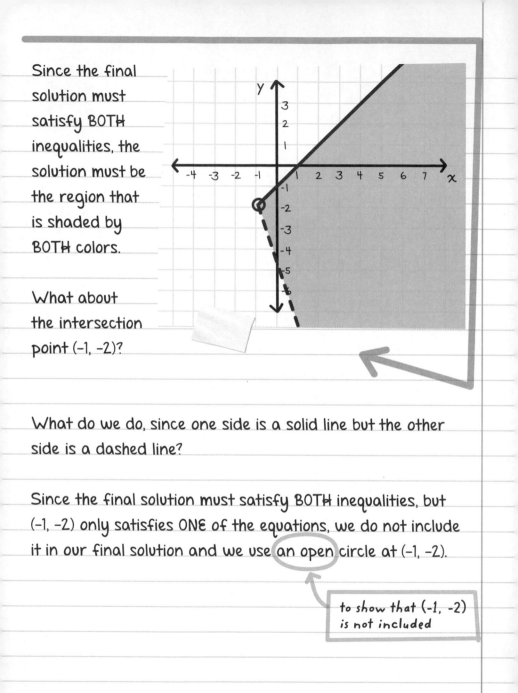

What do we do, since one side is a solid line but the other side is a dashed line?

Since the final solution must satisfy BOTH inequalities, but (-1, -2) only satisfies ONE of the equations, we do not include it in our final solution and we use an open circle at (-1, -2).

to show that (-1, -2) is not included

Graph each of the following systems of linear inequalities to find the solution.

1. $\begin{cases} x + y < 1 \\ x - y > -5 \end{cases}$

2. $\begin{cases} x + y \geq -2 \\ 4x + y \leq 7 \end{cases}$

3. $\begin{cases} 3x - y < 4 \\ 2x + y \leq 6 \end{cases}$

4. $\begin{cases} y > 3 \\ x \geq -5 \end{cases}$

5. $\begin{cases} x + 2y > -7 \\ -x + 3y < -3 \end{cases}$

6. $\begin{cases} -2x + y > 3 \\ 3x + y < -7 \end{cases}$

1.

4.

2.

5.

3.

6.

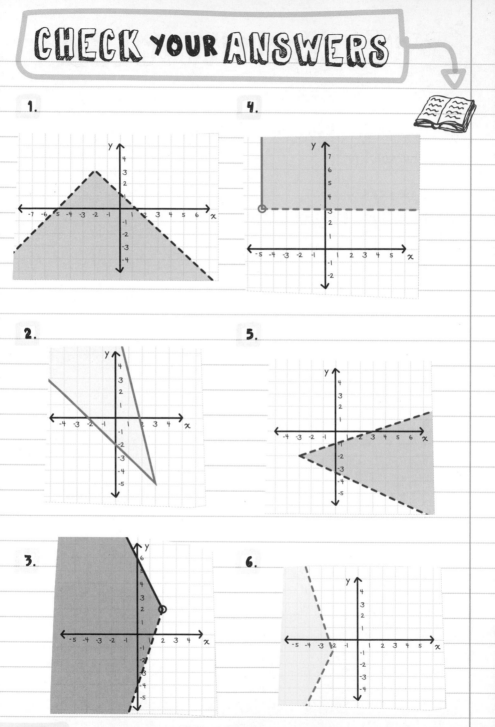

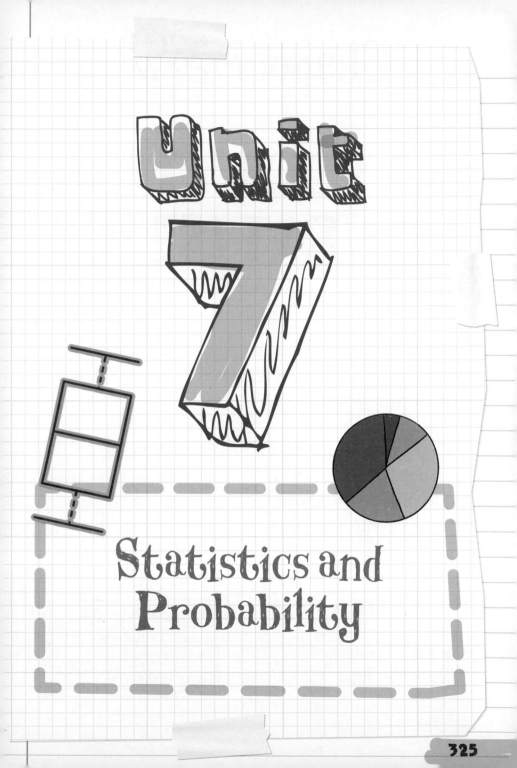

Unit 7

Statistics and Probability

Chapter 39

INTRODUCTION TO STATISTICS

STATISTICS is the organization, presentation, and study of data. DATA is a collection of facts in the form of numbers, words, or descriptions.

Data and statistics are important because they:

- help us identify problems.
- provide evidence to prove our claims.
- help us make informed decisions.

There are two types of data:

- quantitative data
- qualitative data.

> **STATISTICIANS** help us collect, interpret, summarize, and present data.

QUANTITATIVE DATA	
The number of students in math class	1 2 3 4 5 6 7 8
The number of students passing math class	1 2 3 4 5
The number of students passing math class with an A	ME ME ME 1 2 3
The number of students in danger of failing math class	UH-OH SIGH I DON'T WANNA TALK ABOUT IT 1 2 3

QUALITATIVE DATA
Information given that describes something.
Usually this is information that you can observe,
such as appearances, textures, smells, and tastes.

QUALITATIVE DATA

Do the students like math class?	LOVE IT · THE BEST! · YEP · IT'S OKAY
Are students happy?	YOU BET! · ECSTATIC · YEP · I'M OKAY
Are the students friendly?	NO!
Are the students paying attention?	I AM! · ME TOO! · YEP · WHAT DID YOU SAY?

Quantitative and qualitative data can be collected, interpreted, and summarized.

> **THINK:** How many answers are possible?
>
> If there is <u>only one</u> answer, then it's <u>not</u> a statistical question.
>
> If <u>more than one</u> answer is possible, then it <u>is</u> a statistical question.

COLLECTING DATA

A STATISTICAL QUESTION is a question that anticipates having many different responses. Answers that differ have VARIABILITY, which describes how spread out or closely clustered a set of data is.

For example: "How old am I?" This question has only one answer. It is not a statistical question.

"How old are the people in my family?" This question has more than one answer, so it is a statistical question.

The answers to a statistical question are "spread out" and can be very different—so there can be HIGH VARIABILITY— very spread out—or LOW VARIABILITY—closely clustered.

SAMPLING

Sometimes we can gather data from every member in a group. Most of the time that's impossible. Therefore, we use a SAMPLING, taking a small part of a larger group to estimate characteristics about the whole group.

For example, a school has 2,500 students and you want to find out how many consider math their favorite subject. Sampling would entail interviewing a portion of the students and using the findings to draw approximate conclusions about the entire group.

OH BOY. THIS IS GONNA TAKE A LONG TIME!

It is important to make sure that the sample is a good representation of the entire group. For example, you know that the school has 2,500 students, and you randomly choose 50 people. You might find out that 40 of the students are in the same grade. This is not a good sample because the sample is not a true representation of the entire school.

THIS IS MORE LIKE IT!

KEY WORDS IN STATISTICS

Population: the set from which a sample of data is selected

Sample: a representative part of a population

Random sample: a sample obtained from a population in which each element has an equal chance of being selected

Sampling: selecting a small group that represents the entire population

EXAMPLE: One thousand people bought food at concession stands at a theater. You want to find out how many of those people bought vegan snacks. So you ask 20 people if they bought vegan or nonvegan snacks. Of the 20 people, 5 said they bought vegan snacks. Approximately how many people altogether bought vegan snacks at the theater?

Because there are 5 people who bought vegan snacks out of 20, it means that $\frac{5}{20}$ of the sample bought vegan snacks.

Apply this number to the entire population of 1,000 people.

$1,000 \times \frac{5}{20} = 250$

Approximately 250 people bought vegan snacks.

It's vegan!

EXAMPLE: There are 150 members in Kaycee's theater group. Kaycee wants to know how many members would be interested in a summer theater project. Kaycee asks 30 members and finds out that 10 would be interested in the project. Approximately how many members in Kaycee's theater group would be interested in participating in a summer theater project?

Because 10 of 30 members were interested, it means that $\frac{10}{30} = \frac{1}{3}$ of the sample are interested.

$150 \times \frac{1}{3} = 50$

Entire population

Approximately 50 members are interested in the summer theater project.

CHECK YOUR KNOWLEDGE

1. Which of the following questions asks about quantitative data? Which asks about qualitative data?
   A. How many customers are in the grocery store?
   B. What is your favorite color?
   C. What types of cars do the teachers in your school drive?
   D. How many students are going to the game?

2. There are 140 cars in a parking lot. Keisha looks at 15 cars and sees that 2 of those cars are red. Approximately how many cars in the parking lot are red?

3. Maya wants to guess how many marbles are in a box with a height of 18 inches. She knows that there are 32 marbles in a box with a height of 5 inches. Approximately how many marbles are in the first box?

4. Jason has 25 classmates. Fifteen of his classmates had summer internships. If there are a total of 500 students in Jason's school, about how many students had summer internships?

ANSWERS 333

CHECK YOUR ANSWERS

1. **A.** Quantitative
   B. Qualitative
   C. Qualitative
   D. Quantitative

2. Approximately 19 cars (rounded up from 18.67)

3. Approximately 115 marbles (rounded down from 115.2)

4. 300 students had a summer internship.

Chapter 40

MEASURES OF CENTRAL TENDENCY AND VARIATION

MEASURES OF CENTRAL TENDENCY

The group of numbers in collected data is called a SET. You can represent the data in a set using MEASURES OF CENTRAL TENDENCY. A measure of central tendency is a single number that is used to summarize all the data set's values.

For example, a student's grade point average (GPA) is a measure of the central tendency for all the student's grades.

The three most common measures of central tendency are:

1. The MEAN (also called the average) is the central value of a set of numbers. To calculate the mean, add all the numbers, then divide the sum by the number of addends. The mean is most useful when the data values are close together.

EXAMPLE: In 4 games, Fola scored 11, 18, 22, and 10 points. What was Fola's mean score?

Step 1: Add all the numbers.

11 + 18 + 22 + 10 = 61

Step 2: Divide the sum by the number of addends.

The sum is 61.

Number of addends: 4

61 ÷ 4 = 15.25

The mean is 15.25. So, Fola scored an average of 15.25 points in each game.

2. The MEDIAN is the middle number of a set of numbers arranged in increasing order.

EXAMPLE: Jason and his friends competed to see who could jump the most number of times with a jump rope. The number of jumps were 120, 90, 140, 200, and 95. What was the median number of jumps made?

Step 1: Arrange the numbers in order from least to greatest.

90   95   120   140   200

Step 2: Identify the number that falls in the middle of the set.

The middle number is 120.

The median number of jumps was 120.

The greatest value in a data set is called the **MAXIMUM**.

The lowest value is called the **MINIMUM**.

The middle number is called the **MEDIAN**.

When there is no middle number, find the mean of the two items in the middle by adding them together, then dividing by 2.

13   24   40   52

24 + 40 = 64
64 ÷ 2 = 32   The median is 32.

---

3. The MODE is the number in a data set that occurs most often. You can have one mode, more than one, or no modes at all. If no numbers are repeated, we say that there is no mode.

EXAMPLE: The students in a Spanish class received the following test scores: 65, 90, 85, 90, 70, 80, 80, 95, 80, 98. What was the mode of the scores?

Step 1: Arrange the numbers in order.
65, 70, 80, 80, 80, 85, 90, 90, 95, 98

Step 2: Identify the numbers that repeat and how often they repeat.

80 repeats 3 times and 90 repeats 2 times.
The mode is 80. So, a score of 80 on the Spanish test occurred the most.

MEASURES OF VARIATION

Another tool we can use to describe and analyze a data set is MEASURES OF VARIATION, which describes how the values of a data set vary. The main measure of variation is RANGE. Range is the difference between the maximum and minimum values in a data set.

Think: Range = high − low

The range shows how "spread out" a data set is.

EXAMPLE: When asked how many hours they spent over the weekend looking at a screen, students answered:

10 hours, 6 hours, 4 hours, 20 hours, 12 hours, 8 hours, 8 hours, 6 hours, 14 hours

What is the range of hours spent in front of a screen?

Step 1: Identify the maximum value and the minimum value.

Maximum: 20 hours, Minimum: 4 hours

Step 2: Subtract.

20 − 4 = 16

The range is 16 hours.

339

A data value that is significantly less or greater than the other values in the set is called an OUTLIER. An outlier can throw off the mean of a data set and give a (skewed) portrayal of the data.

inaccurate; misleading

EXAMPLE: Five friends ate the following numbers of doughnuts:

Justin: 1 doughnut
Manuel: 10 doughnuts
Sam: 2 doughnuts
Tamara: 2 doughnuts
Frances: 3 doughnuts

Which person seems to be the outlier? Manuel.

Manuel is the outlier because he ate a significantly greater number of doughnuts than his friends.

CHECK YOUR KNOWLEDGE

For questions 1 through 3 find the mean, median, mode, and range for each set of data.

1. 290, 306, 309, 313, 330, 357, 400, 431, 461, 601

2. 6, 11, 20, 4, 1, 15, 10, 8, 5, 1, 2, 12, 4

3. 81, 38, 91, 71, 87, 97, 100, 82, 71, 70

4. Five students recorded the number of minutes they spent reading over the weekend. Their times were: 85 minutes, 90 minutes, 75 minutes, 85 minutes, and 95 minutes. Calculate the mean, median, mode, and range of the data set.

5. Several companies donated funds to a local food bank. The amounts of the donations were $1,200, $1,000, $900, $2,000, and $1,500. Calculate the mean, median, mode, and range of the donations.

ANSWERS

CHECK YOUR ANSWERS

1. Mean: 379.8
   Median: 343.5
   Mode: none
   Range: 311

2. Mean: 7.6
   Median: 6
   Modes: 1 and 4
   Range: 19

3. Mean: 78.8
   Median: 81.5
   Mode: 71
   Range: 62

4. Mean: 86
   Median: 85
   Mode: 85
   Range: 20

5. Mean: $1,320
   Median: $1,200
   Mode: none
   Range: $1,100

Chapter 41

DISPLAYING DATA

Tables are used to present data in list form. But we can also represent data visually with graphs, pie charts, and diagrams. For example, Lena can use a pie chart to visually represent data collected about what sport fellow classmates like best.

a drawing used to represent information

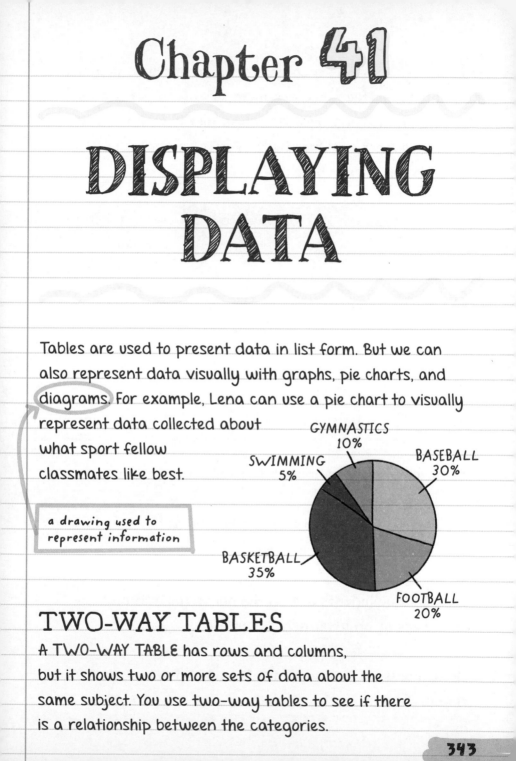

GYMNASTICS
10%

SWIMMING
5%

BASEBALL
30%

BASKETBALL
35%

FOOTBALL
20%

TWO-WAY TABLES

A TWO-WAY TABLE has rows and columns, but it shows two or more sets of data about the same subject. You use two-way tables to see if there is a relationship between the categories.

EXAMPLE: Ms. Misra collects data from students in her class about whether they are members of an after-school club and on the honor roll. Ms. Mirsa wants to find out if there is evidence that members of after-school clubs also tend to be on the honor roll.

	After-school club	No after-school club	Total
On the honor roll	16	8	(16 + 8) = 24
Not on the honor roll	3	4	(3 + 4) = 7
TOTAL	(16 + 3) = 19	(8 + 4) = 12	31

The table can help us answer the following questions.

total number of students

• How many students are on the honor roll but are not members of an after-school club? 8

• How many students are on the honor roll and also members of an after-school club? 16

• How many students are members of an after-school club but are not on the honor roll? 3

The data in the table can be interpreted to mean that if you are a member of an after-school club, you are also likely to be on the honor roll. That section of the table has the highest number of students.

Read two-way tables carefully! Sometimes the relationship they show is that there is <u>no</u> relationship at all!

LINE PLOTS

how often something happens

A **LINE PLOT** shows the frequency of data. It displays data by placing an x above numbers on a number line.

This line plot displays the number of games friends have on their cell phones.

NUMBER OF GAMES ON CELL PHONE

Number of Games

Each x represents 1 friend.

EXAMPLE: Ten students were asked, "How many books did you read over the summer?"

Their responses were: 4, 3, 2, 5, 1, 1, 3, 6, 3, and 2.

Make a line plot to show the recorded data.

First, put the data in numerical order: 1, 1, 2, 2, 3, 3, 3, 4, 5, and 6.

Then draw a line plot to show the numbers of books read over the summer.

Write an x above each response on the line plot

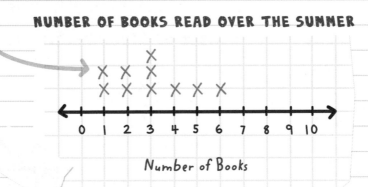

NUMBER OF BOOKS READ OVER THE SUMMER

Number of Books

The line plot tells us that the most common answer (the mode) is 3. The numbers are between 1 and 6, so the range is 5.

HISTOGRAMS

A HISTOGRAM is a graph that shows the frequency of data within equal intervals. It looks like a bar graph, but unlike a bar graph there are no gaps between the vertical or horizontal bars unless there is an interval that has a frequency of 0.

> Since a bar cannot be used to show 0, a blank space is used instead.

This histogram shows the number of customers who visit a store in a 10-hour period that is divided into 2-hour intervals. From the graph we can see the following:

35 customers visited the store between 10 a.m. and 11:59 a.m.

15 customers visited the store between 6 p.m. and 7:59 p.m.

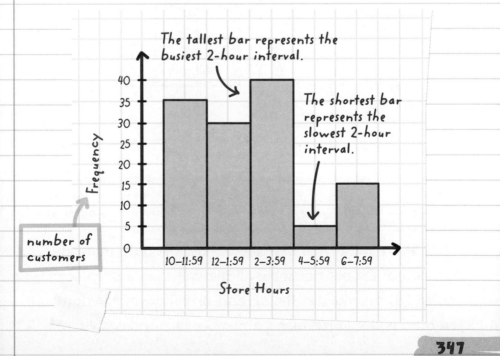

CUSTOMER VISITS TO A STORE

The tallest bar represents the busiest 2-hour interval.

The shortest bar represents the slowest 2-hour interval.

number of customers

Frequency

Store Hours

EXAMPLE: Let's look at the problem on page 346 again. Ten students were asked, "How many books did you read over the summer?"

Their responses were: 4, 3, 2, 5, 1, 1, 3, 6, 3, and 2. Make a histogram to show this data.

First, show the data in numerical order: 1, 1, 2, 2, 3, 3, 3, 4, 5, and 6.

Then draw a bar above each set of responses.

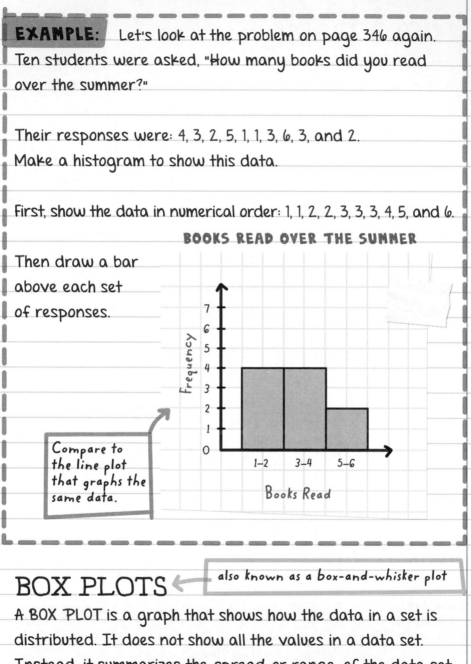

BOOKS READ OVER THE SUMMER

Compare to the line plot that graphs the same data.

BOX PLOTS ← also known as a box-and-whisker plot

A BOX PLOT is a graph that shows how the data in a set is distributed. It does not show all the values in a data set. Instead, it summarizes the *spread*, or range, of the data set. The data is displayed along a number line and is split into

QUARTILES (quarters). The median of the data separates the data into halves. The quartiles are values that divide the data into fourths. The median of the lower half is the LOWER QUARTILE of the data and is represented by Q1. The median of the upper half is the UPPER QUARTILE of the data and is represented by Q3. The size of each section indicates the variability of the data.

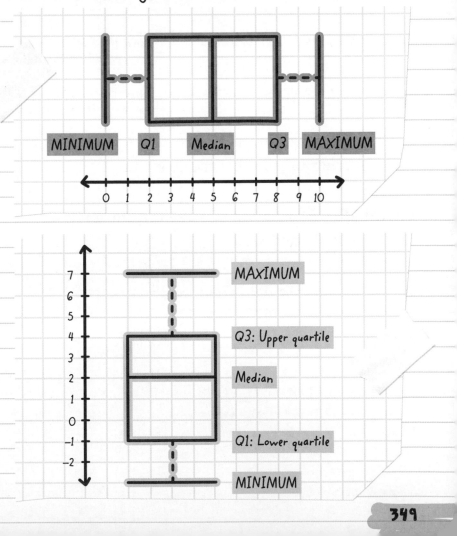

To Make a Box Plot:

1. Arrange the data from the least to the greatest along a number line.

2. Identify the minimum, maximum, median, lower half, and upper half.

3. Identify the lower quartile. ← *Find the median of the lower half of the data.*

4. Identify the upper quartile. ← *Find the median of the upper half of the data.*

5. Mark the upper and lower quartiles on a number line and draw boxes to represent the quartiles.

EXAMPLE: Make a box plot of the data set: 14, 22, 21, 48, 12, 4, 18, 14, 21, 17, and 16.

Step 1: Arrange the data from least to greatest.

minimum   median   maximum

4, 12, 14, 14, 16, 17, 18, 21, 21, 22, 48

Lower half   Upper half

Step 2: Identify the minimum (4), maximum (48), median (17), lower half, and upper half.

Step 3: Calculate the lower quartile by finding the median of the lower half of the data.

Median. This is the beginning of Q1.

- Lower quartile = the median of 4, 12, 14, 14, and 16.

Step 4: Calculate the upper quartile by finding the median of the upper half of the data.

Median. This is the end of Q3.

- Upper quartile = the median of 18, 21, 21, 22, and 48.

Step 5: Plot values above a number line and draw boxes to represent the quartiles.

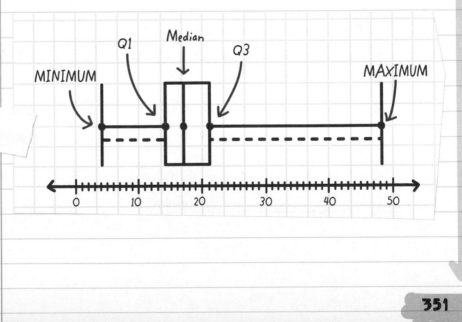

The graph shows:

25% of the data was above 21.
> Q3 up to the maximum

25% of the data was between 17 and 21.
> the median up to Q3

25% of the data was between 14 and 17.
> Q1 up to the median

25% of the data was below 14.
> Q1 down to the minimum

The box plot shows that the right-hand portion of the box appears wider than the left-hand portion of the box. When box graphs are not evenly divided in half, this is known as SKEW.

- If the box plot has a wider right side, the graph is described as SKEWED RIGHT.

- If the box plot has a wider left side, the graph is described as SKEWED LEFT.

- If the box plot is evenly divided, the graph is described as SYMMETRICAL.

SCATTER PLOTS

A SCATTER PLOT is a graph that compares two related sets of data on a coordinate plane. Scatter plots graph data as ORDERED PAIRS.

To make a scatter plot:

1. Decide on a title for the graph.

2. Draw a vertical and horizontal axis.

3. Choose a scale for each axis, using a range and intervals that fit the data.

4. Plot a point for each pair of numbers given as the data.

EXAMPLE: After a test, Mr. Evans asked students how many hours they studied. He recorded their answers, along with their test scores. Make a scatter plot of hours studied and test scores.

Name	Number of Hours Studied	Test Score
Kwan	4.5	90
Anna	1	60
James	4	92

Name	Number of Hours Studied	Test Score
Mike	3.5	88
Latisha	2	76
Serena	5	100
Tyler	3	90
Todd	1.5	72
Chris	3	70
Maya	4	86

To show Kwan's data, mark the point whose horizontal value is 4.5 and whose vertical value is 90. The ordered pair for this data is (4.5, 90).

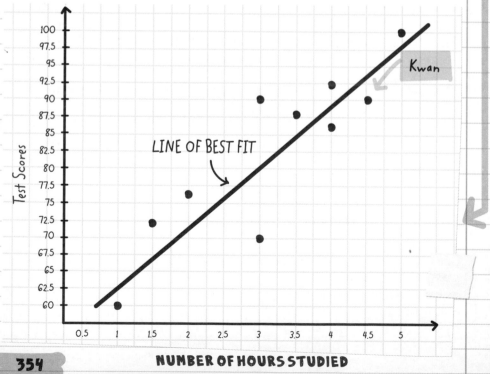

NUMBER OF HOURS STUDIED

By graphing the data on a scatter plot, we can see if there is a relationship between the number of hours studied and test scores. The scores generally go up as the hours of studying go up, so this shows that there is a relationship between test scores and studying.

We can draw a line on the graph that roughly describes the relationship between the two sets of data (number of hours studied and test scores). This line is called the LINE OF BEST FIT (see the red line on the graph). The line of best fit is close to *most* of the data points. It is the best indicator of how the points are related to one another.

> None of the points on this graph lie *on* the line of best fit. That's okay, because the line describes the relationship of *all* the points.

THAT WAS THREE HOURS WELL SPENT.

MAYBE FOR YOU!

Tyler studied for only 3 hours, but still got a 90. Chris also studied for 3 hours, but got a 70. A scatter plot shows the overall relationship between data, while individual ordered pairs (like Tyler's and Chris's) don't show the general trend. Tyler and Chris might be considered OUTLIERS in this situation because they might be considered far from the line of best fit.

separate from the set of data

Scatter plots show relationships called CORRELATIONS.

● **Positive Correlation** As one set of values increases, the other set increases as well.

not necessarily every value

For example, time spent studying and test scores:

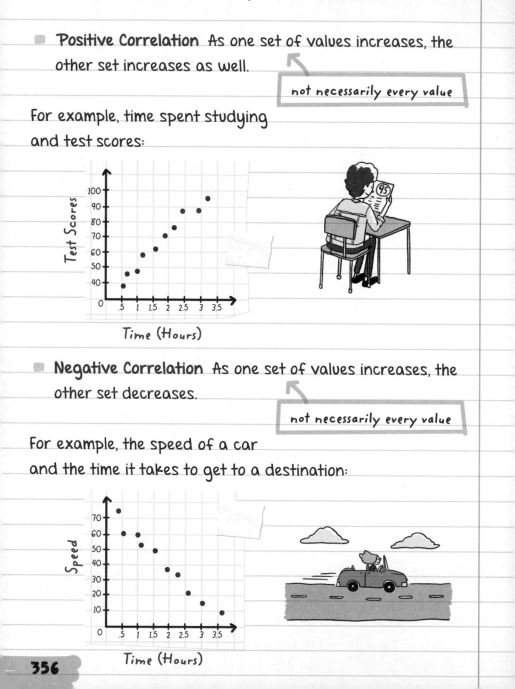

● **Negative Correlation** As one set of values increases, the other set decreases.

not necessarily every value

For example, the speed of a car and the time it takes to get to a destination:

No Correlation The values have no relationship.

For example, a person's shoe size and their musical ability:

1. Answer the questions based on the two-way table below.

	School swim team	Not on school swim team	Total
Summer lifeguard	12	4	(12 + 4) = 16
Not a summer lifeguard	8	20	(8 + 20) = 28
TOTAL	(12 + 8) = 20	(4 + 20) = 24	44

A. How many students are summer lifeguards but are not on the swim team?

B. How many students are on the swim team but are not summer lifeguards?

C. How many students are on the swim team and are also summer lifeguards?

D. What conclusion can you make from the information about a student who is on the swim team in the table?

2. A bookstore asked its customers how many books they bought in the past six months. The answers were 3, 5, 6, 4, 8, 5, 4, 4, 1, 2, 3, 2, 4, 3, 2, 3, and 4. Create a line plot of the data the bookstore found.

3. Answer the questions based on the histogram below.

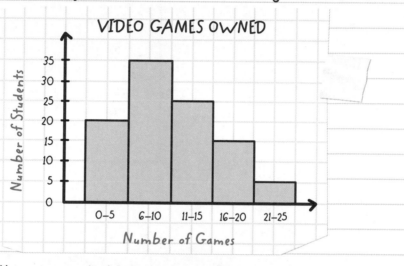

A. How many students were surveyed?

B. In which interval does the greatest frequency occur?

C. How many students have no more than 15 video games?

4. Make a box-and-whisker plot of the data set: 5, 12, 4, 6, 0, 20, 14, 14, 12, and 13. Then complete the questions about the plot.

A. What is the range?

B. What is the median?

C. At what number does the lower quartile begin?

D. At what number does the upper quartile end?

ANSWERS ▶ 359

5. In each of the following scatter plots, state whether there is a positive correlation, a negative correlation, or no correlation.

A.

B.

C.

D.

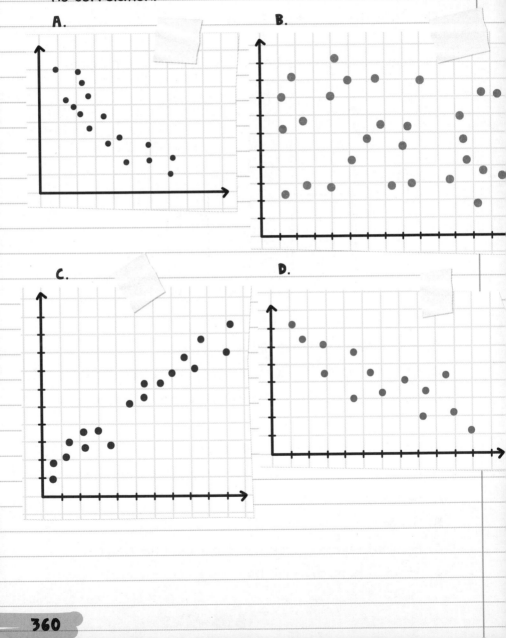

CHECK YOUR ANSWERS

1. **A.** 4

   B. 8

   C. 12

   D. A student who is on the swim team is more likely to also be a summer lifeguard.

2. **BOOKS PURCHASED OVER SIX MONTHS**

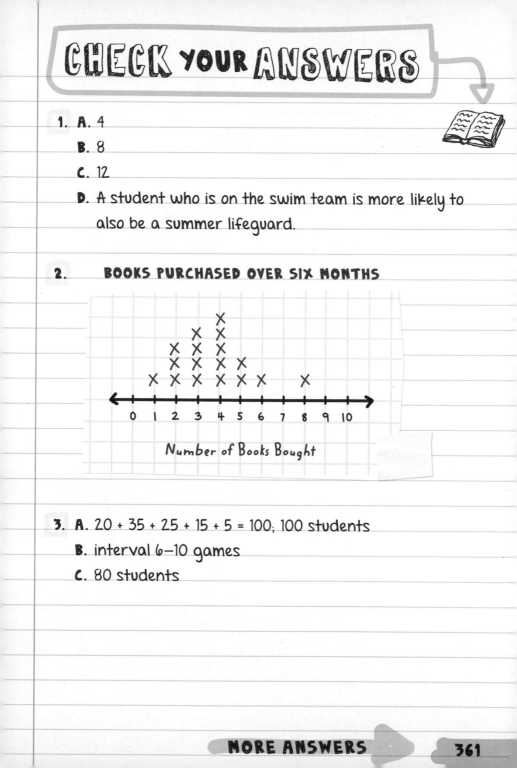

Number of Books Bought

3. **A.** 20 + 35 + 25 + 15 + 5 = 100; 100 students

   B. interval 6–10 games

   C. 80 students

4.

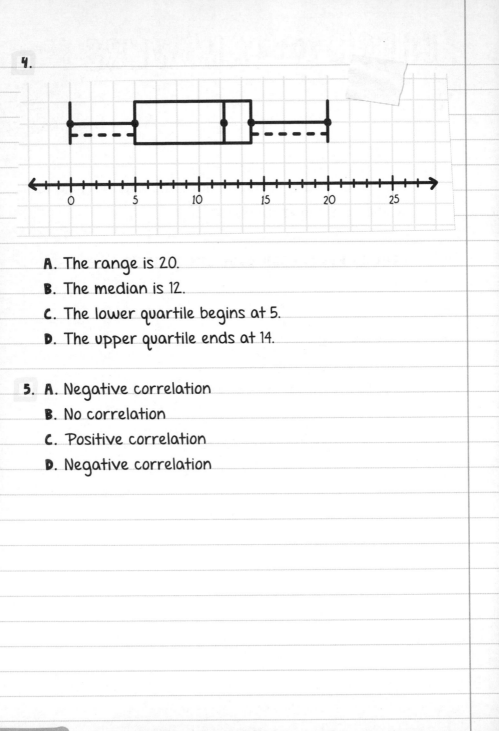

A. The range is 20.

B. The median is 12.

C. The lower quartile begins at 5.

D. The upper quartile ends at 14.

5. A. Negative correlation

B. No correlation

C. Positive correlation

D. Negative correlation

Chapter 42

PROBABILITY

Probability is the likelihood that an event will happen. It is a number between 0 and 1 and can be written as a percent.

> Probability = how likely something will happen

A higher number means that there is a greater likelihood that an event will happen.

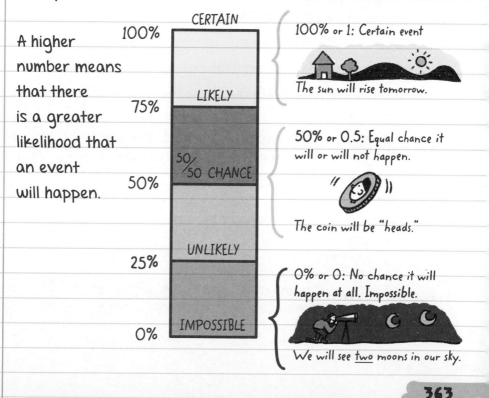

100% — CERTAIN

100% or 1: Certain event

The sun will rise tomorrow.

75% — LIKELY

50% — 50/50 CHANCE

50% or 0.5: Equal chance it will or will not happen.

The coin will be "heads."

25% — UNLIKELY

0% — IMPOSSIBLE

0% or 0: No chance it will happen at all. Impossible.

We will see <u>two</u> moons in our sky.

When we flip two coins they could land on heads or tails.

The ACTION is what is happening.

flipping 2 coins

The OUTCOMES are all of the possible results.

coins landing on heads, heads and tails, or coins landing on tails

The EVENT is any outcome or group of outcomes.

heads and heads, heads and tails, tails and tails

When we flip a coin, both outcomes are equally likely to occur. This feature is called RANDOM.

When trying to find the probability of an event (P), we use a ratio to find out how likely it is that the event will happen.

$$\text{Probability(Event)} = \frac{\text{number of favorable outcomes}}{\text{number of possible outcomes}}$$

EXAMPLE: What is the probability of a coin landing on heads?

$$\text{Probability(Event)} = \frac{\text{number of favorable outcomes}}{\text{number of possible outcomes}}$$

The number of favorable outcomes (landing heads) is 1, and the number of possible outcomes (landing heads or landing tails) is 2.

what we want to happen

$P(\text{Heads}) = \dfrac{1}{2} = 50\%$

So, there is a 50% chance that the coin will land on heads.

EXAMPLE: What is the probability of the spinner landing on blue, considering that the color groups are of equal size and shape?

$\text{Probability(Event)} = \dfrac{\text{number of favorable outcomes}}{\text{number of possible outcomes}}$

$P(\text{Blue}) = \dfrac{1}{5} = 20\%$

There is a 20% probability that the spinner will land on blue.

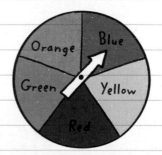

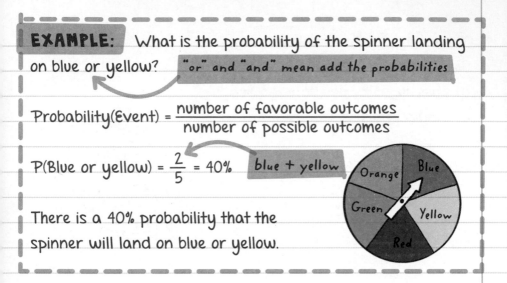

EXAMPLE: What is the probability of the spinner landing on blue or yellow?

"or" and "and" mean add the probabilities

$$\text{Probability(Event)} = \frac{\text{number of favorable outcomes}}{\text{number of possible outcomes}}$$

P(Blue or yellow) = $\frac{2}{5}$ = 40%   blue + yellow

There is a 40% probability that the spinner will land on blue or yellow.

If a probability question is more complicated, we can make a table to list the possible outcomes.

EXAMPLE: Kevin flips a coin twice. What is the probability that he will flip heads twice?

Step 1: Make a table that lists all the possible combinations.

Outcome of the 1st flip	Outcome of the 2nd flip	Combination of the 2 flips
heads	heads	2 heads
heads	tails	1 head, 1 tail
tails	heads	1 tail, 1 head
tails	tails	2 tails

Step 2: Use the formula.

$$\text{Probability(Event)} = \frac{\text{number of favorable outcomes}}{\text{number of possible outcomes}}$$

$$P(\text{2 heads}) = \frac{1}{4} = 25\%$$

The probability that Kevin will flip heads twice is 25%.

A **SAMPLE SPACE** is the collection of all possible outcomes in an experiment. The sample space for Kevin's experiment is heads, heads; heads, tails; tails, heads; tails, tails. When all outcomes of an experiment are equally likely to occur and an event has two or more stages, it is helpful to draw a TREE DIAGRAM.

A **TREE DIAGRAM** is a visual representation that shows all possible outcomes of one or more events.

EXAMPLE: If Keisha rolls a pair of dice twice, what is the probability that she rolls double twos?

Record all possible outcomes in a tree diagram.

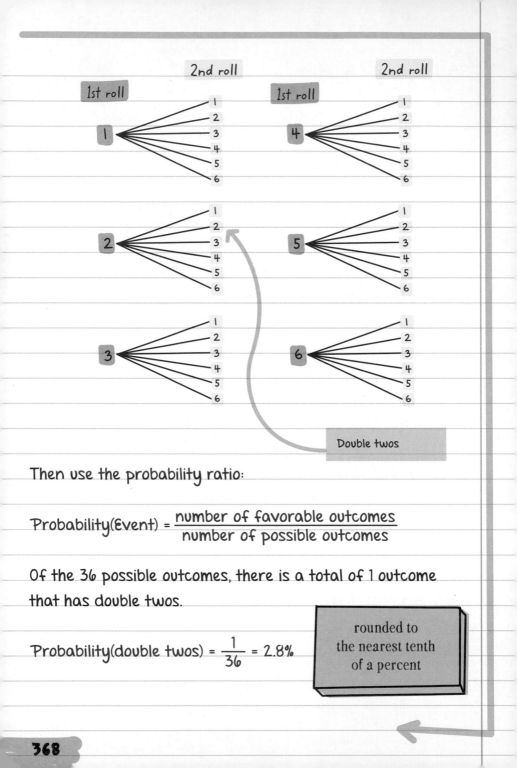

2nd roll

1st roll

1 — 1 2 3 4 5 6

2nd roll

1st roll

4 — 1 2 3 4 5 6

2 — 1 2 3 4 5 6

5 — 1 2 3 4 5 6

3 — 1 2 3 4 5 6

6 — 1 2 3 4 5 6

Double twos

Then use the probability ratio:

Probability(Event) = $\dfrac{\text{number of favorable outcomes}}{\text{number of possible outcomes}}$

Of the 36 possible outcomes, there is a total of 1 outcome that has double twos.

Probability(double twos) = $\dfrac{1}{36}$ = 2.8%

> rounded to the nearest tenth of a percent

The FUNDAMENTAL COUNTING PRINCIPLE states that if there are a ways to do one thing, and b ways to do another thing, then there are **a · b** ways to do both things.

For example, if a jacket comes in 3 colors and 4 sizes, then there are 3 × 4, or 12, possible outcomes for combinations of color and size. The multiplication process is the COUNTING PRINCIPLE.

Instead of listing all the possible combinations, we multiply the possible choices.

EXAMPLE: A coin is tossed 3 times. How many arrangements of heads and tails are possible?

2 choices (heads or tails) and 3 tosses

2 × 3 = 6 possible choices

EXAMPLE: You have 5 pairs of pants and 6 sweaters.

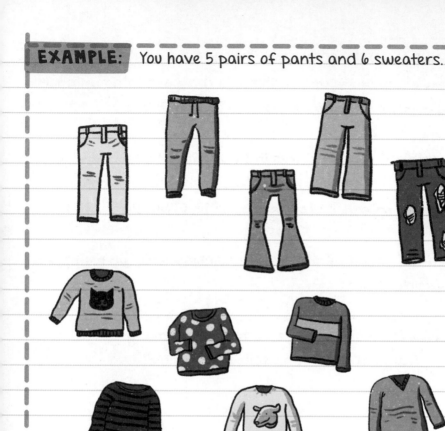

How many outfits can you make?

5 pants and 6 sweaters

5 x 6 = 30

There are 30 possible outfits.

The COMPLEMENT OF AN EVENT is the opposite of the event happening.

Event	Complement
win	lose
float	sink
heads	tails

EVENT: WIN   COMPLEMENT: LOSE

Probability of an event + probability of its complement = 1

OR

Probability of an event + probability of its complement = 100%

In other words, there is a 100% chance that either an event or its complement will happen.

EXAMPLE: If the chance of winning the competition is 45%, then the chance of not winning the competition is 55%.

45% + 55% = 100%

EXAMPLE: The probability that a student in your class is right-handed is 82%. What is the complement of being right-handed, and what is the probability of the complement?

The complement of being right-handed is being left-handed.

P(right-handed) + P(left-handed) = 100%

82% + P(left-handed) = 100%

P(left-handed) = 18%

So, the probability that a student is left-handed is 18%.

CHECK YOUR WORK:

Does P(right-handed) + P(left-handed) = 100%?

82% + 18% = 100% ✓

Use the spinner to answer questions
1 through 3.

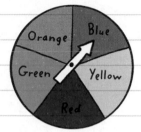

1. What is the probability of
   landing on red?

2. What is the probability of
   landing on yellow or red?

3. What is the probability of not landing on blue?

4. A six-sided number cube has faces with the numbers 1
   through 6 marked on it. What is the probability that the
   number 6 will occur on one toss of the number cube?

5. Kim has 6 types of ice creams and 4 toppings. How many
   different kinds of sundaes can she make?

6. The probability that an athlete on a local basketball
   team is taller than 6 feet 2 inches is 75%. What is the
   probability of the complement?

ANSWERS

CHECK YOUR ANSWERS

1. The probability of landing on red is 20%.

2. The probability of landing on yellow or red is 40%.

3. The probability of not landing on blue is 80%.

4. The probability that 6 will appear is $\frac{1}{6}$ or 16.7%.

5. Kim can make 24 kinds of sundaes.

6. The probability of the complement is 25%.

Chapter 43

COMPOUND EVENTS

A COMPOUND EVENT is an event that consists of two or more single events.

single event + single event = compound event

A compound event can be an INDEPENDENT EVENT or a DEPENDENT EVENT.

INDEPENDENT EVENTS

An INDEPENDENT EVENT is one in which the outcome of one event has no effect on any other event or events.

If the events are independent, multiply the probability of each event.

If A and B are independent events, then

$$P(A \text{ and } B) = P(A) \cdot P(B)$$

EXAMPLE: Drake tosses a coin and a six-sided die at the same time. What is the probability of Drake getting a tails on the coin and a 3 on the die together?

Event A = coin landing on tails

Event B = die landing on 3

First, find the probability of the coin landing on tails: $\frac{1}{2}$.

desired outcome

$$P(A) = \frac{1}{2}$$

possible outcomes

Second, find the probability of the die landing on 3: $\frac{1}{6}$.

$$P(B) = \frac{1}{6}$$

Then, multiply the probabilities to find the probability of both landing on tails and on 3.

P(A and B) = P(A) • P(B)

$\frac{1}{2} \times \frac{1}{6} = \frac{1}{12}$ = approx. 8%

The probability of Drake tossing a coin and getting tails and rolling a die and getting 3 is about 8%.

The example can also be shown as:

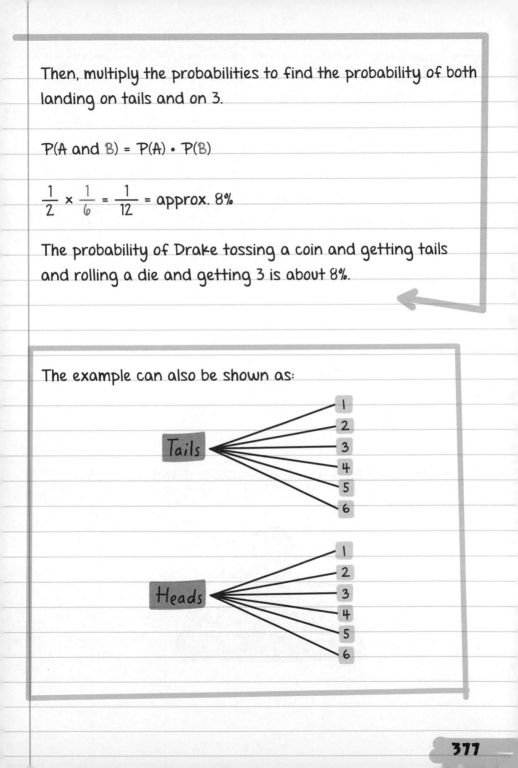

EXAMPLE: Lisette places 10 index cards in a jar. On each of those index cards is written a letter from A through J. Lisette places 5 index cards in a second jar. On each of the 5 cards is written a number from 1 to 5. Letters and numbers are not repeated. Lisette draws one card from each jar. What is the probability that Lisette will draw the letter C and the number 5?

Event A = drawing the card with letter C

Event B = drawing the card with the number 5

P(A and B) = P(A) • P(B)

$$\frac{1}{10} \times \frac{1}{5} = \frac{1}{50} = 2\%$$

The probability that Lisette will draw a C and a 5 is 2%.

DEPENDENT EVENTS

A DEPENDENT EVENT is one in which the first event affects the probability of the second event.

If the events are dependent, multiply the probability of the first event by the probability of the second event after the first event has happened.

If A and B are dependent events, then

$$P(A, \text{ then } B) = P(A) \cdot P(B, \text{ after } A)$$

EXAMPLE: Jamal has a bag of 3 red and 6 yellow gumballs. He removes one of the gumballs at random from the bag and gives it to a friend. He then takes another gumball at random for himself.

What is the probability that Jamal picked a red and then a yellow gumball from the bag?

$$P(A, \text{ then } B) = P(A) \cdot P(B, \text{ after } A)$$

Event A = picking a red gumball
Event B = picking a yellow gumball

$P(A) = P(\text{red gumball}) = \dfrac{3}{9}$ ← number of red gumballs

← total number of gumballs

$P(B) = P(\text{yellow gumball}) = \dfrac{6}{8}$ ← number of yellow gumballs

← total number of remaining gumballs (there is 1 less than before)

P(red gumball, then yellow gumball) =

$$\dfrac{3}{9} \times \dfrac{6}{8} = \dfrac{18}{72} = \dfrac{1}{4} = 25\%$$

The probability of Jamal picking a red and then a yellow gumball is 25%.

EXAMPLE: Two cards are drawn from a deck of 52 cards. The first card is drawn and not replaced. Then a second card is drawn. Find the probability of drawing an ace and then another ace: P(ace, ace).

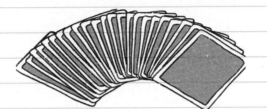

The ace is chosen as the first card. So, there are 51 cards left and 3 of them are aces.

> There are 4 of each type of card in a deck of cards.

$$P(ace, ace) = \frac{4}{52} \times \frac{3}{51} = \frac{12}{2,652} = \frac{1}{221} = 0.45\%$$

The probability of choosing an ace and then another ace is 0.45%.

CHECK YOUR KNOWLEDGE

For problems 1 through 3, determine whether the events are independent or dependent.

1. Picking a red marble from a bag, and without replacing it, picking another red marble from the same bag

2. Choosing two names from a jar without replacement

3. Rolling 2 number cubes at the same time and getting a 6 on each of them

4. Tamara tosses 2 coins. What is the probability that both coins will land on tails?

5. Two cards are drawn from a deck of 52 cards. The first card is not put back before the second card is drawn. What is the probability of:
   A. P(jack, then king)
   B. P(red 2, then black 2)

6. There are 5 cards numbered 1 through 5. Sam selects a card, doesn't replace it, and then selects again. What is P(1, then 3)?

7. Luis has a set of 4 cards made up of 1 yellow card, 1 purple card, and 2 black cards. He randomly picks one card and keeps it. Then he picks a second card. What is the probability that Luis picked first a black card and then a yellow card?

8. Evan has 3 red markers, 4 green markers, 1 yellow marker, and 2 black markers in his pencil case. He picks one marker from the case and does not replace it. Then he picks a second marker. What is the probability of:

A. P(black, then black)

B. P(red, then green)

CHECK YOUR ANSWERS

1. Dependent event

2. Dependent event

3. Independent event

4. $\frac{1}{2} \times \frac{1}{2} = \frac{1}{4}$; probability is 25%

5. A. $\frac{4}{52} \times \frac{4}{51} = \frac{16}{2652} = \frac{4}{663}$; probability is approx. 0.6%

   B. $\frac{2}{52} \times \frac{2}{51} = \frac{4}{2652} = \frac{1}{663}$; probability is approx. 0.15%

6. $\frac{1}{20} = 5\%$

7. $\frac{2}{4} \times \frac{1}{3} = \frac{1}{6}$; probability is approx. 16.7%

8. A. $\frac{2}{10} \times \frac{1}{9} = \frac{2}{90} = \frac{1}{45}$; probability is approx. 2.2%

   B. $\frac{3}{10} \times \frac{4}{9} = \frac{12}{90} = \frac{2}{15}$; probability is approx. 13.3%

Chapter 44

PERMUTATIONS AND COMBINATIONS

A PERMUTATION is an arrangement of things in which the order IS important.

A permutation is like an ordered combination.

A COMBINATION is an arrangement in which order is NOT important.

Think: Permutation → positioning

PERMUTATIONS WITH REPETITION

When an arrangement has a certain number of possibilities (*n*), then we have that number (*n*) of choices each time.

For example, if $n = 3$, this means we have 3 choices each time.

So if we could choose 4 times, then the arrangement would be $3 \times 3 \times 3 \times 3$.

Choosing a number (r) of a set of objects that have n different types can be written as n^r.

number of times

number of things to choose from

For example, if we want to create a 3-digit number, where each digit can be chosen from the numbers 1, 2, 3, 4, or 5, then the permutation would be $5 \times 5 \times 5$ or 5^3.

REPETITION: the number of choices stays the same each time. Selections can be repeated and order matters. For example, 113, 131, and 311 are different permutations..

EXAMPLE: Maya can write a 5-digit code from 10 possible numbers to set the code on her lock. For each of Maya's selected numbers, she can choose from the digits 0, 1, 2, 3, 4, 5, 6, 7, 8, and 9. How many possible permutations can Maya choose from?

Since the order matters and Maya can repeat the digits:

$10 \times 10 \times 10 \times 10 \times 10$ or 10^5

Maya can choose from 10 digits for each of her 5 code numbers.

Maya can choose from 100,000 permutations.

HEY, CAN YOU HELP ME WITH MY PERMUTATION LOCK?

PERMUTATIONS WITHOUT REPETITION

For each permutation that doesn't allow repetition, we must reduce the number of available choices each time to avoid repetition.

In how many ways could 6 colored beads be selected if we do not want to repeat a color?

The choices are reduced each time. So the first choice is 6, and the second choice is 5, and the third is 4, etc.

$6 \times 5 \times 4 \times 3 \times 2 \times 1 = 720$

There are 720 permutations. We can write this mathematically using FACTORIAL FUNCTIONS.

The factorial function (!) means to multiply all whole numbers from a given number down to 1.

This is read as "five factorial." 5! means $5 \times 4 \times 3 \times 2 \times 1$

Note: $0! = 1$

FACTORIAL FUNCTIONS: There is no repetition of choices, and order matters.

EXAMPLE: Nico displays 7 medals in his room. In how many different ways can Nico arrange the medals in a row?

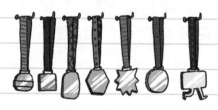

$7! = 7 \times 6 \times 5 \times 4 \times 3 \times 2 \times 1 = 5,040$

There are 5,040 different ways that Nico can arrange his medals in a row.

To select fewer than the total number of objects when order matters, use the formula:

number of things to choose from

$$\frac{n!}{(n-r)!}$$

number of objects chosen

So if we wanted to select only 3 of the 6 beads from the earlier example, we could write the number of permutations as:

$$\frac{6!}{(6-3)!} = \frac{6!}{3!} = \frac{6 \times 5 \times 4 \times \cancel{3} \times \cancel{2} \times \cancel{1}}{\cancel{3} \times \cancel{2} \times \cancel{1}} = 120$$

There are 120 permutations.

There are other ways to write this **PERMUTATION FORMULA**:

$$P(n, r) \rightarrow {_n}P_r$$

This means the number of permutations of n things taken r at a time.

So, $P(6, 3)$ or $_6P_3$ represents the number of permutations of 6 things taken 3 at a time.

EXAMPLE: Jordan is at an ice cream parlor and has a choice of 5 ice cream flavors. How many 3-scoop arrangements can he make for his sundae?

$_5P_3$ or $P(5, 3)$ means 5 things taken 3 at a time, or $5 \times 4 \times 3$.

There are 60 different sundaes that Jordan can make.

COMBINATIONS WITHOUT REPETITION

A combination is a group of objects in which order does not matter.

The combination formula is a modification of the permutation formula:

$$_nC_r = \frac{_nP_r}{r!}$$ We can also use the notation $C(n, r)$.

Use permutations to find the number of combinations.

First, find the number of permutations by selecting a certain number of objects, $_nP_r$.

Then divide the number of permutations by the number of selected objects, $r!$

For example, how many combinations can be made when 4 numbers are selected out of 8 numbers?

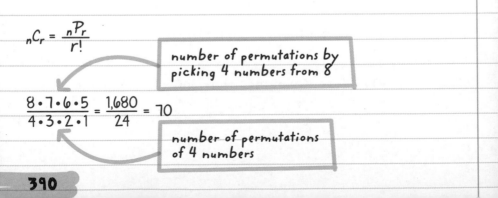

$$_nC_r = \frac{_nP_r}{r!}$$

number of permutations by picking 4 numbers from 8

$$\frac{8 \cdot 7 \cdot 6 \cdot 5}{4 \cdot 3 \cdot 2 \cdot 1} = \frac{1,680}{24} = 70$$

number of permutations of 4 numbers

EXAMPLE: Jaz is having dessert at a restaurant. She wants to choose the combination plate, which allows a choice of 2 different desserts from a menu of 4 desserts. Jaz can choose from cheesecake, apple pie à la mode, chocolate mousse, a cheese plate and a fruit plate. From how many dessert combinations can Jaz choose?

Step 1: Find the number of permutations by selecting a certain number of objects.

Step 2: Divide by the number of selected objects.

$$_nC_r = \frac{_nP_r}{r!} = \frac{\text{permutations of 2 from 4}}{\text{permutations of 2}} = \frac{4 \cdot 3}{2 \cdot 1} = \frac{12}{2} = 6$$

Jaz can choose 6 dessert combinations.

1. There are 9 students on the debate team. The debate coach is picking the first 3 presenters. How many ways can the coach arrange the presentation order of the first 3 debaters?

2. How many ways are there to arrange 5 books on a shelf?

3. A keypad has 10 digits. How many 4-digit personal identification codes can be made if no digit is repeated?

4. Three students are standing in line. How many different ways can the students arrange themselves in line?

5. Glen has 5 T-shirts. How many ways can he choose 1 T-shirt for Monday, 1 T-shirt for Tuesday, and 1 T-shirt for Wednesday if he doesn't repeat any T-shirt?

6. Glenn has 5 T-shirts. How many ways can he choose a group of 3 T-shirts if he doesn't repeat any T-shirt?

7. How many ways can you choose 2 beach balls from a selection of 20 beach balls?

8. A team is choosing its uniform colors. They can choose from red, gold, black, green, purple, silver, blue, orange, white, and red. How many different 2-color combinations could the team choose?

CHECK YOUR ANSWERS

1. $9 \times 8 \times 7 = 504$ ways

2. $5 \times 4 \times 3 \times 2 \times 1 = 120$ ways

3. $10 \times 9 \times 8 \times 7 = 5{,}040$

4. $3 \times 2 \times 1 = 6$ ways

5. Since order matters we use permutations:
$$_nP_r = \frac{5!}{(5-3)!} = 5 \times 4 \times 3 = 60 \text{ ways}$$

6. Since order doesn't matter, we use combinations:
$$_nC_r = \frac{_nP_r}{r!} = {_5C_3} = 5 \times 4 \times \frac{5 \times 4 \times 3}{3 \times 2 \times 1} = \frac{60}{6} = 10 \text{ ways}$$

7. $_nC_r = \dfrac{_nP_r}{r!} = {_{20}C_2} = \dfrac{20 \cdot 19}{2 \cdot 1} = \dfrac{380}{2} = 190$ ways

8. $_{10}C_2 = \dfrac{10 \cdot 9}{2 \cdot 1} = \dfrac{90}{2} = 45$ different combinations

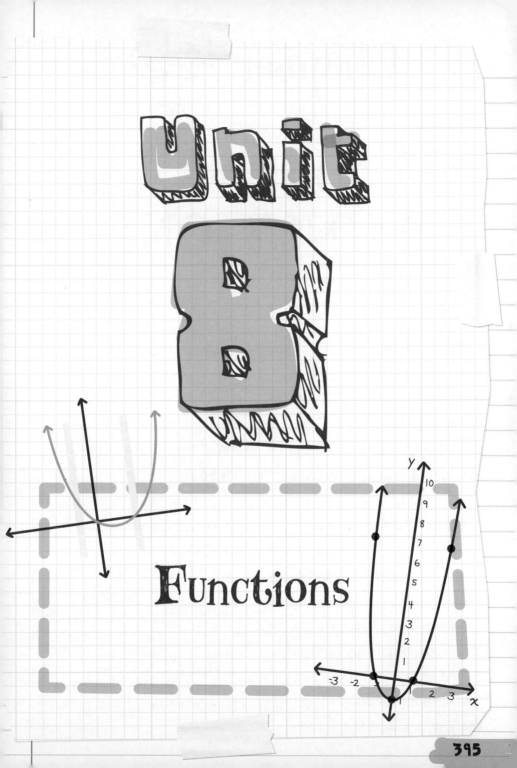

Unit

8

Functions

Chapter 45

RELATIONS AND FUNCTIONS

A **RELATION** is a set of input and output values (ordered pairs).

Whenever there is a relation between two sets, the set of all the input elements is called the **DOMAIN** and the set of all the output elements is called the **RANGE**.

A **FUNCTION** is a mathematical relationship between two variables, an INDEPENDENT VARIABLE and a DEPENDENT VARIABLE, where there is *only one* output for each input. You can call the values input and output, or *x* and *y*. (In many cases, the *output* is represented by the *y*-value and the *input* is

> stands alone: unaffected by other variables

> depends on the independent variables

represented by the x-value. But this is not always true.)

In a function, the value of y is dependent on the value of x.

> A function is a special relationship where each element of the domain is paired with exactly one element in the range.

You can represent a function in a table, in a graph, in words, or as a diagram.

> Relations can be any kind of relationship between sets of numbers, but functions are a special kind of relation where there is only one y-value for each x-value.

EXAMPLE: Is the relation (-4, -2), (-1, 4), (0, 6), (2, 10) a function?

Use a diagram to show the relationship between all the values of the domain and all the values of the range.

Domain (input)   Range (output)

-4 ————————————→ -2
-1 ————————————→ 4
0 —————————————→ 6
2 ————————————→ 10

Each input (in the domain) has only one output (in the range). This relation *is* a function because all the input values are unique.

(5,8) (-2,1)

398

EXAMPLE: Is the relation (6, 0), (–2, 7), (1, 5), (–3, 7) a function?

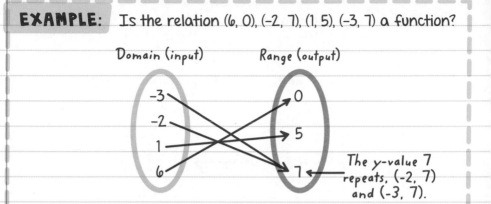

Domain (input)   Range (output)

–3
–2
1
6

0
5
7

The y-value 7 repeats, (-2, 7) and (-3, 7).

This relation *is* a function because each input (in the domain) has only one output (in the range). All the input values are unique.

Even though there are y-values that repeat, this is still a function.

IMPORTANT NOTE
For a function:
It IS NOT okay for the x-values to repeat.
It IS okay for the y-values to repeat.

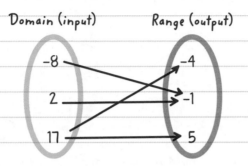
Another way to easily determine if a relation is a function is
to graph it on the coordinate plane and do a VERTICAL LINE
TEST (OR VLT). This is a test where you draw any vertical
line (or more) on the graph: If your vertical line touches
more than one point of the relation, it's not a function.

The vertical line test validates that none of the *x*-values
repeat, and a relation is a function if none of the domain
numbers (*x*-coordinates) repeat.

Vertical line tests:

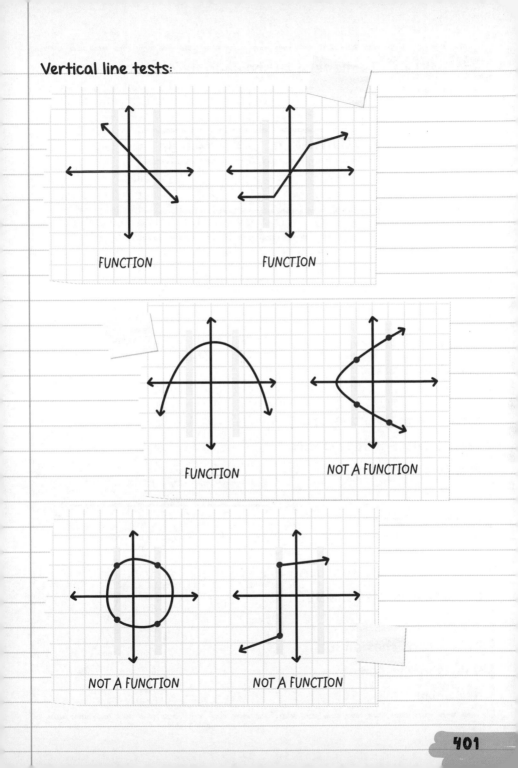

FUNCTION

FUNCTION

FUNCTION

NOT A FUNCTION

NOT A FUNCTION

NOT A FUNCTION

Is the relation shown in the table below a function?

DOMAIN (x)	RANGE (y)
-4	8
-2	4
0	0
2	-4
4	-8

Graph the relation on the coordinate plane.

Then use the vertical line test to check if the relation is a function or not.

Is this a function?

This relation *is* a function because it passes the VLT.

This means that all the values in the domain are unique.

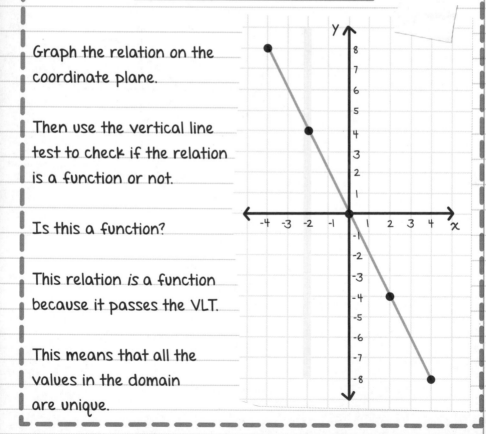

EXAMPLE: Is the relation shown in the table below a function?

DOMAIN (x)	RANGE (y)
-5	3
-5	6
-2	3
1	5
4	2
4	6

Graph the relation on the coordinate plane.

Then use the vertical line test to check if the relation is a function or not.

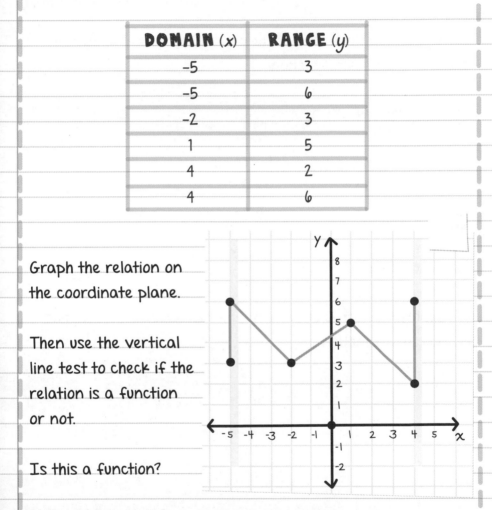

Is this a function?

This relation is *not* a function because a vertical line can be drawn that touches two or more points, so it fails the VLT.

This means that there are values in the domain that repeat.

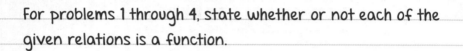
For problems 1 through 4, state whether or not each of the given relations is a function.

1. (3, 5), (2, 0), (7, 8), (12, 1)

2. (4, –9), (8, 7), (–5, 2), (8, 0)

3. (–0.6, 3.7), (4.1, 5.9), (5.9, –2.8), (–7.3, 8.2)

4. (0, –5), (8, –7), (0, 5)

For problems 5 through 8, state whether or not the graphed relation is a function.

5.

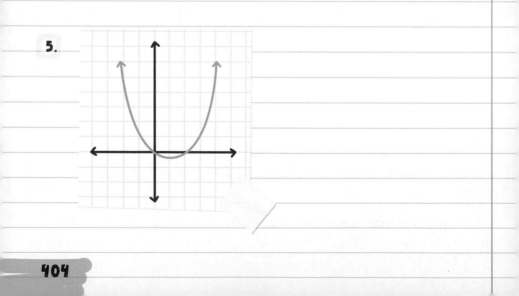

6.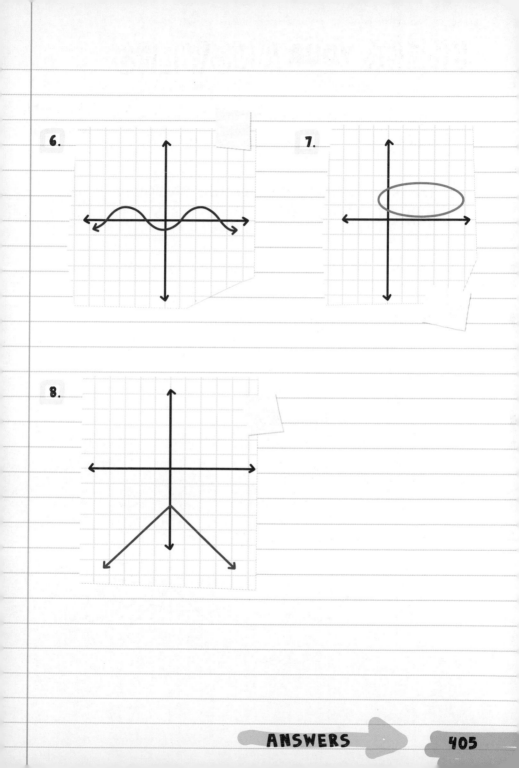

7.

8.

1. This is a function because none of the x-values repeat.

2. This is not a function because the x-value 8 has more than one y-value.

3. This is a function because none of the x-values repeat.

4. This is not a function because the x-value 0 has more than one y-value.

5. 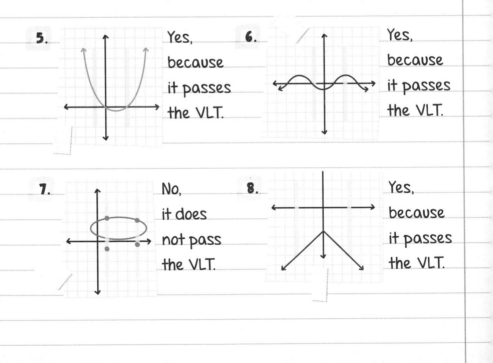 Yes, because it passes the VLT.

6. Yes, because it passes the VLT.

7. No, it does not pass the VLT.

8. Yes, because it passes the VLT.

Chapter 46

FUNCTION NOTATION

Functions can be represented by graphs, tables, and equations. They can also be represented by FUNCTION NOTATION, a shortened way to write functions.

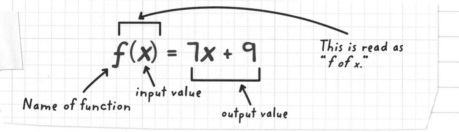

$$f(x) = 7x + 9$$

This is read as "f of x."

Name of function

input value

output value

We usually use the letter f to represent a function, but any letter can be used.

The input is the variable inside the parentheses.

EVALUATING FUNCTIONS is the process of substituting a number into the input to find the output.

For example, $f(x) = -3x + 10$ when $x = 2$ means we need to find the value of $f(x)$. We substitute the given value into the input to find the output.

$f(x) = -3x + 10$ First, substitute 2 for the variable x.

$f(2) = -3(2) + 10$

$f(2) = -6 + 10$ Then, calculate.

$\therefore f(2) = 4$ represents "therefore"

EXAMPLE: Evaluate $g(h) = h^2 - 1$ when $h = -3$.

$g(h) = h^2 - 1$ Substitute -3 for h.

$g(-3) = (-3)^2 - 1$

$g(-3) = 9 - 1$ Calculate.

$\therefore g(-3) = 8$

Sometimes the input can be an algebraic expression, but the steps are still the same.

EXAMPLE: Evaluate $f(x) = 2x + 7$ when $x = 3a + b$.

$f(x) = 2x + 7$ Substitute $3a + b$ for x.

$f(3a + b) = 2(3a + b) + 7$ Use the Distributive Property to calculate.

$\therefore f(3a + b) = 6a + 2b + 7$

EXAMPLE: Evaluate $j(p) = 2n - 3p$ when $p = 5m + 2n$.

$j(p) = 2n - 3p$ Substitute $5m + 2n$ for p.

$j(5m + 2n) = 2n - 3(5m + 2n)$

$j(5m + 2n) = 2n - 15m - 6n$

                         Distribute and then combine like terms.

$j(5m + 2n) = -15m - 4n$

We can use function notation to solve for an input value.

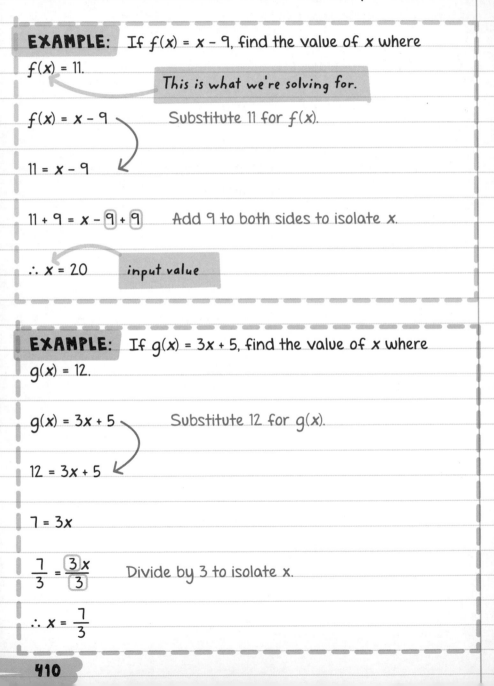

EXAMPLE: If $f(x) = x - 9$, find the value of x where $f(x) = 11$.

This is what we're solving for.

$f(x) = x - 9$ Substitute 11 for $f(x)$.

$11 = x - 9$

$11 + 9 = x - \boxed{9} + \boxed{9}$ Add 9 to both sides to isolate x.

$\therefore x = 20$ input value

EXAMPLE: If $g(x) = 3x + 5$, find the value of x where $g(x) = 12$.

$g(x) = 3x + 5$ Substitute 12 for $g(x)$.

$12 = 3x + 5$

$7 = 3x$

$\dfrac{7}{3} = \dfrac{\boxed{3}x}{\boxed{3}}$ Divide by 3 to isolate x.

$\therefore x = \dfrac{7}{3}$

EXAMPLE: If $j(x) = \dfrac{2x-5}{7}$, find the value of x where $j(x) = -3$.

$j(x) = \dfrac{2x-5}{7}$ Substitute −3 for $j(x)$.

$-3 = \dfrac{2x-5}{7}$

$-3(7) = \dfrac{2x-5}{7}(7)$ Multiply both sides by 7.

$-21 = 2x - 5$ Add 5 to both sides.

$-16 = 2x$

$\therefore x = -8$

EXAMPLE: If $p(a) = a^2 - 5$, find the value of a where $p(a) = 11$.

$p(a) = a^2 - 5$ Substitute 11 for $p(a)$.

$11 = a^2 - 5$ Add 5 to both sides.

$16 = a^2$ Take the square root of both sides.

$\therefore a = 4$ or -4 $(4 \times 4) = 16$ and $(-4 \times -4) = 16$

CHECK YOUR KNOWLEDGE

For problems 1 through 5, evaluate each function.

1. $f(x) = x - 7$ when $x = 5$

2. $g(x) = -6x + 9$ when $x = -2$

3. $h(a) = a^2 + 4$ when $a = -3$

4. $k(p) = p^2 - 5p$ when $p = 6$

5. $j(x) = 9x^2 - 6x + 1$ when $x = -2$

For problems 6 through 10, find the value of each of the following variables.

6. If $f(x) = x + 3$, find the value of x where $f(x) = -2$.

7. If $m(n) = -9 + \dfrac{1}{2}n$, find the value of n where $m(n) = 3$.

8. If $p(t) = \dfrac{8t + 7}{3}$, find the value of t where $p(t) = -3$.

9. If $k(s) = s^2 - 7$, find the value of s where $k(s) = 18$.

10. If $j(a) = a^3 + 11$, find the value of a where $j(a) = 38$.

CHECK YOUR ANSWERS

1. $f(5) = -2$

2. $g(-2) = 21$

3. $h(-3) = 13$

4. $k(6) = 6$

5. $j(-2) = 49$

6. $x = -5$

7. $n = 24$

8. $t = -2$

9. $s = 5$ or -5 ($5 \times 5 = 25$ and $-5 \times -5 = 25$)

10. $a = 3$

Chapter 47

APPLICATION OF FUNCTIONS

Functions can be graphed and evaluated. **LINEAR FUNCTIONS** are functions whose graphs are straight lines. **NONLINEAR FUNCTIONS** are functions whose graphs are NOT straight lines, and they are NOT in the form $y = mx + b$.

An example of a nonlinear function is a QUADRATIC EQUATION. In a quadratic equation, the input variable (x) is squared (x^2). The result is a **PARABOLA**, which is a U-shaped curve.

More on this later!

Parabolas

To make an input/output chart and graph $y = x^2$, calculate the given input data to find the output. Use the values to plot a coordinate point.

INPUT (x)	FUNCTION $y = x^2$	OUTPUT (y)	COORDINATE POINTS (x, y)
-3	$y = (-3)^2$	9	(-3, 9)
-2	$y = (-2)^2$	4	(-2, 4)
-1	$y = (-1)^2$	1	(-1, 1)
0	$y = (0)^2$	0	(0, 0)
1	$y = (1)^2$	1	(1, 1)
2	$y = (2)^2$	4	(2, 4)
3	$y = (3)^2$	9	(3, 9)

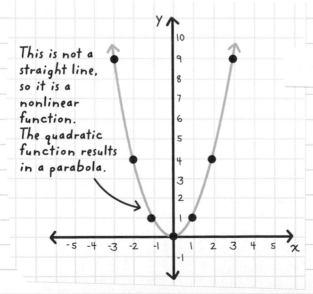

This is not a straight line, so it is a nonlinear function.
The quadratic function results in a parabola.

EXAMPLE: Graph $y = 2x^2 - 1$ by making a table that shows the relation between some x-values and y-values.

INPUT (x)	FUNCTION $y = 2x^2 - 1$	OUTPUT (y)	COORDINATE POINTS (x, y)
-2	$y = 2(-2)^2 - 1$ $y = 2(4) - 1$ $y = 7$	7	(-2, 7)
-1	$y = 2(-1)^2 - 1$ $y = 2(1) - 1$ $y = 1$	1	(-1, 1)
0	$y = 2(0)^2 - 1$ $y = 2(0) - 1$ $y = -1$	-1	(0, -1)
1	$y = 2(1)^2 - 1$ $y = 2(1) - 1$ $y = 1$	1	(1, 1)
2	$y = 2(2)^2 - 1$ $y = 2(4) - 1$ $y = 7$	7	(2, 7)

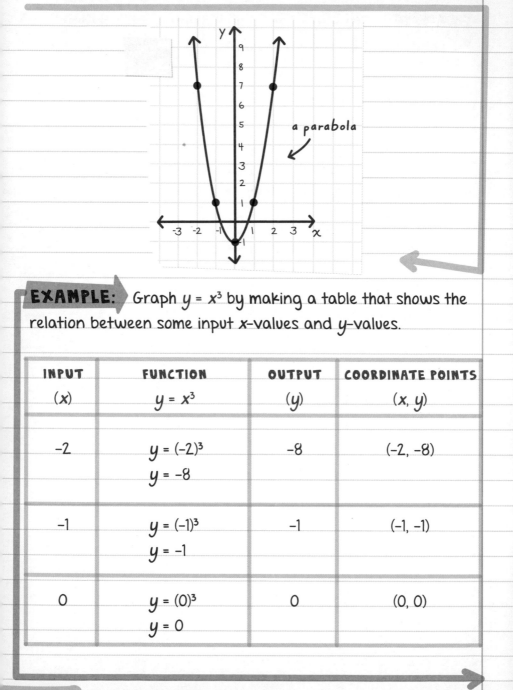

a parabola

EXAMPLE: Graph $y = x^3$ by making a table that shows the relation between some input x-values and y-values.

INPUT (x)	FUNCTION $y = x^3$	OUTPUT (y)	COORDINATE POINTS (x, y)
–2	$y = (-2)^3$ $y = -8$	–8	(–2, –8)
–1	$y = (-1)^3$ $y = -1$	–1	(–1, –1)
0	$y = (0)^3$ $y = 0$	0	(0, 0)

1	$y = (1)^3$ $y = 1$	1	(1, 1)
2	$y = (2)^3$ $y = 8$	8	(2, 8)

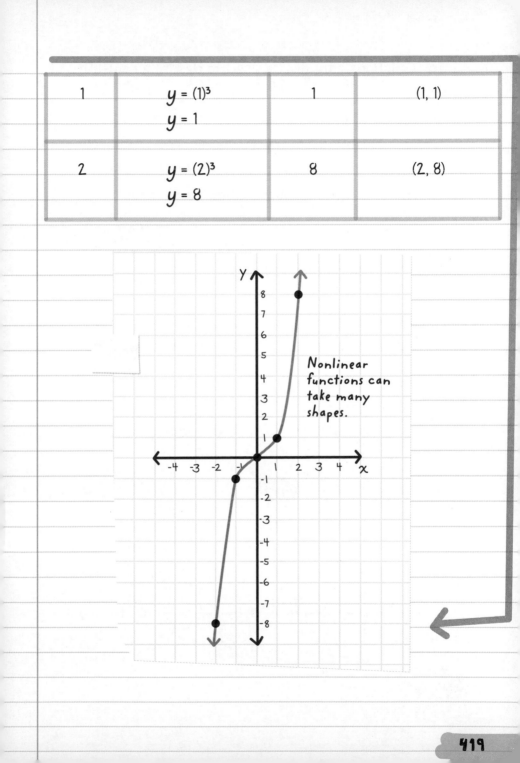

Nonlinear functions can take many shapes.

Nonlinear functions can also be used to describe real-life situations.

EXAMPLE: Javier rides a roller coaster. The graph below displays Javier's height on the roller coaster above (sea level) (in feet), after a specific amount of time (in seconds).

Sea level = x-axis

At what times is the roller coaster at a height of 200 feet above sea level?

Note: For each coordinate, the x-value is the number of seconds, and the y-value is the height in feet.

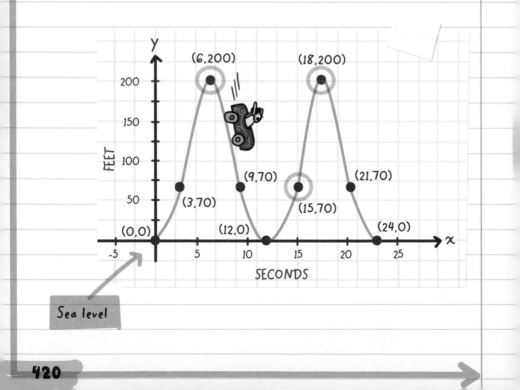

Sea level

The graph shows that the roller coaster reaches a height of 200 feet twice.

The roller coaster is 200 feet above sea level at **6 seconds** and at **18 seconds**.

Approximately at what height is the roller coaster after 7 seconds?

Since 7 seconds is between 6 seconds and 9 seconds, our answer needs to be in between 200 feet and 70 feet.

After 7 seconds, the roller coaster with Javier is at **approximately 175 feet** above sea level.

1. Complete the table. Then graph $y = x^2 - 3$.

INPUT (x)	FUNCTION $y = x^2 - 3$	OUTPUT (y)	COORDINATE POINTS (x, y)
-2			
-1			
0			
1			
2			

2. Complete the table. Then graph $y = \frac{1}{2}x^3 + 4$.

INPUT (x)	FUNCTION $y = \frac{1}{2}x^3 + 4$	OUTPUT (y)	COORDINATE POINTS (x, y)
-2			
-1			
0			
1			
2			

For problems 3 through 5, use the information provided below.

Tanya leaves her home and walks to the park. She rests at the park for a while and then runs home. The graph below displays the distance that Tanya is away from her home (in miles) after a specific amount of time (in hours).

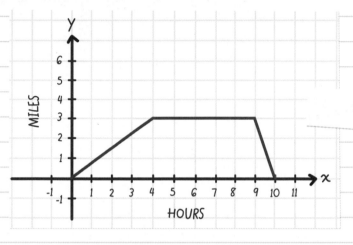

3. How far away is Tanya from her home after 5 hours?

4. Approximately at what time is Tanya 3 miles away from home?

5. After how many hours does Tanya arrive home from the park?

1.

INPUT (x)	FUNCTION $y = x^2 - 3$	OUTPUT (y)	COORDINATE POINTS (x, y)
–2	$y = (-2)^2 - 3$ $y = 4 - 3; y = 1$	1	(–2, 1)
–1	$y = (-1)^2 - 3$ $y = 1 - 3; y = -2$	–2	(–1, –2)
0	$y = (0)^2 - 3$ $y = 0 - 3; y = -3$	–3	(0, –3)
1	$y = (1)^2 - 3$ $y = 1 - 3; y = -2$	–2	(1, –2)
2	$y = (2)^2 - 3$ $y = 4 - 3; y = 1$	1	(2, 1)

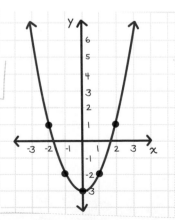

2.

INPUT (x)	FUNCTION $y = \frac{1}{2}x^3 + 4$	OUTPUT (y)	COORDINATE POINTS (x, y)
-2	$y = \frac{1}{2}(-2)^3 + 4$ $y = \frac{1}{2}(-8) + 4$ $y = 0$	0	$(-2, 0)$
-1	$y = \frac{1}{2}(-1)^3 + 4$ $y = \frac{1}{2}(-1) + 4$ $y = \frac{7}{2}$	$\frac{7}{2}$	$\left(-1, \frac{7}{2}\right)$
0	$y = \frac{1}{2}(0)^3 + 4$ $y = \frac{1}{2}(0) + 4$ $y = 4$	4	$(0, 4)$
1	$y = \frac{1}{2}(1)^3 + 4$ $y = \frac{1}{2}(1) + 4$ $y = \frac{9}{2}$	$\frac{9}{2}$	$\left(1, \frac{9}{2}\right)$

INPUT (x)	FUNCTION $y = \frac{1}{2}x^3 + 4$	OUTPUT (y)	COORDINATE POINTS (x, y)
2	$y = \frac{1}{2}(2)^3 + 4$ $y = \frac{1}{2}(8) + 4$ $y = 8$	8	(2, 8)

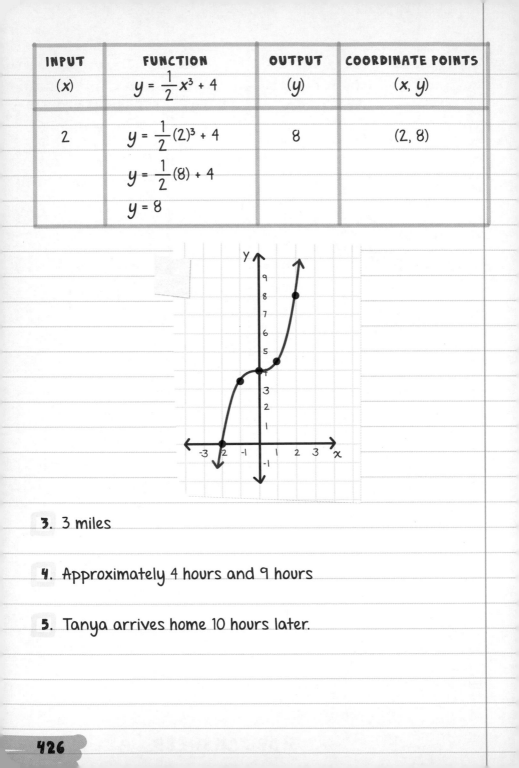

3. 3 miles

4. Approximately 4 hours and 9 hours

5. Tanya arrives home 10 hours later.

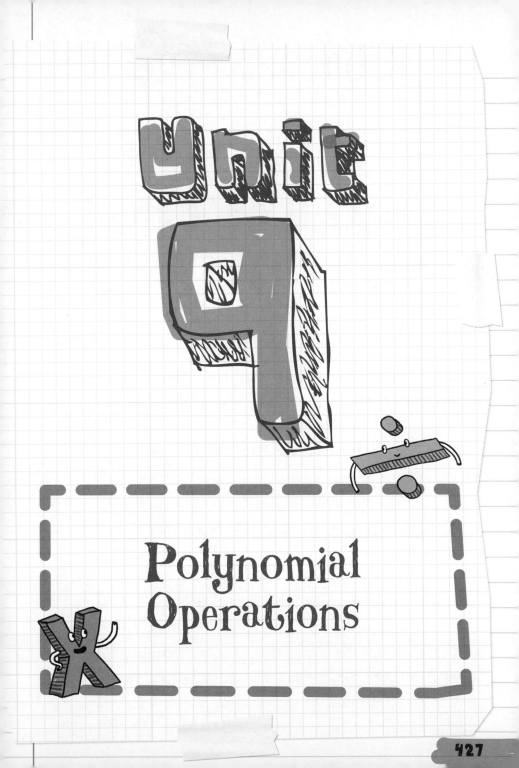

Unit 9

Polynomial Operations

Chapter 48

ADDING AND SUBTRACTING POLYNOMIALS

A MONOMIAL is an expression that has 1 term.

For example: $38m$

> $mono = one$

A BINOMIAL is an expression that has 2 terms.

For example: $-7y + \dfrac{1}{2}$

> $bi = two$

A TRINOMIAL is an expression that has 3 terms.

For example: $8a^2 - \dfrac{3}{5}ab + 6b^2$

> $tri = three$

Expressions can also have more than 3 terms.

A POLYNOMIAL is an expression of more than two algebraic terms that is the sum (or difference) of several terms that contain different powers of the same variable(s).

MONOMIAL

BINOMIAL:
A TYPE OF
POLYNOMIAL

TRINOMIAL:
A TYPE OF
POLYNOMIAL

Examples of polynomials:

$38m \quad -7y + \dfrac{1}{2}$

$8a^2 - \dfrac{3}{5} ab + 6b^2$

$\sqrt{3} \, xyz^3 - \dfrac{9}{8} abc^5 + 7k - 4m + 2.6$

Expressions can be simplified by *combining like terms*.
In the same way, we can **simplify** polynomials by **combining like terms** using addition and subtraction.

> Like terms have the same
> variables (sometimes with more
> than one variable, like 7*ab*)
> raised to the same powers.

To add or subtract polynomials:

Step 1: Rewrite the expression by "distributing" the addition or subtraction so the parentheses do not need to be included.

Step 2: Combine like terms.

Step 3: Write the polynomial in descending order for x.

For example, $22x + 5x^3 + 6 \longrightarrow 5x^3 + 22x + 6$.

Remember the Distributive Property!
A positive sign or a negative sign in front
of a polynomial is just like distributing 1 or –1:
$-(7x - 9y) = -1(7x - 9y) = -7x + 9y$ The result has no parentheses.

EXAMPLE: Find the sum and/or difference.
$(3x + 5y) + (7x - 9y)$. Simplify your answer.

$= (3x + 5y) + (7x - 9y)$ Distribute the + sign to both $7x$ and $-9y$:
$\qquad\qquad\qquad\qquad +(7x) = 7x$ and $+(-9y) = -9y$

$= 3x + 5y + 7x - 9y$

$= 3x + 7x + 5y - 9y$ Simplify by combining like terms.
$\qquad\qquad\qquad\qquad 3x + 7x = 10x$ and $5y - 9y = -4y$

$= 10x - 4y$

EXAMPLE: Find the sum and/or difference.
$(8a^2 + 11a) - (19a - 5)$. Simplify your answer.

$= (8a^2 + 11a) - (19a - 5)$ Distribute the − sign to both $19a$ and −5.
Subtract by adding the opposite of the
subtrahend. $-(19a) = -19a$ and $-(-5) = 5$

$= 8a^2 + 11a - 19a + 5$ Simplify by combining like terms.
$11a - 19a = -8a$

$= 8a^2 - 8a + 5$

EXAMPLE: Find the sum and/or difference.
$(3m^2 + n) - (5n - 6m^2)$. Simplify your answer.

$= (3m^2 + n) - (5n - 6m^2)$ Distribute the − sign to both
$5n$ and $-6m^2$.

$= 3m^2 + n - 5n + 6m^2$

$= 3m^2 + 6m^2 + n - 5n$ Simplify by combining like terms.
$n - 5n = -4n$ and $3m^2 + 6m^2 = 9m^2$

$= 9m^2 - 4n$

EXAMPLE: Find the sum and/or difference.

$(9a + 10b + 14c) + (8a + 2b + 5c)$. Simplify your answer.

$= (9a + 10b + 14c) + (8a + 2b + 5c)$ Distribute the + sign to 8a, 2b, and 5c.

$= 9a + 10b + 14c + 8a + 2b + 5c$

$= 9a + 8a + 10b + 2b + 14c + 5c$ Simplify by combining like terms.

$= 17a + 12b + 19c$

EXAMPLE: Find the sum and/or difference.

$(0.7a + 9a^2 - 6) - (5 + 4a + 2.6a^2)$. Simplify your answer.

$= (0.7a + 9a^2 - 6) - (5 + 4a + 2.6a^2)$ Distribute the – sign to 5, 4a, and $2.6a^2$.

$= 0.7a + 9a^2 - 6 - 5 - 4a - 2.6a^2$

$= 0.7a - 4a + 9a^2 - 2.6a^2 - 6 - 5$ Simplify by combining like terms.

$= -3.3a + 6.4a^2 - 11$

$= 6.4a^2 - 3.3a - 11$ ← Always write your answer in descending order.

EXAMPLE: Find the sum and/or difference.

$(3m^2 - 6n + 7mn) - (9mn - 4) + (2n + 8m^2 - 1)$.

Simplify your answer.

$= (3m^2 - 6n + 7mn) - (9mn - 4)$

$+ (2n + 8m^2 - 1)$

Distribute the – sign to $9mn$ and -4, and the + sign to $2n$, $8m^2$, and -1.

$= 3m^2 - 6n + 7mn - 9mn + 4 + 2n + 8m^2 - 1$

$= 3m^2 + 8m^2 - 6n + 2n + 7mn - 9mn + 4 - 1$

$= 11m^2 - 4n - 2mn + 3$

$= 11m^2 - 2mn - 4n + 3$

Don't forget to sort your variables alphabetically: mn comes before n.

EXAMPLE: Jared has a rectangular block of wood. He wants to measure a piece of string that wraps around the perimeter of the block of wood. However, Jared doesn't have a ruler with him. He only has a pen and an eraser. He discovers that the length of the block of wood is the same length as 9 erasers put end to end and that the width of the block of wood is the same as 4 pens put end to end. Find how long the string should be.

Let e represent the length of an eraser.
Let p represent the length of a pen.

The length of the block of wood is: $9 \cdot e = 9e$.
The width of the block of wood is: $4 \cdot p = 4p$.

Perimeter = length + width + length + width

$= 9e + 4p + 9e + 4p$

$= 18e + 8p$

$9e$

$4p$ $\quad$ $4p$

$9e$

Therefore, the length of the string is: $18e + 8p$.

Find the sum and/or difference of each polynomial and simplify your answer.

1. $(3x^2 - 6x) + (4x^2 - 11x)$

2. $(3k^2 - 8) + (-4k - 5)$

3. $(8w^9 - 5z - wz^3) + (8wz^3 + 4w^9)$

4. $(2p^3 - 5pq^2 + 7pq) + (11p^2q - 4pq - 3)$

5. $(8x - 5y) - (7x - 9y)$

6. $(7m^5 + 0.7y - 1) - (6y + m^5 - 12)$

7. $(6z + 9t^2 + 7tz) - (4tz - 3t^2 + 5z + 8)$

8. $(\frac{1}{2}s + 4st - 7t^2) - (3s + st) - (6st - \frac{1}{4}t^2)$

9. $(6a^5 - 7abc + 9b^2c - 8) + (5b^2c + 8abc - 4) - (4a^5 + 9a^4 - 3ab)$

10. Adam is finding a square's perimeter. He discovers that the length of one side is the same length as 2 pennies and 5 dimes set side by side. What is the perimeter of the square?

CHECK YOUR ANSWERS

1. $7x^2 - 17x$

2. $3k^2 - 4k - 13$

3. $12w^9 + 7wz^3 - 5z$

4. $2p^3 + 11p^2q - 5pq^2 + 3pq - 3$

5. $x + 4y$

6. $6m^5 - 5.3y + 11$

7. $12t^2 + 3tz + z - 8$

8. $-\dfrac{5}{2}s - 3st - \dfrac{27}{4}t^2$

9. $2a^5 - 9a^4 + 3ab + abc + 14b^2c - 12$

10. If p represents the length of a penny and d represents the length of a dime, the perimeter is: $8p + 20d$.

Chapter 49

MULTIPLYING AND DIVIDING EXPONENTS

You can simplify numeric and algebraic expressions that contain more than one exponent by combining the exponents. The only requirement is that the **BASE** must be the **SAME**.

$3^2 \cdot 3^9$ **CAN** be simplified ⟶ The bases, 3 and 3, are the same.

$8^5 \cdot 7^4$ **CANNOT** be simplified ⟶ The bases, 8 and 7, are not the same.

$4^5 \div 3^5$ **CANNOT** be simplified ⟶ The bases, 4 and 3, are not the same even though the exponents are the same.

Multiplying Exponents with the Same Base

You can multiply exponents with the same base by adding:

$$x^a \cdot x^b = x^{a+b}$$

When multiplying exponents with the same base:

1. Write the common base.

2. ADD the exponents.

EXAMPLE: Simplify $5^2 \cdot 5^6$.

$= 5^2 \cdot 5^6$ ← The exponents can be added because the bases are the same.

$= 5^{2+6}$　　　　Add the exponents.

$= 5^8$

Check:

$5^2 \cdot 5^6 = 5 \cdot 5 \cdot 5 \cdot 5 \cdot 5 \cdot 5 \cdot 5 \cdot 5 = 5^8$

Dividing Exponents with the Same Base

You can divide exponents with the same base
by subtracting:

$$x^a \div x^b = x^{a-b}$$

When dividing exponents with the same base:

1. write the common base.

2. SUBTRACT the exponents.

EXAMPLE: Simplify $8^7 \div 8^3$.

$= 8^7 \div 8^3$ ← The exponents can be subtracted
because the bases are the same.

$= 8^{7-3}$ Subtract the exponents.

$= 8^4$

Check:

$$8^7 \div 8^3 = \frac{8^7}{8^3} = \frac{8 \cdot 8 \cdot 8 \cdot 8 \cdot \cancel{8} \cdot \cancel{8} \cdot \cancel{8}}{\cancel{8} \cdot \cancel{8} \cdot \cancel{8}} = 8^4$$

EXAMPLE: Simplify $(-2)^9 \div (-2)$.

$= (-2)^9 \div (-2)$ ← The exponents can be subtracted because the bases are the same.

$= (-2)^9 \div (-2)^1$ ← Whenever an exponent is not written, it means that the exponent is 1.

$= (-2)^{9-1}$ Subtract the exponents.

$= (-2)^8$

EXAMPLE: Simplify $6^{12} \div 6^9 \div 6^5$.

$= 6^{12} \div 6^9 \div 6^5$ ← The bases are the same.

$= 6^{12-9-5}$ Subtract the exponents.

$= 6^{-2}$

Another way to write this is: $6^{-2} = \dfrac{1}{6^2} = \dfrac{1}{36}$

We can multiply **and** divide exponents in the same expression.

Remember to use the correct Order of Operations!

For example: to simplify the expression $9^7 \cdot 9^3 \div 9^2$:

1. Add the first two exponents because the bases are multiplied.

$$= 9^{7+3} \div 9^2$$

$$= 9^{10} \div 9^2$$

2. Then subtract the next exponent from the sum, because the bases are divided.

$$= 9^{10-2}$$

Simplified:

$$= 9^8$$

EXAMPLE: Simplify:

$(-3)^7 \div (-3)^9 \cdot (-3)^{10} \cdot (-3)^5 \div (-3)^{-2}$.

$(-3)^7 \div (-3)^9 \cdot (-3)^{10} \cdot (-3)^5 \div (-3)^{-2}$ ⟵—— The bases are the same.

$= (-3)^{7-9} \cdot (-3)^{10} \cdot (-3)^5 \div (-3)^{-2}$ ⟵—— Subtract the first two exponents.

$= (-3)^{-2} \cdot (-3)^{10} \cdot (-3)^5 \div (-3)^{-2}$

$= (-3)^{-2+10} \cdot (-3)^5 \div (-3)^{-2}$ ⟵—— Add the difference and the next exponent.

$= (-3)^8 \cdot (-3)^5 \div (-3)^{-2}$

$= (-3)^{8+5} \div (-3)^{-2}$ ⟵—— Add the sum to the next exponent.

$= (-3)^{13} \div (-3)^{-2}$

$= (-3)^{13-(-2)}$ ⟵—— Subtract the last exponent from the difference.

$= (-3)^{15}$

CHECK YOUR KNOWLEDGE

Simplify each expression.

1. $7^2 \cdot 7^8$

2. $9^3 \div 9^1$

3. $(-12)^2 \div (-12)^{-9}$

4. $3^8 \cdot 3^6 \div 3^9$

5. $(-5)^7 \div (-5)^6 \cdot (-5)^3$

Solve.

6. Mr. Jones asks Ahmed, Brian, Celia, and Dee to simplify $3^5 \cdot 3^7$. These are their answers:

Ahmed: $3^5 \cdot 3^7 = (3 + 3)^{5 + 7} = 6^{12}$.

Brian: $3^5 \cdot 3^7 = (3 \cdot 3)^{5 + 7} = 9^{12}$.

Celia: $3^5 \cdot 3^7 = 3^{5 + 7} = 3^{12}$.

Dee: $3^5 \cdot 3^7 = 3^{5 \cdot 7} = 3^{35}$.

Who is correct?

CHECK YOUR ANSWERS

1. 7^{10}

2. 9^2

3. $(-12)^{11}$

4. 3^5

5. $(-5)^4$

6. Celia's answer is correct.

Chapter 50

MULTIPLYING AND DIVIDING MONOMIALS

We can multiply and divide monomials using the same approach we use to multiply and divide exponents.

- If the bases are the **same**, you **can** simplify the monomials.

- If the bases are **different**, you **cannot** simplify the monomials.

To simplify the expression $a^3 \cdot 2b^5$:

1. Look at the bases: Are they the same?

2. If the bases are the **same**, **combine** the exponents.

$a^3 \cdot 2b^5$ The two bases, a and b, are different.

$= 2a^3b^5$

EXAMPLE: Simplify $x^2 \cdot 2xy \cdot x^4$.

$x^2 \cdot 2xy \cdot x^4$

$= 2 \cdot x^{2+1+4} \cdot y$ Combine the exponents for the base x. The exponent for the y base cannot be combined.

$= 2x^7y$

EXAMPLE: Simplify $3m^{-4}n^7 \cdot 5m^6n^2$.

$3m^{-4}n^7 \cdot 5m^6n^2$ Combine the exponents for the base m.

Combine the exponents for the base n.

The exponents for m and n cannot be combined.

$= 3 \cdot 5 \cdot m^{-4+6} \cdot n^{7+2}$

$= 3 \cdot 5 \cdot m^2n^9$ Multiply the constants: $3 \cdot 5 = 15$.

$= 15m^2n^9$

EXAMPLE: Simplify $21x^6y^{10} \div 7x^4y^3$.

$21x^6y^{10} \div 7x^4y^3$

$21 \div 7 = 3$ Divide the coefficients.

$= 3x^{6-4} \, y^{10-3}$ Combine the exponents for the base x.

Combine the exponents for the base y.

The exponents for x and y cannot be combined.

$= 3x^2y^7$

$3a^5 \div 10a^9$

$= \dfrac{3}{10} a^{5-9}$

$= \dfrac{3}{10} a^{-4}$

To make the simplification easier to see, you can also write the solution as:

$3a^5 \div 10a^9 = \dfrac{3a^5}{10a^9}$

$= \dfrac{3}{10a^{-4}}$

An exponent inside the parentheses and another outside the parentheses is called a POWER OF A POWER. A power of a power can be simplified by multiplying the exponents. It looks like this:

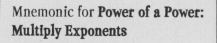

Mnemonic for **Power of a Power: Multiply Exponents**

Powerful **O**rangutans **P**ropelled **M**ultiple **E**lephants.

$$(x^a)^b = x^{a \cdot b}$$

EXAMPLE: Simplify $(3a^7b^4)^2$.

$(3a^7b^4)^2$

$= 3^{1 \cdot 2} \cdot a^{7 \cdot 2} \cdot b^{4 \cdot 2}$ Multiply each exponent inside the parentheses by the exponent on the outside.

$= 3^2 a^{14} b^8$

$= 9a^{14} b^8$

EXAMPLE: Simplify $(5a^3b^4)^2 \cdot (2a^5b)^3$.

$(5a^3b^4)^2 \cdot (2a^5b)^3$ First, expand each monomial.

$= (5^{1 \cdot 2} a^{3 \cdot 2} b^{4 \cdot 2}) \cdot (2^{1 \cdot 3} a^{5 \cdot 3} b^{1 \cdot 3})$

$= (5^2 a^6 b^8) \cdot (2^3 a^{15} b^3)$ Next, multiply the monomials.

$= (25a^6 b^8) \cdot (8a^{15} b^3)$

$= 25 \cdot 8 \cdot a^{6 + 15} \cdot b^{8 + 3}$

$= 200a^{21} b^{11}$

EXAMPLE: Simplify $(2p^3q)^4 \div (4p^6q^2)^3$.

$(2p^3q)^4 \div (4p^6q^2)^3$ First, expand each monomial.

$= (2^{1 \cdot 4}p^{3 \cdot 4}q^{1 \cdot 4}) \div (4^{1 \cdot 3}p^{6 \cdot 3}q^{2 \cdot 3})$

$= (2^4 p^{12} q^4) \div (4^3 p^{18} q^6)$

$= (16p^{12} q^4) \div (64p^{18} q^6)$ Next, divide the monomials.

$= 16 \div 64 \cdot p^{12-18} \cdot q^{4-6} = \frac{1}{4} p^{-6} q^{-2} \left[\text{or } \frac{1}{4p^6q^2} \right]$

EXAMPLE: Simplify $(2x^4y^{-5})^{-3} \div (5x^9y^{-7})^2$.

$(2x^4y^{-5})^{-3} \div (5x^9y^{-7})^2$ Expand each monomial.

$= (2^{1 \cdot (-3)}x^{4 \cdot (-3)}y^{-5 \cdot (-3)}) \div (5^{1 \cdot 2}x^{9 \cdot 2}y^{-7 \cdot 2})$

$= (2^{-3}x^{-12}y^{15}) \div (5^2 x^{18} y^{-14})$

$= (\frac{1}{8} x^{-12}y^{15}) \div (25x^{18}y^{-14})$ Divide the monomials.

$= \frac{1}{8} \div 25 \cdot x^{-12-18} \cdot y^{15-(-14)}$

$= \frac{1}{200} x^{-30} y^{29} \left[\text{or } \frac{y^{29}}{200x^{30}} \right]$

CHECK YOUR KNOWLEDGE

Simplify each expression. Write your answer using only positive exponents.

1. $x^4 y^7 \cdot x^3 y^5$

2. $3a^4 b^2 c^6 \cdot (-2a^5 b)$

3. $(12x^5 y^{-8} z^4) \div (-15x^9 y^3 z)$

4. $(3x^3)^2$

5. $(8m^{-3} n^{-4})^2 \div (4m^{-5} n^2)^3$

Solve.

6. Mrs. Smith asks Ming and Nathan to simplify $(5a^2)^3$.
   These are their answers:
   Ming: $(5a^2)^3 = 5^3 \cdot (a)^{2^3} = 125a^8$.
   Nathan: $(5a^2)^3 = 5^3 \cdot (a)^{2 \cdot 3} = 125a^6$.

   Who is correct?

ANSWERS

1. $x^7 y^{12}$

2. $-6a^9 b^3 c^6$

3. $-\dfrac{4z^3}{5x^4 y^{11}}$

4. $9x^6$

5. $\dfrac{m^9}{n^{14}}$

6. Nathan is correct.

Chapter 51

MULTIPLYING AND DIVIDING POLYNOMIALS

We can use the Distributive Property to multiply polynomials. To simplify the expression $x^2(x^3 + 7y)$:

$x^2(x^3 + 7y)$

First, use the Distributive Property. Multiply each of the terms inside the parentheses by the term outside the parentheses.

$= (x^2 \cdot x^3) + (x^2 \cdot 7y)$

Then, multiply exponents with the same base by adding the exponents.

$= x^{2+3} + 7x^2y$

$= x^5 + 7x^2y$

These are NOT like terms, so they cannot be combined.

Multiplying a monomial (x^2) by a binomial $(x^3 + 7y)$ looks like this:

$$x^2(x^3 + 7y)$$

	x^3	$7y$
x^2	$x^2 \cdot x^3 = x^5$	$x^2 \cdot 7y = 7x^2y$

Answer: $x^2(x^3 + 7y) = x^5 + 7x^2y$

EXAMPLE: Simplify $a^3b(a^2b^7 + ab^4)$.

$= a^3b(a^2b^7 + ab^4)$ Use the Distributive Property.

$= (a^3b \cdot a^2b^7) + (a^3b \cdot ab^4)$ Multiply exponents by using addition.

$= (a^{3+2}b^{1+7}) + (a^{3+1}b^{1+4})$

$= a^5b^8 + a^4b^5$

EXAMPLE: Simplify $(x + 9)(x + 7)$.

$= (x + 9)(x + 7)$

$= (x \cdot x) + (x \cdot 7) + (9 \cdot x) + (9 \cdot 7)$

$= x^2 + 7x + 9x + 63$ Combine like terms.

$= x^2 + 16x + 63$

EXAMPLE: Simplify $(x^3y + x^2y^4)(x^5y^7 - xy^2)$.

$= (x^3y + x^2y^4)(x^5y^7 - xy^2)$

$= (x^3y \cdot x^5y^7) - (x^3y \cdot xy^2) + (x^2y^4 \cdot x^5y^7) - (x^2y^4 \cdot xy^2)$

$= (x^{3+5}y^{1+7}) - (x^{3+1}y^{1+2}) + (x^{2+5}y^{4+7}) - (x^{2+1}y^{4+2})$

$= x^8y^8 - x^4y^3 + x^7y^{11} - x^3y^6$

Multiplying a binomial by another binomial is also called the FOIL Method:

First, Outer, Inner, Last

1. Multiply the FIRST terms within each parentheses.

2. Multiply the Outer terms of the parentheses.

3. Multiply the Inner terms of the parentheses.

4. Multiply the Last terms of the parentheses.

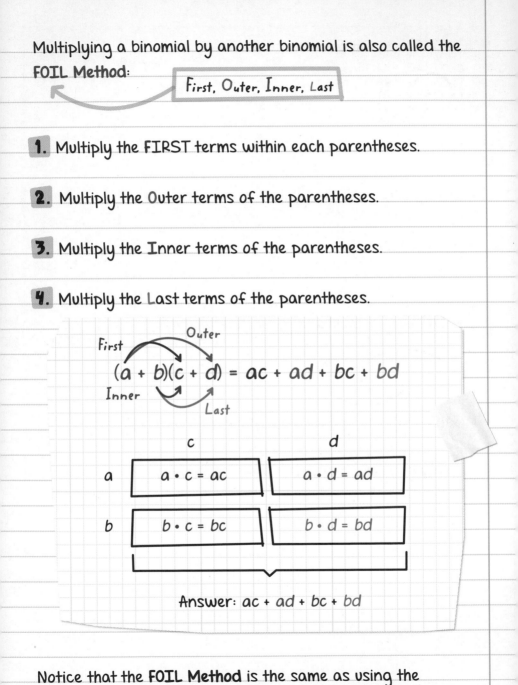

$$(a + b)(c + d) = ac + ad + bc + bd$$

	c	d
a	a · c = ac	a · d = ad
b	b · c = bc	b · d = bd

Answer: $ac + ad + bc + bd$

Notice that the **FOIL Method** is the same as using the Distributive Property for multiplying two binomials!

We can divide a **polynomial** by a **monomial** by separating the expression into separate fractions.

EXAMPLE: Simplify $(a^{10}b^4 - a^8b^5) \div (a^2b^3)$.

$(a^{10}b^4 - a^8b^5) \div (a^2b^3)$

Split into separate fractions by dividing each of the 2 terms by a^2b^3.

$$= \frac{a^{10}b^4}{a^2b^3} - \frac{a^8b^5}{a^2b^3}$$

$= (a^{10-2}b^{4-3}) - (a^{8-2}b^{5-3})$

Subtract to simplify:
$10 - 2 = 8; \ 4 - 3 = 1$
$8 - 2 = 6; \ 5 - 3 = 2$

$= a^8b - a^6b^2$

EXAMPLE: Simplify $(8x^3y^7 - 9x^{12}y^5) \div (6x^{10}y^{11})$.

$(8x^3y^7 - 9x^{12}y^5) \div (6x^{10}y^{11})$

Divide each of the 2 terms by $6x^{10}y^{11}$.

$= \dfrac{8x^3y^7}{6x^{10}y^{11}} - \dfrac{9x^{12}y^5}{6x^{10}y^{11}}$

$= \left(\dfrac{8}{6} x^{3-10}y^{7-11}\right) - \left(\dfrac{9}{6} x^{12-10}y^{5-11}\right)$

Subtract to simplify:
3 – 10 = –7; 7 – 11 = –4
12 – 10 = 2; 5 – 11 = –6

$= \dfrac{4}{3} x^{-7}y^{-4} - \dfrac{3}{2} x^2 y^{-6} \quad \left[\text{or } \dfrac{4}{3x^7y^4} - \dfrac{3x^2}{2y^6}\right]$

CHECK YOUR KNOWLEDGE

Simplify each of the expressions. Write your answer using only positive exponents.

1. $xy(x^3y^5 - x^7)$

2. $3m^2n^3(-5m + 7m^6n^4)$

3. $(x + 2y)(3x - 4y)$

4. $(a^2b - ab^2)(ab + a^5b^3)$

5. $(3x^5y^4 - xy^3)(y^2 + 5xy)$

6. $(3p^3 - 2q^5)(2p^6 + 5q^8)$

7. $(x^5y^3 + x^9y^6) \div (xy)$

8. $(a^{13}b^4 + a^8b^{10}) \div (a^6b^3)$

9. $(6m^{10}n^3 - 8m^2n) \div (2m^8n)$

10. $(3x^5y^2z^7 - 10x^6yz + 8xy^9z^2) \div (-6x^2yz^4)$

CHECK YOUR ANSWERS

1. $x^4y^6 - x^8y$

2. $-15m^3n^3 + 21m^8n^7$

3. $3x^2 + 2xy - 8y^2$

4. $a^3b^2 + a^7b^4 - a^2b^3 - a^6b^5$

5. $3x^5y^6 + 15x^6y^5 - xy^5 - 5x^2y^4$

6. $6p^9 + 15p^3q^8 - 4p^6q^5 - 10q^{13}$

7. $x^4y^2 + x^8y^5$

8. $a^7b + a^2b^7$

9. $3m^2n^2 - \dfrac{4}{m^6}$

10. $-\dfrac{1}{2}x^3yz^3 + \dfrac{5x^4}{3z^3} - \dfrac{4y^8}{3xz^2}$

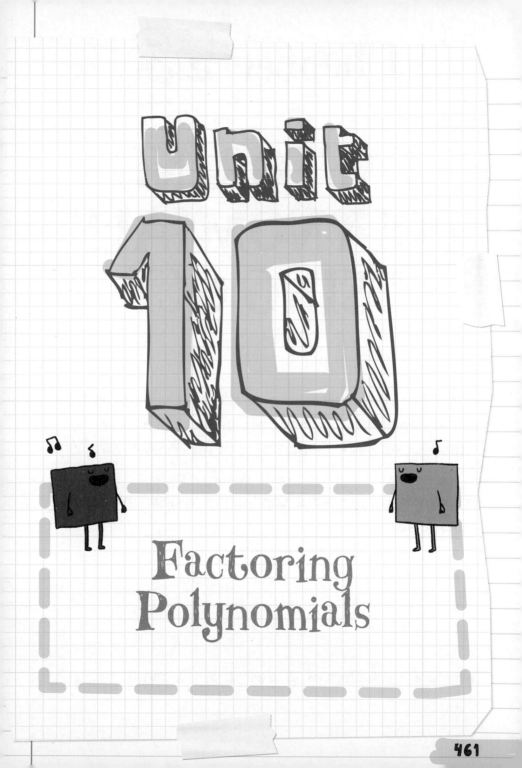

Unit 10

10

Factoring Polynomials

Chapter 52

FACTORING POLYNOMIALS USING GCF

An integer (whole number) can be broken down into its FACTORS. Factors of a number are integers that when multiplied with other integers give us the original number.

For example, the number 12 can be broken down into the following factors:

1 and 12: $1 \cdot 12 = 12$
2 and 6: $2 \cdot 6 = 12$
3 and 4: $3 \cdot 4 = 12$

Therefore, the factors of 12 are: 1, 2, 3, 4, 6, and 12.

Many polynomials can be broken down into factors that you multiply together to get the original polynomial.

For example, the monomial $6x$ can be broken down into:

$\quad$ 1 and $6x$: $1 \cdot 6x = 6x$
$\quad$ 2 and $3x$: $2 \cdot 3x = 6x$
$\quad$ 3 and $2x$: $3 \cdot 2x = 6x$
$\quad$ 6 and x: $6 \cdot x = 6x$

Therefore, the factors of $6x$ are: 1, 2, 3, 6, x, $2x$, $3x$, and $6x$.

EXAMPLE: State the factors of the monomial $7y^3$.

- 1 and $7y^3$: $1 \cdot 7y^3 = 7y^3$

- 7 and y^3: $7 \cdot y^3 = 7y^3$

- y and $7y^2$: $y \cdot 7y^2 = 7y^3$

- $7y$ and y^2: $7y \cdot y^2 = 7y^3$

So, the factors of $7y^3$ are: 1, $7y^3$, 7, y^3, y, $7y^2$, $7y$, and y^2.

We can arrange the factors in order of the exponents:
1, 7, y, $7y$, y^2, $7y^2$, y^3, and $7y^3$.

Write the factors of the monomial 6ab.

1 and 6ab: $1 \cdot 6ab = 6ab$
2 and 3ab: $2 \cdot 3ab = 6ab$
3 and 2ab: $3 \cdot 2ab = 6ab$
6 and ab: $6 \cdot ab = 6ab$
a and 6b: $a \cdot 6b = 6ab$
2a and 3b: $2a \cdot 3b = 6ab$
3a and 2b: $3a \cdot 2b = 6ab$
6a and b: $6a \cdot b = 6ab$

So, the factors of 6ab are: 1, 2, 3, 6, a, 2a, 3a, 6a, b, 2b, 3b, 6b, ab, 2ab, 3ab, and 6ab.

When finding the factors of a polynomial, ask: "What can be multiplied together to end up with the original polynomial?"

EXAMPLE: Tanya is given the expression $ax + ay$.

Tanya says, "The factors of $ax + ay$ are: 1, a, $(x + y)$, and $(ax + ay)$."

Is Tanya correct?

Multiply some of the expressions together, to see if we end up with the original polynomial:

$1 \cdot (ax + ay) = ax + ay$ ✓

$a \cdot (x + y) = ax + ay$ ✓

So the factors of $ax + ay$ are: 1, a, $(x + y)$, and $(ax + ay)$.

Therefore, Tanya is correct.

> The process of rewriting polynomials into their factors is called FACTORIZATION.

GCF OF POLYNOMIALS

When we look at two integers, we can ask: "What is the greatest factor that these two integers share?" This process is called FINDING THE GREATEST COMMON FACTOR, or FINDING THE GCF.

EXAMPLE: Find the GCF of 12 and 20.

- The factors of 12 are: 1, 2, 3, 4, 6, and 12.

- The factors of 20 are: 1, 2, 4, 5, 10, and 20.

Therefore, the GCF of 12 and 20 is: 4.

We can find the GCF of polynomials in the same way.

EXAMPLE: Find the GCF of ax and ay.

- The factors of ax are: 1, ax, a, and x.

- The factors of ay are: 1, ay, a, and y.

Therefore, the GCF of ax and ay is: a.

EXAMPLE: Find the GCF of 4xy and 6xz.

- The factors of 4xy are: 1, 2, 4, x, $2x$, 4x, y, 2y, 4y, xy, 2xy, and 4xy.

- The factors of 6xz are: 1, 2, 3, 6, x, $2x$, 3x, 6x, z, 2z, 3z, 6z, xz, 2xz, 3xz, and 6xz.

Therefore, the GCF of 4xy and 6xz is: 2x.

Listing all the factors of a monomial often takes too long.

There is a more efficient way to find the GCF of two monomials:

1. Find the GCF of the coefficients.

2. Find the highest power of each of the variables that appears within every monomial.

3. Multiply. The GCF is the product of the first two steps.

EXAMPLE: Find the GCF of $8a^2b^7$ and $12a^5b^3$.

Step 1: Find the GCF of the coefficients.

The coefficients are 8 and 12, and the GCF of the coefficients is 4.

Step 2: Find the greatest exponent of each of the variables within the monomials.

The monomials share both a and b:

The highest power of a that both $8a^2b^7$ and $12a^5b^3$ contain is a^2.

The highest power of b that both $8a^2b^7$ and $12a^5b^3$ contain is b^3.

Step 3: Multiply. The GCF is the product of steps 1 and 2.
$4 \cdot a^2 \cdot b^3 = 4a^2b^3$

EXAMPLE: Find the GCF of $10p^5q^9r^2$, $4p^{11}q^4r^3$, and $9p^{13}q^8rs^7$:

Step 1: Find the GCF of the coefficients.

The coefficients are 10, 4, and 9. The GCF of the coefficients is: 1.

Step 2: Find the greatest exponent of each of the variables within the monomials.

The monomials share p, q, and r:

> They do not all contain s.

- The highest power of p that they all contain is: p^5.

- The highest power of q that they all contain is: q^4.

- The highest power of r that they all contain is: r.

Step 3: Multiply the above steps.
$1 \cdot p^5 \cdot q^4 \cdot r = p^5 q^4 r$

FACTORING POLYNOMIALS

Once we find the GCF of several terms of a polynomial, we can factor the entire polynomial.

Ask yourself: "If I factor out the GCF from each of the terms, what factors remain?"

We use this answer to write the polynomial as the product of the GCF and another factor.

To factor a polynomial:

Step 1: Find the GCF of all the terms in the polynomial.

Step 2: For each of the terms, find the remaining factor after you divide by the GCF.

Step 3: Write your answer as the product of the GCF and the sum (or difference) of the remaining factors.

For example to factor $ax + ay$:

Step 1: Find the GCF of the terms ax and ay:

Since a is the only common factor, the GCF is a.

Step 2: For each of the terms, find the remaining factor after you divide by a.

- For the term ax: $\dfrac{ax}{a} = x$

- For the term ay: $\dfrac{ay}{a} = y$

Step 3: Write the answer as the product of a and the sum of x and y.

$$ax + ay = a(x + y)$$

EXAMPLE: Factor $6x^9y^7 - 10x^4y^{15}$

Step 1: Find the GCF of the terms $6x^9y^7$ and $10x^4y^{15}$.

Since the terms are $6x^9y^7$ and $10x^4y^{15}$, the GCF is: $2x^4y^7$.

Step 2: For each of the terms, find the remaining factor after you divide by $2x^4y^7$.

- For the term $6x^9y^7$: $\dfrac{6x^9y^7}{2x^4y^7} = 3x^5$

- For the term $10x^4y^{15}$: $\dfrac{10x^4y^{15}}{2x^4y^7} = 5y^8$

Step 3: Write the answer as the product of $2x^4y^7$ and the difference of $3x^5$ and $5y^8$.

$$6x^9y^7 - 10x^4y^{15} = 2x^4y^7(3x^5 - 5y^8)$$

Polynomial factorization is the "opposite" of polynomial multiplication. When we multiply polynomials, we are "expanding" the polynomial. But when we factor polynomials, we are "collapsing" the polynomial.

Polynomial multiplication   Polynomial factorization

For example:

$8x^2y - 6xy^3$ can be factored into: $2xy(4x - 3y^2)$.

Multiplying $2xy(4x - 3y^2)$ becomes:

$2xy(4x - 3y^2) = 2xy \cdot 4x - 2xy \cdot 3y^2$

$= 8x^2y - 6xy^3$

For problems 1 through 4, find the GCF of each expression.

1. $cx + cy$

2. $8m - 6n$

3. $10a^2b + 8a^3b^2$

4. $12m^2n^5p^4 - 8mn^3p^5 + 20mp^2$

For problems 5 through 8, factor each expression.

5. $km + kn$

6. $30x^5 - 12x^3$

7. $16a^3b^7 - 12a^2b^6$

8. $18f^{20}g^{12}h^{16} - 15f^4g^8h^{24}$

9. Lisa wants to fully factor the expression $12x^7y^9 - 16x^{10}y^4$. She factors it to $2x^7y^2(6y^7 - 8x^3y^2)$. Is Lisa correct? Explain.

CHECK YOUR ANSWERS

1. c

2. 2

3. $2a^2b$

4. $4mp^2$

5. $k(m + n)$

6. $6x^3(5x^2 - 2)$

7. $4a^2b^6(4ab - 3)$

8. $3f^4g^8h^{16}(6f^{16}g^4 - 5h^8)$

9. No, Lisa did not use the GCF, so her answer is not fully factored.

Chapter 53

FACTORING POLYNOMIALS USING GROUPING

Another way to factor is to rewrite an expression into separate groups, where each of the groups could have a GCF that we can use to factor. This method is called FACTORING BY GROUPING.

To factor by grouping:

Step 1: Use parentheses to combine the terms into different groups.

Step 2: Factor each of the groups separately, using the GCF of each group.

Step 3: Factor the entire polynomial by using the GCF of all the terms.

475

For example, to fully factor

$ax + ay + bx + by$:

> The four terms ax, ay, bx, and by do not share a GCF.

1. Use parentheses to group the terms into two different groups.

$ax + ay + bx + by$
$(ax + ay) + (bx + by)$

2. Find the GCF of each of the two groups:

a is the GCF of the first group.
b is the GCF of the second group.

$a(x + y) + b(x + y)$

3. Since the two terms $a(x + y)$ and $b(x + y)$ share the GCF $(x + y)$, factor out $(x + y)$.

$(x + y)(a + b)$

Factoring by grouping is the only way to factor the polynomials. We cannot use the previous methods of finding a GCF of all the terms.

EXAMPLE: Factor $pq - 3q + 4p - 12$.

$pq - 3q + 4p - 12$

$= (pq - 3q) + (4p - 12)$ ← | Use parentheses to group the terms into two different groups.

$= q(p - 3) + 4(p - 3)$ Since the two terms $q(p - 3)$ and $4(p - 3)$ share the GCF $(p - 3)$, factor out $(p - 3)$.

$= (p - 3)(q + 4)$

Be careful that your signs are correct when you factor out a negative sign.

For example, factor $mx - my - nx + ny$.

$= (mx - my) - (nx - ny)$

Remember the rule for multiplying integers: $- \cdot - = +$

$= m(x - y) - n(x - y)$

$= (x - y)(m - n)$ ← **Use the correct mathematical operation.**

If all the terms share a GCF, factor out the GCF first.

EXAMPLE: Factor $12m^5n^2 - 8m^4n^2 + 9m^3n^5 - 6m^2n^5$.

$12m^5n^2 - 8m^4n^2 + 9m^3n^5 - 6m^2n^5$

$= m^2n^2(12m^3 - 8m^2 + 9mn^3 - 6n^3)$ The GCF of all the terms is m^2n^2.

$= m^2n^2[4m^2(3m - 2) + 3n^3(3m - 2)]$ Use grouping for the terms in the parentheses.

Do the calculations inside the square brackets first.

$= m^2n^2[(3m - 2)(4m^2 + 3n^3)]$

$= m^2n^2(3m - 2)(4m^2 + 3n^3)$

For 1 through 6, factor each expression.

1. $x^2 + 5x + xy + 5y$

2. $3fm - gm + 6fn - 2gn$

3. $10a^2 + 14a - 15ab - 21b$

4. $5ac - 15ad - bc + 3bd$

5. $2m + 7am - 6n - 21an$

6. $30am^2 - 40amn + 16bmn - 12bm^2$

7. Chuck is asked to factor the expression:
$8x^5y^6 - 2x^3y^9 - 24x^5y^4 + 6x^3y^7$.

Line 1: $= 8x^5y^6 - 2x^3y^9 - 24x^5y^4 + 6x^3y^7$

Line 2: $= (8x^5y^6 - 2x^3y^9) - (24x^5y^4 + 6x^3y^7)$

Line 3: $= 2x^3y^6(4x^2 - y^3) - 6x^3y^4(4x^2 + y^3)$

Line 4:   The two terms do not share a GCF,
so it cannot be factored.

Is Chuck correct? If not, where did he make an error?

CHECK YOUR ANSWERS

1. $(x + 5)(x + y)$

2. $(3f - g)(m + 2n)$

3. $(5a + 7)(2a - 3b)$

4. $(c - 3d)(5a - b)$

5. $(2 + 7a)(m - 3n)$

6. $2m(3m - 4n)(5a - 2b)$

7. No. Chuck made an error on line 2 because the sign is wrong inside the second parentheses. The correct term should be $(24x^5y^4 - 6x^3y^7)$.

Chapter 54

FACTORING TRINOMIALS WHEN $a = 1$

The trinomial of $ax^2 + bx + c$ is made up of three terms.

> Think of a as 1. In this case, x^2, ax^2, and $1x^2$ are the same.

- The coefficient, a, of the first term is 1.
- The constants are b and c.

Examples of trinomials when $a = 1$:

$$x^2 - 5x + 14 \qquad x^2 + x - 2 \qquad x^2 + 6x + 1$$

Many of these types of trinomials can be factored as the product of two binomials.

For example, the trinomial $x^2 + 7x + 12$ can be factored into $(x + 3)(x + 4)$.

How can we verify that?

If $x^2 + 7x + 12$ can be factored into $(x + 3)(x + 4)$, this means that the reverse should also be true: $(x + 3)(x + 4)$ should equal $x^2 + 7x + 12$.

$(x + 3)(x + 4) \overset{?}{=} x^2 + 7x + 12$

$(x + 3)(x + 4) \overset{?}{=} x^2 + 4x + 3x + 12$ Use the FOIL Method.

$\overset{?}{=} x^2 + 7x + 12$ ✓

This process proves that it is possible for a trinomial in the form $x^2 + bx + c$ to be factored as the product of two binomials.

How do we find those two binomials?

Let's assume that the trinomial $x^2 + bx + c$ can be factored into the product of two binomials. We can use shapes to represent the unknown terms:

1. $x^2 + bx + c = (\square + \triangle)(\bigcirc + \star)$ Using the FOIL Method, we know that **both $\square$ and $\bigcirc$ must be** x, because $x \cdot x = x^2$.

2. $x^2 + bx + c = (x + \triangle)(x + \stackrel{\star}{\star})$ Using the FOIL Method, we know that **both** $\triangle$ and $\stackrel{\star}{\star}$ must be constants whose product is the constant c because $\triangle \cdot \stackrel{\star}{\star} = c$.

> This is the "Last" part of the FOIL Method.

$x^2 + bx + c = (x + d)(x + e)$ Let the constants be d and e. Therefore, $d \cdot e = c$.

$x^2 + bx + c = (x + d)(x + e)$ Using the FOIL Method, we know that the sum of $x \cdot e = ex$ and $d \cdot x = dx$ must be equal to bx.

> These are "Inner" and "Outer" parts of the FOIL Method.

Therefore, if $x^2 + bx + c$ can be factored as $(x + d)(x + e)$, we are looking for two numbers (d and e).

- The sum of the two numbers equals b.
- The product of the two numbers equals c.

EXAMPLE: Factor $x^2 + 8x + 15$.

$x^2 + 8x + 15$ Which two numbers when multiplied equal 15 and when added equal 8? The numbers are 3 and 5.

$= (x + 3)(x + 5)$ ← You could also write the answer as $(x + 5)(x + 3)$.

EXAMPLE: Factor $x^2 + 10x + 24$.

$x^2 + 10x + 24$ Which two numbers when multiplied equal 24 and when added equal 10? The numbers are 4 and 6.

$= (x + 4)(x + 6)$

EXAMPLE: Factor $x^2 + 5x + 6$.

$x^2 + 5x + 6$ Which two numbers when multiplied equal 6 and when added equal 5? The numbers are 2 and 3.

$= (x + 2)(x + 3)$

Since both numbers are positive, it means that:

- *c* is positive because a positive number times a positive number = a positive number.

- *b* is positive because a positive number plus a positive number = a positive number.

If either one or both of the two factors are negative numbers, follow the same steps.

To factor $x^2 - 10x + 21$:

$x^2 - 10x + 21$ Ask: "Which two numbers multiply to 21 and add up to -10? -3 and -7."

$= (x - 3)(x - 7)$ ⟵   You could also write the answer as $(x - 7)(x - 3)$.

EXAMPLE: Factor $x^2 - 12x + 11$.

$= x^2 - 12x + 11$ Which two numbers when multiplied equal 11 and when added equal -12? The numbers are -1 and -11.

$= (x - 1)(x - 11)$

485

EXAMPLE: Factor $a^2 - 18a + 32$.

$a^2 - 18a + 32$ Which two numbers multiply to 32 and add up to −18? The numbers are −16 and −2.

> Be careful! The first term of the expression is a^2, so the first terms of the binomial must be a.

$= (a - 16)(a - 2)$

EXAMPLE: Factor $x^2 + 2x - 35$.

$x^2 + 2x - 35$ Which two numbers multiply to −35 and add up to 2? The numbers are −5 and 7.

$= (x - 5)(x + 7)$ ← You could also write the answer as $(x + 7)(x - 5)$.

EXAMPLE: Factor $x^2 - 2x - 35$.

$= x^2 - 2x - 35$ Which two numbers multiply to −35 and add up to −2? The numbers are 5 and −7.

$= (x + 5)(x - 7)$ ← You could also write the answer as $(x - 7)(x + 5)$.

EXAMPLE: Factor $y^2 + 8y - 48$.

$= y^2 + 8y - 48$

$= (y - 4)(y + 12)$

Not all trinomials are factorable.

For example, $x^2 + 5x + 3$ is not factorable. No two numbers have a product of 3 and add up to 5.

Another example is $x^2 + 10x - 16$. No two numbers have a product of -16 and add up to 10.

Be careful!

Make sure that you use the correct signs for each of the factors.

The answer $(x + 7)(x - 5)$ is **NOT** the same as $(x - 7)(x + 5)$!

$(x + 7)(x - 5) = x^2 + 2x - 35$

These are not the same answers!

$(x - 7)(x + 5) = x^2 - 2x - 35$

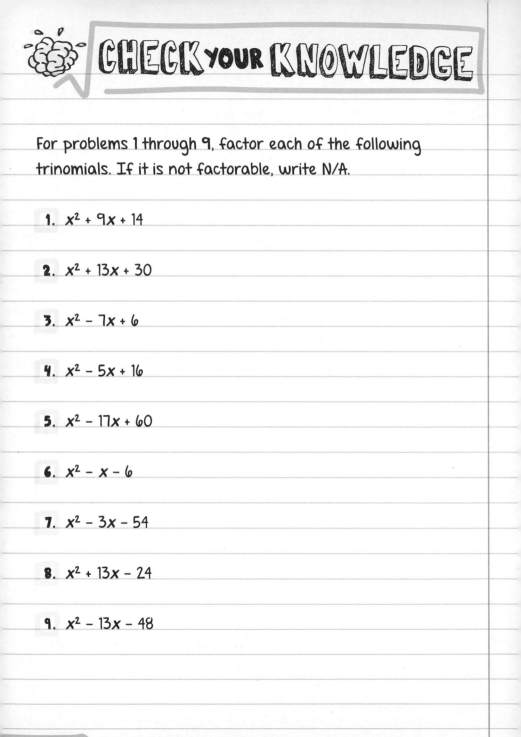

CHECK YOUR KNOWLEDGE

For problems 1 through 9, factor each of the following trinomials. If it is not factorable, write N/A.

1. $x^2 + 9x + 14$

2. $x^2 + 13x + 30$

3. $x^2 - 7x + 6$

4. $x^2 - 5x + 16$

5. $x^2 - 17x + 60$

6. $x^2 - x - 6$

7. $x^2 - 3x - 54$

8. $x^2 + 13x - 24$

9. $x^2 - 13x - 48$

10. Mr. Lee asks Linda and Maleek to factor $x^2 - 3x - 28$.

Linda says: "$x^2 - 3x - 28$ can be factored as either $(x - 7)(x + 4)$ or $(x + 7)(x - 4)$."

Maleek says: "$x^2 - 3x - 28$ can be factored as either $(x - 7)(x + 4)$ or $(x + 4)(x - 7)$."

Who is correct?

CHECK YOUR ANSWERS

1. $(x + 2)(x + 7)$

2. $(x + 3)(x + 10)$

3. $(x - 1)(x - 6)$

4. N/A

5. $(x - 5)(x - 12)$

6. $(x + 2)(x - 3)$

7. $(x - 9)(x + 6)$

8. N/A

9. $(x + 3)(x - 16)$

10. Maleek is correct.

Chapter 55

FACTORING TRINOMIALS WHEN $a \neq 1$

Some trinomials have the form $ax^2 + bx + c$, where the coefficient, a, of the first term is not 1. Examples:

$$5x^2 + 17x + 6 \qquad 5x^2 - 28x - 12 \qquad 6a^2 + a - 12$$

Many of these types of trinomials can be factored into the product of two binomials. So, $ax^2 + bx + c$ can be factored to $(dx + e)(fx + g)$.

This means that we need to find 4 numbers d, e, f, and g, where:

$$ax^2 + bx + c = (dx + e)(fx + g)$$

$$= (d \cdot f)x^2 + (d \cdot g + e \cdot f)x + (e \cdot g)$$

Since $ax^2 + bx + c = (dx + e)(fx + g) = (d \cdot f)x^2 + (d \cdot g + e \cdot f)x + (e \cdot g)$, we need to find four numbers d, e, f, and g, where:

- $a = d \cdot f$
- $c = e \cdot g$
- $b = d \cdot g + e \cdot f$

$a = d \cdot f$

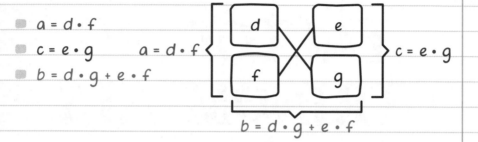

$c = e \cdot g$

$b = d \cdot g + e \cdot f$

So, to factor $2x^2 + 7x + 5$, which four numbers work for d, e, f, and g?

- $a = d \cdot f = 2$
- $c = e \cdot g = 5$
- $b = d \cdot g + e \cdot f = 7$

$2 \cdot 1$

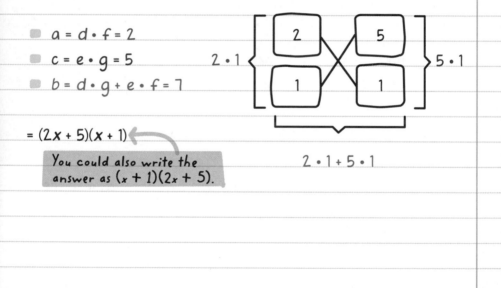

$5 \cdot 1$

$= (2x + 5)(x + 1)$

You could also write the answer as $(x + 1)(2x + 5)$.

$2 \cdot 1 + 5 \cdot 1$

492

Factor each of the following trinomials. If the trinomial is not factorable, write N/A.

1. $3x^2 + 16x + 5$

2. $7x^2 + 17x + 6$

3. $6x^2 + 31x + 35$

4. $3x^2 - 10x + 8$

5. $2x^2 - 15x + 28$

6. $4x^2 - 16x + 15$

7. $6x^2 + 17x + 5$

8. $20x^2 - 44x - 15$

9. $6x^2 - 5x + 14$

CHECK YOUR ANSWERS

1. $(x + 5)(3x + 1)$

2. $(7x + 3)(x + 2)$

3. $(3x + 5)(2x + 7)$

4. $(3x - 4)(x - 2)$

5. $(x - 4)(2x - 7)$

6. $(2x - 3)(2x - 5)$

7. $(2x + 5)(3x + 1)$

8. $(10x + 3)(2x - 5)$

9. N/A

Chapter 56

FACTORING USING SPECIAL FORMULAS

There are several formulas that we can use to factor some polynomials.

DIFFERENCE OF TWO SQUARES FORMULA

Use the Difference of Two Squares formula when subtracting two squares.

$x^2 - y^2 = (x + y)(x - y)$ ⟵ This can also be written as $(x - y)(x + y)$.

When working with this formula, ask:

"Is the first term a perfect square? Is the second term also a perfect square?" ⟵ A perfect square is when you multiply something by itself.

If they are both perfect squares, then you can use the formula.

For example, to factor $a^2 - 81b^2$, a^2 can be written as: $a^2 = (a)^2$, and $81b^2$ can be written as $(9b)^2$.

$= (a)^2 - (9b)^2$

WE'RE PERFECT TOGETHER.

$= (a + 9b)(a - 9b)$

Pay attention to the operations (addition and/or subtraction)!

EXAMPLE: Factor $25a^6b^{14} - 4c^2d^8$.

$25a^6b^{14} - 4c^2d^8$ $25a^6b^{14}$ can be written as: $25a^6b^{14} = (5a^3b^7)^2$, and $4c^2d^8$ can be written as: $4c^2d^8 = (2cd^4)^2$, so we can use the Difference of Two Squares formula.

$= (5a^3b^7)^2 - (2cd^4)^2$

$= (5a^3b^7 - 2cd^4)(5a^3b^7 + 2cd^4)$

496

PERFECT SQUARE TRINOMIAL FORMULA

We use the Perfect Square Trinomial formula to factor trinomials into a factor that is squared. Ask: "If I multiply $x \cdot y$ and then double it, do I get the middle term, $2xy$ in the original expression?"

$x^2 + 2xy + y^2 = (x + y)^2$

$x^2 - 2xy + y^2 = (x - y)^2$

If the following conditions are met, then use the perfect square trinomial formula:

- The first term is a perfect square $(x)^2$.
- The second term is a perfect square $(y)^2$.
- Multiplying $x \cdot y$, and then doubling it, results in the middle term.

For example to factor $a^2 + 6a + 9$.

$a^2 + 6a + 9$	a^2 can be written as $(a)^2$
$= a^2 + 2 \cdot a \cdot 3 + (3)^2$	9 can be written as $(3)^2$
$= (a + 3)^2$	$(a \cdot 3) \cdot 2 = 6a$, so we can use the Perfect Square Trinomial formula.

EXAMPLE: Factor $4m^2 - 20mn + 25n^2$.

$4m^2 - 20mn + 25n^2$ $4m^2$ can be written as: $(2m)^2$,

$= (2m)^2 - 2 \cdot 2m \cdot 5n + (5n)^2$ $25n^2$ can be written as: $(5n)^2$, and $(2m \cdot 5n) \cdot 2 = 20mn$

$= (2m - 5n)^2$

Make sure you are using the correct sign.

EXAMPLE: Factor $16x^6 + 40x^3y^7 + 25y^{14}$

$16x^6 + 40x^3y^7 + 25y^{14}$ $16x^6$ can be written as: $(4x^3)^2$,

$= (4x^3)^2 + 2 \cdot 4x^3 \cdot 5y^7 + (5y^7)^2$ $25y^{14}$ can be written as: $(5y^7)^2$, and $(4x^3 \cdot 5y^7) \cdot 2 = 40x^3y^7$

$= (4x^3 + 5y^7)^2$

498

SUM OF TWO CUBES AND DIFFERENCE OF TWO CUBES FORMULAS

We can use the Sum of Two Cubes and the Difference of Two Cubes formulas when we are ADDING two cubes:

$$x^3 + y^3 = (x + y)(x^2 - xy + y^2)$$

Or when we are SUBTRACTING two cubes:

$$x^3 - y^3 = (x - y)(x^2 + xy + y^2)$$

Ask "Is the first term a perfect cube? Is the second term also a perfect cube?"

when you multiply a number by itself 3 times

For example, to factor $a^3 + 8b^3$:

$a^3 + 8b^3$ a^3 can be written as: $(a)^3$, and $8b^3$ can be written as: $(2b)^3$.

$2b \times 2b \times 2b$

$= (a)^3 + (2b)^3$

$= (a + 2b)[(a)^2 - a \cdot 2b + (2b)^2]$

$= (a + 2b)(a^2 - 2ab + 4b^2)$

EXAMPLE: Factor $125 - m^9n^{12}$

$125 - m^9n^{12}$ 125 can be written as: 5^3

                              m^9n^{12} can be written as $(m^3n^4)^3$.

$= (5)^3 - (m^3n^4)^3$

$= (5 - m^3n^4)[(5)^2 + 5 \cdot m^3n^4 + (m^3n^4)^2]$

$= (5 - m^3n^4)(25 + 5m^3n^4 + m^6n^8)$

EXAMPLE: Factor $27x^3y^{12} - 64z^{21}$

$27x^3y^{12} - 64z^{21}$ $27x^3y^{12}$ can be written as: $(3xy^4)^3$, and

                             $64z^{21}$ can be written as: $(4z^7)^3$.

$= (3xy^4)^3 - (4z^7)^3$

$= (3xy^4 - 4z^7)[(3xy^4)^2 + (3xy^4) \cdot (4z^7) + (4z^7)^2]$

$= (3xy^4 - 4z^7)(9x^2y^8 + 12xy^4z^7 + 16z^{14})$

Notice that there is a **SUM of TWO CUBES** formula and a **DIFFERENCE of TWO CUBES** formula and a **DIFFERENCE of TWO SQUARES** formula, but there is <u>NO</u> "Sum of Two Squares" formula.

We can combine all the different methods of factoring.

EXAMPLE: Factor $18ax^2 - 32a$.

$= 18ax^2 - 32a$ The GCF of $18ax^2$ and $32a$ is: $2a$.

$= 2a(9x^2 - 16)$ Use the Difference of Two Squares formula. $9x^2$ and 16 are perfect squares.

$= 2a[(3x)^2 - (4)^2]$

$= 2a(3x + 4)(3x - 4)$

EXAMPLE: Factor $x^4 - 81 + 6x^3 - 54x$.

$x^4 - 81 + 6x^3 - 54x$

$= x^4 - 81 + 6x^3 - 54x$ Use grouping.

$= (x^4 - 81) + (6x^3 - 54x)$ Use the Difference of Two Squares formula for the first parentheses,

$= (x^2 - 9)(x^2 + 9) + 6x(x^2 - 9)$ Use GCF of $6x$ for the second parentheses.

$= (x^2 - 9)(x^2 + 9 + 6x)$ The GCF is $x^2 - 9$.

$= (x^2 - 9)(x^2 + 6x + 9)$ Use the Difference of Two Squares formula for the first parentheses.

$= (x - 3)(x + 3)(x + 3)^2$ Use the Perfect Square Trinomial formula for the second parentheses.

$= (x - 3)(x + 3)^3$

Always check for the GCF first. This will make your factorization more efficient.

Fully factor each of the following trinomials. If the trinomial is not factorable, write N/A.

1. $m^2 - 121$

2. $9x^2 + 6xy + y^2$

3. $64 - a^3b^6$

4. $25p^2 - 15pq + 9q^2$

5. $25f^{16} - 36g^{36}$

6. $27a^6 + 64b^3c^{15}$

7. $121p^4q^{10} - 66p^2q^5r^4 + 9r^8$

8. $4m^2n^8 - 36n^2p^8$

9. $8a^8b^4 - 40a^5b^6 + 50a^2b^8$

10. $16a^6b^3 + 54b^{18}c^3$

1. $(m + 11)(m - 11)$

2. $(3x + y)^2$

3. $(4 - ab^2)(16 + 4ab^2 + a^2b^4)$

4. N/A

5. $(5f^8 - 6g^{18})(5f^8 + 6g^{18})$

6. $(3a^2 + 4bc^5)(9a^4 - 12a^2bc^5 + 16b^2c^{10})$

7. $(11p^2q^5 - 3r^4)^2$

8. $4n^2(mn^3 - 3p^4)(mn^3 + 3p^4)$

9. $2a^2b^4(2a^3 - 5b^2)^2$

10. $2b^3(2a^2 + 3b^5c)(4a^4 - 6a^2b^5c + 9b^{10}c^2)$

Unit 11

Radicals

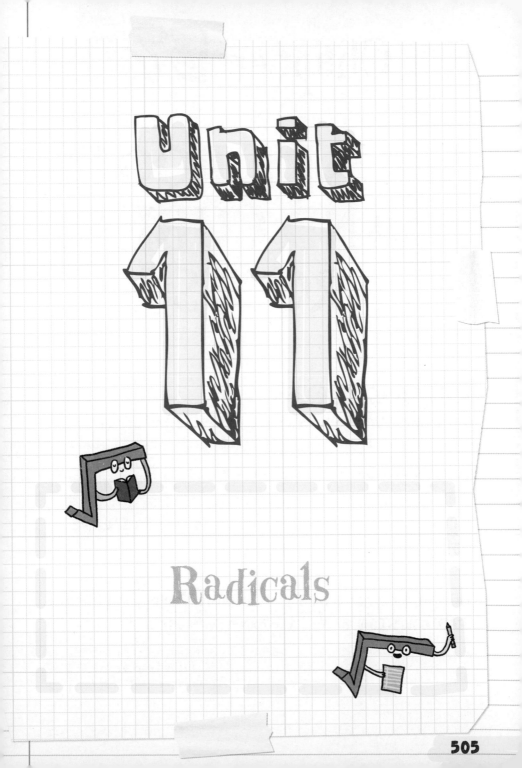

Chapter 57

SQUARE ROOTS AND CUBE ROOTS

SQUARE ROOTS

When we SQUARE a number, we raise it to the power of 2.

Examples: $3^2 = 3 \times 3 = 9$ $8^2 = 8 \times 8 = 64$

> Read as "eight squared."

The opposite of squaring a number is to take its SQUARE ROOT.

The square root of a number is indicated by putting it inside a RADICAL SIGN, or $\sqrt{}$. For example: $\sqrt{49}$

> This is read as the "square root of 49."

When simplifying a square root, ask:
"What number times itself equals the
number inside the radical sign?"

For example, to simplify $\sqrt{16}$, ask: What number times itself equals 16?

$$\sqrt{16} = \sqrt{4 \times 4}$$

$$= \sqrt{4^2} = 4$$

Notice that a square root and a square "cancel" each other out.

EXAMPLE: Simplify $\sqrt{81}$.

$$\sqrt{81}$$

$$= \sqrt{9 \times 9} \qquad \text{What number times itself equals 81?}$$

$$= \sqrt{9^2} = 9$$

EXAMPLE: Simplify $\sqrt{-9}$.

Since there is no number that multiplied by itself equals -9, there is no answer!

We know that 4 × 4 = 16 and (-4) × (-4) = 16.

This means that 16 has two square roots: 4 and -4.

Even though the two square roots of 16 are 4 and -4, 4 is called the PRINCIPAL SQUARE ROOT, which is the nonnegative square root.

Whenever we see the square root symbol, we should write only the principal square root.

PERFECT SQUARES

A PERFECT SQUARE is a number that is the square of a rational number.

The square root of a perfect square is always a *rational number.*

The square root of a positive number that is not a perfect square is an *irrational number.*

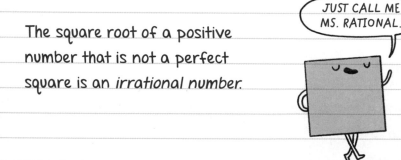

JUST CALL ME MS. RATIONAL.

Example:

- Is the simplified form of $\sqrt{144}$ a rational number or an irrational number?

  Since $144 = 12^2$, this means that 144 is a perfect square.

  Therefore, the simplified form of $\sqrt{144}$ is a rational number 12.

- Is the simplified form of $\sqrt{\dfrac{49}{36}}$ a rational number or an irrational number?

  Since $\dfrac{49}{36} = \left(\dfrac{7}{6}\right)^2$, this means that $\dfrac{49}{36}$ is a perfect square.

  Therefore, the simplified form of $\sqrt{\dfrac{49}{36}}$ is a rational number $\dfrac{7}{6}$.

- Is the simplified form of $\sqrt{20}$ a rational number or an irrational number?

  Since $\sqrt{20} = 4.472$, this means that 20 is not a perfect square.

  Therefore, the simplified form of $\sqrt{20}$ is an irrational number 4.472.

CUBE ROOTS

When we CUBE a number, we raise it to the power of 3.

Examples of cube roots:

$$2^3 = 2 \times 2 \times 2 = 8$$

$$4^3 = 4 \times 4 \times 4 = 64$$

The opposite of cubing a number is to take its CUBE ROOT.

The cube root of a number is indicated by putting it inside a radical sign with a raised 3 to the left of the radical: $\sqrt[3]{}$

When simplifying a cube root, ask: "What number multiplied by itself three times equals the number inside the radical sign?"

For example, to simplify $\sqrt[3]{125}$, ask: What number times itself three times equals 125?

$$\sqrt[3]{125} = \sqrt[3]{5 \times 5 \times 5}$$

$$= \sqrt[3]{5^3} = 5 \longleftarrow$$

Notice that a cube root and a cube "cancel" each other out!

EXAMPLE: Simplify $\sqrt[3]{\dfrac{1}{27}}$.

What number times itself three times equals $\dfrac{1}{27}$?

$$\sqrt[3]{\frac{1}{27}} = \sqrt[3]{\frac{1}{3} \times \frac{1}{3} \times \frac{1}{3}}$$

$$= \sqrt[3]{\left(\frac{1}{3}\right)^3} = \frac{1}{3}$$

Perfect Cubes

A PERFECT CUBE is a number that is the cube of a rational number. Perfect cubes can be positive or negative numbers.

EXAMPLE: Is 125 a perfect cube?

$125 = 5 \times 5 \times 5 = 5^3$

125 is the cube of a rational number. Therefore, 125 is a perfect cube.

EXAMPLE: Is 9 a perfect cube?

9 is NOT the cube of a rational number. Therefore, 9 is NOT a perfect cube.

For problems 1 through 9, simplify each of the radicals.
If the answer is not a rational number, write N/A.

1. $\sqrt{64}$

2. $\sqrt{1}$

3. $\sqrt{-25}$

4. $\sqrt{169}$

5. $\sqrt{0}$

6. $\sqrt[3]{-216}$

7. $\sqrt[3]{25}$

8. $\sqrt{\dfrac{121}{9}}$

9. $\sqrt[3]{-\dfrac{1000}{27}}$

10. Ms. Wong asks her class to simplify $\sqrt[3]{-64}$.

Adam says: "64 is a perfect square, so the answer is 8."
Brianna says: "-64 is not a perfect square, so the answer is N/A." Carlos says: "64 is a perfect cube, so the answer is 4." Damon says: "-64 is not a perfect cube, so the answer is N/A." Eddie says: "-64 is a perfect cube, so the answer is -4."

Who is correct?

ANSWERS 513

CHECK YOUR ANSWERS

1. 8

2. 1

3. N/A

4. 13

5. 0

6. −6

7. N/A

8. $\dfrac{11}{3}$

9. $-\dfrac{10}{3}$

10. Everyone is correct except for Damon. Adam gives the principle root, so he is the most correct.

Chapter 58

SIMPLIFYING RADICALS

We can simplify the square root of perfect squares and the cube roots of perfect cubes.

For example:

$$\sqrt{25} = \sqrt{5 \times 5} = 5 \qquad \sqrt[3]{-64} = \sqrt[3]{(-4) \times (-4) \times (-4)} = -4$$

We can also simplify the square root of a number that is not a perfect square and simplify the cube root of a number that is not a perfect cube.

Steps to simplify the SQUARE ROOT of any number:

Step 1: Ask: "What is the GREATEST factor of the number that is a *perfect square?*"

Step 2: Use multiplication to rewrite the number as the product of two factors.

Step 3: Simplify the square root.

For example, to simplify $\sqrt{18}$, ask: What is the GREATEST factor of 18 that is a perfect square? 9.

$$\sqrt{18} = \sqrt{9 \times 2}$$

9 is a perfect square, so take the square root: $\sqrt{9} = 3$

$= 3\sqrt{2}$ ← The second factor.

Square root of the greatest factor.

This is read as "3 root 2" or "3 rad 2." Both are equal to $3 \times \sqrt{2}$.

EXAMPLE: Simplify $\sqrt{75}$.

$= \sqrt{75}$ What is the GREATEST factor of 75 that is a perfect square? 25

$= \sqrt{25 \times 3}$ Since 25 is a perfect square, $\sqrt{25} = 5$.

$= 5\sqrt{3}$

We use the same process to simplify cube roots.

EXAMPLE: Simplify $\sqrt[3]{40}$.

$= \sqrt[3]{40}$ What is the GREATEST factor of 40 that is a perfect cube? 8

$2 \times 2 \times 2$

$= \sqrt[3]{8 \times 5}$ Since 8 is a perfect cube, $\sqrt[3]{8} = 2$.

$= 2\sqrt[3]{5}$ This is read as "two times the cube root of 5."

EXAMPLE: Simplify $\sqrt[3]{-128}$.

$= \sqrt[3]{-128}$ What is the LARGEST factor of -128 that is a perfect cube? -64

$= \sqrt[3]{-64 \times 2}$ Since -64 is a perfect cube, $\sqrt[3]{-64} = -4$.

$= -4\sqrt[3]{2}$

$= \sqrt[3]{\dfrac{1}{54}}$ What is the GREATEST factor of $\dfrac{1}{54}$ that is a perfect cube? $\dfrac{1}{27}$

$= \sqrt[3]{\dfrac{1}{27} \times \dfrac{1}{2}}$ Since $\dfrac{1}{27}$ is a perfect cube, $\sqrt[3]{\dfrac{1}{27}} = \dfrac{1}{3}$

$= \dfrac{1}{3}\sqrt[3]{\dfrac{1}{2}}$

Be sure to choose the greatest factor when simplifying.

For example, when simplifying $\sqrt{48}$, we could choose both 4 and 16 because both are perfect square factors of 48.

But we need to choose the GREATEST factor, so we choose 16:

$\sqrt{48} = \sqrt{16 \times 3} = 4\sqrt{3}$

> Finding the largest square root is not always easy. You can use a factor tree when the largest factor that is a perfect square is not obvious.

For problems 1 through 10, simplify each radical. If the radical cannot be simplified further, write N/A.

1. $\sqrt{45}$

2. $\sqrt{10}$

3. $\sqrt{300}$

4. $\sqrt{72}$

5. $\sqrt{63}$

6. $\sqrt{32}$

7. $\sqrt[3]{16}$

8. $\sqrt[3]{81}$

9. $\sqrt[3]{45}$

10. $\sqrt[3]{500}$

CHECK YOUR ANSWERS

1. $3\sqrt{5}$

2. N/A

3. $10\sqrt{3}$

4. $6\sqrt{2}$

5. $3\sqrt{7}$

6. $4\sqrt{2}$

7. $2\sqrt[3]{2}$

8. $3\sqrt[3]{3}$

9. N/A

10. $5\sqrt[3]{4}$

Chapter 59

ADDING AND SUBTRACTING RADICALS

COMPONENTS OF A RADICAL

Each radical is made up of two components: the index and the radicand.

Index $\longrightarrow$ $\sqrt[3]{-16}$ $\longleftarrow$ Radicand

So, for $\sqrt[3]{-16}$, the index is 3 and the radicand is -16.

> Even though we do not write the index for square roots, the index is 2.
>
> So $\sqrt{15}$ is actually $\sqrt[2]{15}$.

Since $13\sqrt[8]{200}$ represents $13 \times \sqrt[8]{200}$, the index is 8 and the radicand is 200.

ADDING AND SUBTRACTING RADICALS

You can only add or subtract radicals that have the same index and the same radicand.

If two radicals do not have the same index and the same radicand, then they CANNOT be combined.

EXAMPLE: Simplify $7\sqrt[3]{5} + 4\sqrt[3]{5}$.

$7\sqrt[3]{5} + 4\sqrt[3]{5}$ Both radicals share the same index, 3, and the same radicand, 5, so the radicals can be combined.

$7\sqrt[3]{5} + 4\sqrt[3]{5}$ Do not add the index or radicand.

$= 7 + 4 = 11$

$= 11\sqrt[3]{5}$

EXAMPLE: Simplify $9\sqrt{5} - 6\sqrt{5}$.

$= 9\sqrt{5} - 6\sqrt{5}$ Both radicals share the same index, 2, and the same radicand, 5, so the radicals can be combined.

$= 3\sqrt{5}$ $9 - 6 = 3$

Sometimes radicals can be combined if we simplify them separately first.

For example, $\sqrt{12} + 8\sqrt{3}$ cannot be combined because they do not share the same radicand. However, we can simplify each radical separately:

$= \sqrt{12} + 8\sqrt{3}$ Simplify $\sqrt{12}$ to $2\sqrt{3}$, giving it has the same radicand as the other number.

$= 2\sqrt{3} + 8\sqrt{3}$ The radicals can be combined in this form, because they share the same index, 2, and the same radicand, 3.

$= 10\sqrt{3}$ Add the radicals. Keep the index and the radicand the same. 2 + 8 = 10

EXAMPLE: Simplify $\sqrt[3]{128} - \sqrt[3]{54} + \sqrt[3]{24}$.

The radicals cannot be combined in this form, because they do not share the same radicand.

$= \sqrt[3]{128} - \sqrt[3]{54} + \sqrt[3]{24}$ Simplify $\sqrt[3]{128}$ to $4\sqrt[3]{2}$.
Simplify $\sqrt[3]{54}$ to $3\sqrt[3]{2}$.
Simplify $\sqrt[3]{24}$ to $2\sqrt[3]{3}$.

$= 4\sqrt[3]{2} - 3\sqrt[3]{2} + 2\sqrt[3]{3}$ Only the first two radicals can be combined because they share the same index and radicand.

$= \sqrt[3]{2} + 2\sqrt[3]{3}$ The radicals cannot be combined further.

1. What is the index and radicand of $\sqrt[3]{11}$?

2. What is the index and radicand of $9\sqrt{20}$?

For problems 3 through 6, simplify each radical expression.

3. $\sqrt{13} + 6\sqrt{13}$

4. $5\sqrt{14} - 8\sqrt{14}$

5. $\sqrt{3} + \sqrt{75}$

6. $\sqrt{45} - \sqrt{80}$

7. Sal is looking at a map of Texas. He notices that the three cities of Dallas, Houston, and San Antonio form a triangle on the map. Mr. Green tells Sal that the distance on the map from Dallas to Houston is $\sqrt{175}$ inches, the distance from Houston to San Antonio is $\sqrt{112}$ inches, and the distance from San Antonio to Dallas is $\sqrt{162}$ inches. Sal draws the triangle that connects the three cities. What is the perimeter of the triangle?

ANSWERS

CHECK YOUR ANSWERS

1. Index: 3; radicand: 11

2. Index: 2; radicand: 20

3. $7\sqrt{13}$

4. $-3\sqrt{14}$

5. $6\sqrt{3}$

6. $-\sqrt{5}$

7. Perimeter of the triangle: $(\sqrt{175} + \sqrt{112} + \sqrt{162}) = (5\sqrt{7} + 4\sqrt{7} + 9\sqrt{2}) = (9\sqrt{7} + 9\sqrt{2})$ inches.

Chapter 60

MULTIPLYING AND DIVIDING RADICALS

You can only multiply or divide radicals that have the same index.

If all the indexes are the same, we can rewrite the problem into a single radical and multiply and divide the radicands.

EXAMPLE: Simplify $\sqrt{5} \cdot \sqrt{7}$.

$\sqrt{5} \cdot \sqrt{7}$

Both radicals share the same index, 2, so the radicals can be multiplied and can be written as a single radical.

$= \sqrt{5 \cdot 7} = \sqrt{35}$

We multiply the radicands 5 and 7.

$= \sqrt[3]{2} \cdot 6\sqrt[3]{5}$ Both radicals share the same index, 3, so the radicals can be multiplied and written as a single radical.

$= 6\sqrt[3]{2 \cdot 5}$ Multiply the radicands 2 and 5.

$= 6\sqrt[3]{10}$ ←   Be careful! 6 is not a radicand, so do not put it inside the radical.

Follow the same process for division. For example, to simplify $12\sqrt[5]{21} \div 6\sqrt[5]{3}$:

$= 12\sqrt[5]{21} \div 6\sqrt[5]{3}$ Both radicals share the same index, 5, so the radicals can be divided and written as a single radical.

$12 \div 6 = 2$ ←

Be careful! 12 and 6 are not radicands, so do not put the 2 inside the radical.

$= 2\sqrt[5]{21 \div 3}$

$= 2\sqrt[5]{7}$

RATIONALIZING THE DENOMINATOR

When we write rational expressions that involve radicals, we do not want our final answer to contain a radical in the denominator. We multiply both the numerator and the denominator by the same number so that the radical is removed from the denominator. This process is called RATIONALIZING THE DENOMINATOR.

For example, we can simplify $\dfrac{6}{\sqrt{7}}$ by rationalizing the denominator.

$\dfrac{6}{\sqrt{7}}$ Multiply both the numerator and denominator by $\sqrt{7}$, so the radical is removed from the denominator.

$$= \frac{6 \times \sqrt{7}}{\sqrt{7} \times \sqrt{7}}$$

$$= \frac{6\sqrt{7}}{7}$$

EXAMPLE: Simplify the expression $\frac{8}{\sqrt{20}}$ by rationalizing the denominator.

$= \frac{8}{\sqrt{20}}$ Multiply both the numerator and denominator by $\sqrt{20}$, so the radical is removed from the denominator.

$= \frac{8 \times \sqrt{20}}{\sqrt{20} \times \sqrt{20}}$

$= \frac{8\sqrt{20}}{20}$ Simplify the radical.

$= \frac{8 \cdot 2\sqrt{5}}{20}$

$= \frac{16\sqrt{5}}{20}$

$= \frac{4\sqrt{5}}{5}$

CHECK YOUR KNOWLEDGE

For problems 1 through 7, simplify each of the expressions.

1. $\sqrt{7} \cdot \sqrt{3}$

2. $\sqrt[3]{3} \cdot \sqrt[3]{18}$

3. $7\sqrt{8} \cdot 2\sqrt{10}$

4. $\sqrt{45} \div \sqrt{5}$

5. $\sqrt{8} \div \sqrt{32}$

6. $10\sqrt[3]{42} \div \sqrt[3]{7}$

7. $2\sqrt[3]{6} \cdot 8\sqrt[3]{16} \div 4\sqrt[3]{3}$

For problems 8 and 9, simplify the expression by rationalizing the denominator.

8. $\dfrac{9}{\sqrt{5}}$

9. $\dfrac{10}{\sqrt{8}}$

10. The height of a rectangle is $7\sqrt[3]{4}$ feet and the length is $9\sqrt[3]{18}$ feet. What is the area of the rectangle?

ANSWERS

CHECK YOUR ANSWERS

1. $\sqrt{21}$

2. $3\sqrt[3]{2}$

3. $14\sqrt{80} = 14 \times 4\sqrt{5} = 56\sqrt{5}$

4. 3

5. $\dfrac{1}{2}$

6. $10\sqrt[3]{6}$

7. $8\sqrt[3]{4}$

8. $\dfrac{9\sqrt{5}}{5}$

9. $\dfrac{5\sqrt{2}}{2}$

10. The area of the box is $126\sqrt[3]{9}$ ft².

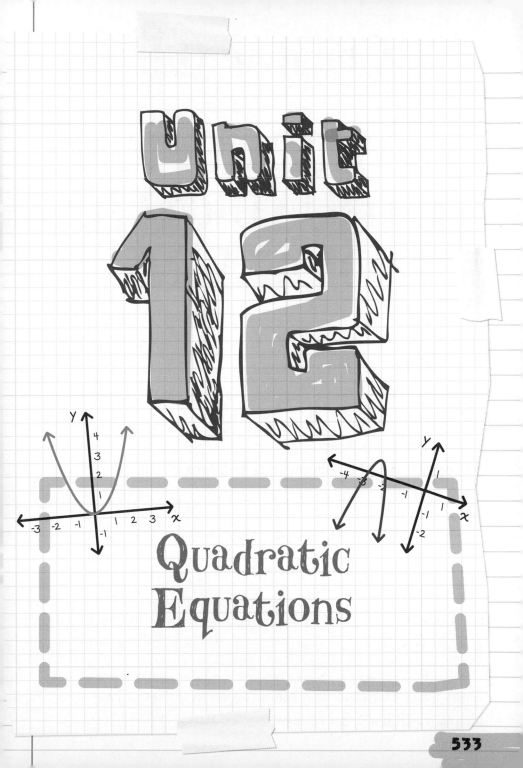

Unit 12

Quadratic Equations

Chapter 61

INTRODUCTION TO QUADRATIC EQUATIONS

A QUADRATIC EQUATION is an equation that has a variable to the second power but no variable higher than the second power.

A quadratic equation always has this form:

$$y = ax^2 + bx + c,$$
$$\text{where } a \neq 0$$

For example, state the values of a, b, and c for the equation $y = 3x^2 - 5x + 7$.

Since quadratic equations have the form $y = ax^2 + bx + c$, where $a \neq 0$: $a = 3$, $b = -5$, and $c = 7$.

EXAMPLE: Is $y = 4x^2 - x + \frac{1}{3}$ an example of a quadratic equation?

Since the highest power is 2, and $a = 4$, $b = -1$, and $c = \frac{1}{3}$, it is a quadratic equation.

EXAMPLE: Is $y = 12x + 5$ an example of a quadratic equation?

The equation does not have an ax^2 part.

The highest power is 1, and $a = 0$, $b = 12$, and $c = 5$.

Since $a = 0$, this means that the equation is **NOT** a quadratic equation.

This equation is actually a linear equation: $y = mx + b$.

EXAMPLE: Is $y = 9x^3 + x^2 - x + 8$ an example of a quadratic equation?

The highest power of the exponent is **NOT** 2.

This means that the equation is **NOT** a quadratic equation.

The equation is called a CUBIC EQUATION because it includes a cubic polynomial: $9x^3$.

All quadratic equations have solutions. We can test a solution by substituting the value into the variable.

EXAMPLE: Is $x = 2$ a solution for $x^2 - 5x + 6 = 0$?

$(2)^2 - 5(2) + 6 \overset{?}{=} 0$ Substitute 2 for x.

$0 \overset{?}{=} 0$

Both sides of the equation
are the same,
so $x = 2$ is a solution.

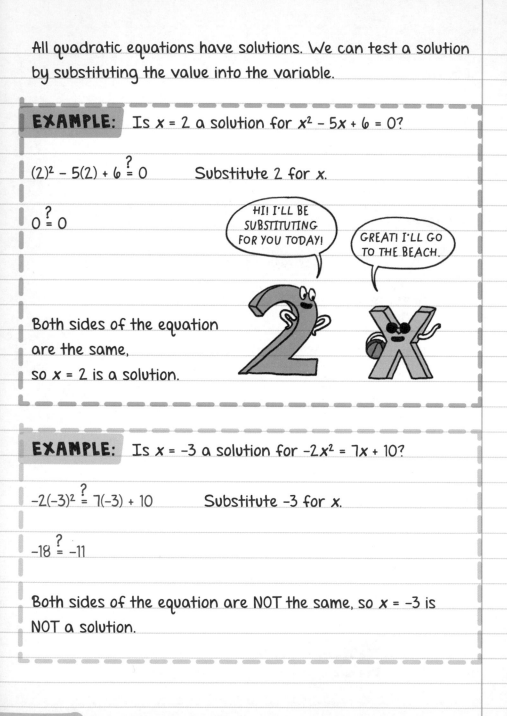

> HI! I'LL BE SUBSTITUTING FOR YOU TODAY!

> GREAT! I'LL GO TO THE BEACH.

EXAMPLE: Is $x = -3$ a solution for $-2x^2 = 7x + 10$?

$-2(-3)^2 \overset{?}{=} 7(-3) + 10$ Substitute -3 for x.

$-18 \overset{?}{=} -11$

Both sides of the equation are NOT the same, so $x = -3$ is NOT a solution.

The shape of a graphed quadratic function is a PARABOLA, a U-shaped curve. Many parabolas open either upward or downward.

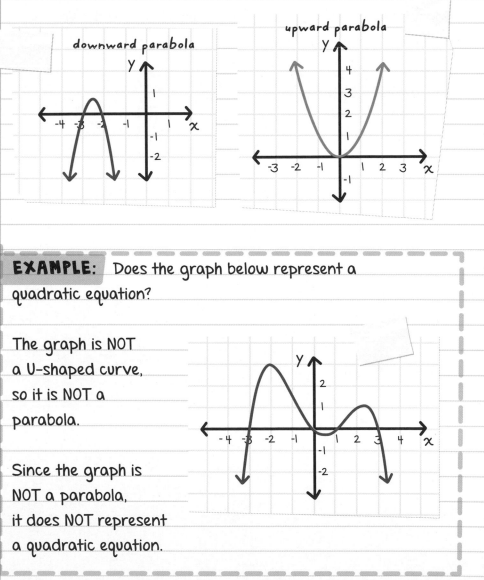

downward parabola

upward parabola

EXAMPLE: Does the graph below represent a quadratic equation?

The graph is NOT a U-shaped curve, so it is NOT a parabola.

Since the graph is NOT a parabola, it does NOT represent a quadratic equation.

For problems 1 and 2, state the values of a, b, and c for the given quadratic equation.

1. $y = 8x^2 - 2x + 9$

2. $y = -\dfrac{1}{3}x^2 + 4$

For problems 3 through 6, state whether or not the given equation is a quadratic equation.

3. $y = x^2 + 3x - 15$

4. $y = 6x^5 - 0.7x + \pi$

5. $y = 9x$

6. $y = -\dfrac{4}{3}x^2$

For problems 7 and 8, state whether or not the graph represents a quadratic equation.

7.

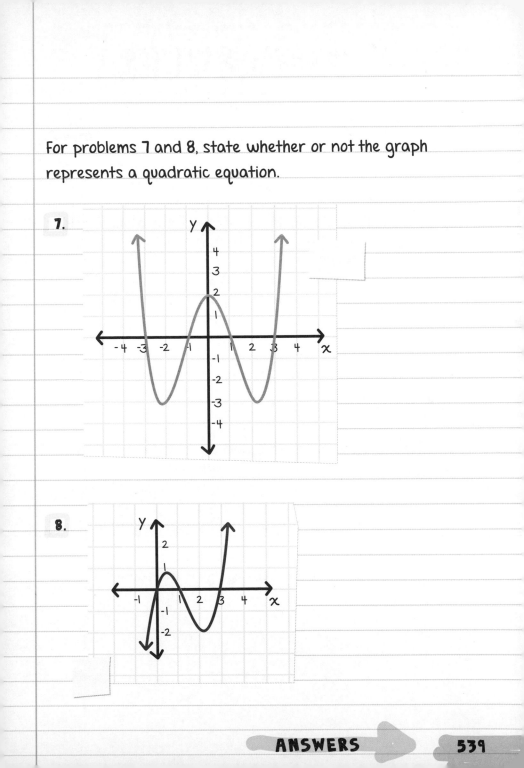

8.

CHECK YOUR ANSWERS

1. $a = 8$, $b = -2$, and $c = 9$

2. $a = -\dfrac{1}{3}$, $b = 0$, and $c = 4$

3. Since the highest power is 2 and $a \neq 0$, it is a quadratic equation.

4. Since the highest power is not 2, it is not a quadratic equation.

5. Since the highest power is not 2, it is not a quadratic equation.

6. Since the highest power is 2 and $a \neq 0$, it is a quadratic equation.

7. The graph does not represent a quadratic equation.

8. The graph does not represent a quadratic equation.

Chapter 62

SOLVING QUADRATIC EQUATIONS BY FACTORING

There are times when we are not given a number to substitute for a variable in a quadratic equation. When this happens, we must solve for the variable.

There are different methods for solving quadratic equations. One way to solve a quadratic equation is by **factoring**.

After factoring a quadratic equation, we use the ZERO-PRODUCT PRINCIPLE, two numbers that when multiplied have a product of zero.

Zero-Product Principle
If $a \bullet b = 0$, then either $a = 0$ or $b = 0$.

If we multiply two numbers that equal 0, then either the first number equals 0 or the second number equals 0.

EXAMPLE: Solve the equation $xy = 0$.

$xy = 0$ Apply the Zero-Product Principle.

So, either $x = 0$ or $y = 0$.

So, if $(x - 2)(y - 5) = 0$ then $(x - 2) = 0$ or $(y - 5) = 0$

For $(x - 2)$ to equal 0, x would need to equal 2.

For $(y - 5)$ to equal 0, y would need to equal 5.

EXAMPLE: Solve the equation $(a - 3)(b + 5) = 0$.

$(a - 3)(b + 5) = 0$ Apply the Zero-Product Principle.

$a - 3 = 0$ or $b + 5 = 0$ Solve each of the linear equations.

$3 - 3 = 0$, so, $a = 3$ or
$-5 + 5 = 0$, so, $b = -5$

FACTORING QUADRATIC EQUATIONS

When solving quadratic equations using factoring, ask:
"Can this equation be factored?"

If a quadratic equation can be factored, we factor the equation. Then we use the Zero-Product Principle to find the solution.

TO SOLVE QUADRATIC EQUATIONS BY FACTORING:

1. Rewrite the quadratic equation into the form $ax^2 + bx + c = 0$.

Make sure that the right-hand side (RHS) equals 0.

2. Factor the left-hand side (LHS).

Use whichever factoring techniques can be applied to the expression.

3. Use the Zero-Product Principle to solve the equation.

EXAMPLE: Solve the equation $x^2 + 3x - 10 = 0$.

$x^2 + 3x - 10 = 0$ Factor the left-hand side (LHS).

$(x + 5)(x - 2) = 0$ Apply the Zero-Product Principle.

$x + 5 = 0$ or $x - 2 = 0$ Solve each of the linear equations.

$x = -5$ or $x = 2$

Remember to use all the rules of factoring, such as factoring out the GCF first, whenever possible.

EXAMPLE: Solve the equation $6x^2 - 4x - 10 = 0$.

$6x^2 - 4x - 10 = 0$ First, factor the GCF: 2.
$2(3x^2 - 2x - 5) = 0$ Factor $3x^2 - 2x - 5$.
$2(3x - 5)(x + 1) = 0$

$2 = 0$ ⟵ This is never true.

$3x - 5 = 0$ or $x = \dfrac{5}{3}$
$x + 1 = 0$ or $x = -1$

So the solution is $x = \dfrac{5}{3}$ or $x = -1$.

544

Another way to simplify this equation is to divide by the GCF.

$6x^2 - 4x - 10 = 0$ First, divide by the GCF: 2.

$$\frac{6x^2}{2} = 3x^2$$

$$\frac{4x}{4} = 2x$$

$$\frac{10}{2} = 5$$

$3x^2 - 2x - 5 = 0$

Before using the Zero-Product Principle, don't forget that the right-hand side (RHS) must be zero!

EXAMPLE: Solve the equation $2x^2 - 11x = -12$.

$2x^2 - 11x = -12$

$2x^2 - 11x + 12 = 0$

$(2x - 3)(x - 4) = 0$

$2x - 3 = 0$ or $x - 4 = 0$

$x = \dfrac{3}{2}$ or $x = 4$

EXAMPLE: Solve the equation $4x^2 = 20 - 2x^2 - 7x$.

$4x^2 = 20 - 2x^2 - 7x$

Rewrite the expression so the RHS equals 0.

$6x^2 + 7x - 20 = 0$

$(3x - 4)(2x + 5) = 0$

$3x - 4 = 0$ or $2x + 5 = 0$

$x = \dfrac{4}{3}$ or $x = -\dfrac{5}{2}$

EXAMPLE: Solve the equation $x^2 - 16x = -64$.

$x^2 - 16x = -64$

Rewrite the expression so the RHS equals 0.

$x^2 - 16x + 64 = 0$

The LHS is a perfect square trinomial!

$(x - 8)(x - 8) = 0$

$x - 8 = 0$ or $x - 8 = 0$

Since the two linear equations are the same, you write it only once.

$x - 8 = 0$

$x = 8$

EXAMPLE: Solve the equation $10 - 9x = 3x - 4x^2 + 1$.

$10 - 9x = 3x - 4x^2 + 1$

Rewrite the expression so the RHS equals 0.

$4x^2 - 12x + 9 = 0$

The LHS is a perfect square trinomial!

$(2x - 3)(2x - 3) = 0$

$2x - 3 = 0$

$x = \dfrac{3}{2}$

You can use the Zero-Product Principle only if the product equals **ZERO**!

- You can simplify $(x - 4)(x + 3) = 0$ into:
  $x - 4 = 0$ or $x + 3 = 0$
  But you **CANNOT** simplify $(x - 4)(x + 3) = 2$ into:
  $x - 4 = 2$ or $x + 3 = 2$
- You need to first rewrite the equation so that the RHS equals 0.

EXAMPLE: Solve the equation $(x + 1)(x + 4) = 10$.

$(x + 1)(x + 4) = 10$ Use the FOIL Method to expand the LHS.

$x^2 + 5x + 4 = 10$

$x^2 + 5x - 6 = 0$

$(x + 6)(x - 1) = 0$

$x + 6 = 0$ or $x - 1 = 0$

$x = -6$ or $x = 1$

When we are solving quadratic equations, why do we write the solution using the word *or* instead of *and*?

Remember what we learned about the words *or* and *and* when we solved compound inequalities:

- The word **AND** is used when we are using the *intersections* of the solutions. In other words, we look at the overlap of the solutions on a number line.
- The word **OR** is used when we are using the *union* of the solutions. In other words, we look at what happens when we put together the solutions on a number line.

When we solve quadratic equations, the solutions are specific numbers, not intervals. So when we graph the solutions on a number line, there is no overlap.

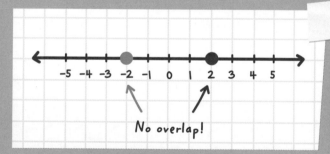

No overlap!

If we use **AND**, the final solution would be "no solution" because there is no overlap.

That is why we use the word **OR** in the final solution.

For problems 1 through 9, solve each of the quadratic equations by using factoring.

1. $x^2 + 7x + 10 = 0$

2. $x^2 - 4x - 21 = 0$

3. $2x^2 + 9x + 4 = 0$

4. $3x^2 + 10x - 8 = 0$

5. $6x^2 - 13x - 28 = 0$

6. $x^2 = 4x + 32$

7. $4x^2 + 6x = 10$

8. $(x - 3)(x + 4) = 8$

9. $(3x - 4)(2x + 5) = -10$

10. Ms. Fung asks Eric to solve the equation $(x - 4)(x - 2) = 3$. Here are Eric's steps:

Line 1: $(x - 4)(x - 2) = 3$
Line 2: $x - 4 = 3$ or $x - 2 = 3$
Line 3: $x = 7$ or $x = 5$

Ms. Fung says that Eric's answer is wrong. On which line did Eric first make an error?

CHECK YOUR ANSWERS

1. $x = -2$ or $x = -5$

2. $x = 7$ or $x = -3$

3. $x = -\dfrac{1}{2}$ or $x = -4$

4. $x = \dfrac{2}{3}$ or $x = -4$

5. $x = -\dfrac{4}{3}$ or $x = \dfrac{7}{2}$

6. $x = -4$ or $x = 8$

7. $x = -\dfrac{5}{2}$ or $x = 1$

8. $x = -5$ or $x = 4$

9. $x = \dfrac{5}{6}$ or $x = -2$

10. Eric made an error in line 2, because he applied the Zero-Product Principle when the RHS did not equal 0.

Chapter 63

SOLVING QUADRATIC EQUATIONS BY TAKING SQUARE ROOTS

When we are given quadratic equations that involve perfect squares, we can find the solution by taking the square root from both sides.

To find the solutions to the equation $x^2 = 64$, ask: "What number multiplied by itself equals 64?" Note that there may be more than one solution. The answer is: 8 and -8.

In written form it would look like this: Solve $x^2 = 64$.

To solve, we might take the square root of both sides: $\sqrt{x^2} = \sqrt{64}$.

Whenever you see the square root symbol, write only the principal square root: $x = 8$.

However, this does not show the negative solution.

Therefore, when we solve quadratic equations by taking square roots, we use the SQUARE ROOT PROPERTY. This property lists both the principal square root and the negative value.

Square Root Property:

If $a^2 = b$, then $a = \pm\sqrt{b}$

EXAMPLE: Solve $x^2 = 9$.

$x^2 = 9$ Take the square root of both sides and include the ± sign on the right-hand side.

$\sqrt{x^2} = \pm\sqrt{9}$

$x = \pm3$ ← This means that the solutions are: $x = 3$ or $x = -3$.

EXAMPLE: Solve $y^2 = \dfrac{64}{121}$.

$y^2 = \dfrac{64}{121}$ Take the square root of both sides and include the ± sign on one side.

$$\sqrt{y^2} = \pm\sqrt{\frac{64}{121}}$$

$$y = \pm\frac{8}{11}$$

EXAMPLE: Solve $x^2 = 20$.

$x^2 = 20$ Take the square root of both sides and include the $\pm$ sign on one side.

$x = \pm\sqrt{20}$ Simplify the radical.

$x = \pm 2\sqrt{5}$

We can also use the Square Root Property when the LHS contains more than just a variable.

EXAMPLE: Solve $(m - 3)^2 = 7$.

$(m - 3)^2 = 7$ Take the square root of both sides and include the $\pm$ sign on one side.

$\sqrt{(m-3)^2} = \pm\sqrt{7}$ Solve for the variable m.

$m - 3 = \pm\sqrt{7}$

$m - 3 + 3 = +3 \pm \sqrt{7}$

$m = 3 \pm \sqrt{7}$

EXAMPLE: Solve $(k + 4)^2 = 9$.

$(k + 4)^2 = 9$ Take the square root of both sides and include the $\pm$ sign on one side.

$\sqrt{(k+4)^2} = \pm\sqrt{9}$

$k + 4 = \pm 3$

$k + 4 - 4 = -4 \pm 3$

$k = -4 + 3$ or $k = -4 - 3$

$k = -1$ or $k = -7$

Before you use the Square Root Property, don't forget to first isolate the squared part, then take the square root of both sides!

EXAMPLE: Solve $3k^2 = 48$.

$3k^2 = 48$

$\dfrac{3k^2}{3} = \dfrac{48}{3}$ Since only k is being squared, we first isolate k^2 by dividing both sides by 3.

$k^2 = 16$

$k = \pm\sqrt{16}$

$k = \pm 4$

EXAMPLE: Solve $3(x + 1)^2 - 7 = 11$.

$3(x + 1)^2 - 7 = 11$

$3(x + 1)^2 = 18$ Since only $(x + 1)$ is being squared, we first isolate $(x + 1)^2$.

$(x + 1)^2 = 6$

$x + 1 = \pm\sqrt{6}$

$x = -1 \pm\sqrt{6}$

CHECK YOUR KNOWLEDGE

For problems 1 through 9, solve each of the quadratic equations by using the Square Root Property.

1. $x^2 = 144$

2. $b^2 = \dfrac{9}{49}$

3. $3y^2 = 75$

4. $\dfrac{1}{2}x^2 = 50$

5. $a^2 - 4 = 5$

6. $10x^2 + 1 = x^2 + 5$

7. $(x + 1)^2 = 15$

8. $(x - 5)^2 = 18$

9. $\dfrac{1}{2}(p + 7)^2 - 6 = 19$

10. Mr. Brown asks Lina to solve the equation:

$9x^2 - 2x - 1 = 15 - 2x$.

Here are Lina's steps:

Line 1: $9x^2 - 2x - 1 = 15 - 2x$

Line 2: $9x^2 = 16$

Line 3: $9x = \pm 4$

Line 4: $x = \pm \dfrac{4}{9}$

Mr. Brown says that Lina's answer is wrong. On which line did Lina first make an error?

ANSWERS

CHECK YOUR ANSWERS

1. $x = \pm 12$

2. $b = \pm\dfrac{3}{7}$

3. $y = \pm 5$

4. $x = \pm 10$

5. $a = \pm 3$

6. $x = \pm\dfrac{2}{3}$

7. $x = -1 \pm \sqrt{15}$

8. $x = 5 \pm 3\sqrt{2}$

9. $p = -7 \pm 5\sqrt{2}$

10. Lina made an error on line 3 because she did not isolate the x^2 term first, or alternately, did not turn it into something being squared $(3x)^2 = \pm 16$.

Chapter 64

SOLVING QUADRATIC EQUATIONS BY COMPLETING THE SQUARE

We can use the SQUARE ROOT PROPERTY to solve quadratic equations that contain a perfect square.

Not every quadratic equation has a perfect square that you can easily see.

We can rewrite any quadratic equation into a perfect square using a process called COMPLETING THE SQUARE.

I'M PERFECT IN EVERY WAY.

What number should be added to $x^2 + 6x$ to get a perfect square?

9 because $x^2 + 6x + 9$ is a perfect square: $(x + 3)^2$

What number should be added to $x^2 - 10x$ to get a perfect square?

25 because $x^2 - 10x + 25$ is a perfect square: $(x - 5)^2$

If we have the quadratic expression $x^2 + bx$, we can obtain a perfect square using these steps:

Step 1: Calculate the value of $\frac{b}{2}$.

Step 2: Square that value.

Step 3: Add this value to the expression.

EXAMPLE: What number should be added to $x^2 + 8x$ to obtain a perfect square?

Since the expression is $x^2 + 8x$, this means that $b = 8$:

Step 1: Calculate the value of $\frac{b}{2}$: $\left(\frac{8}{2}\right) = 4$

Step 2: Square that value: $(4)^2 = 16$

Therefore, 16 should be added to $x^2 + 8x$.

$x^2 + 8x + 16$ is a perfect square: $(x + 4)^2$

EXAMPLE: What number should be added to $x^2 + \frac{2}{3}x$ to obtain a perfect square?

Since the expression is $x^2 + \frac{2}{3}x$, this means that $b = \frac{2}{3}$:

Step 1: Calculate the value of $\frac{b}{2}$: $\left(\frac{\frac{2}{3}}{2}\right) = \frac{2}{3} \div 2$

$= \frac{2}{3} \times \frac{1}{2} = \frac{1}{3}$

Step 2: Square that value: $\left(\frac{1}{3}\right)^2 = \frac{1}{9}$

Therefore, $\frac{1}{9}$ should be added to $x^2 + \frac{2}{3}x$.

$x^2 + \frac{2}{3}x + \frac{1}{9}$ is a perfect square: $\left(x + \frac{1}{3}\right)^2$

We can use the Completing the Square method to find solutions to quadratic equations.

> If we have the quadratic equation $x^2 + bx = c$, we can obtain the solution using these steps:
>
> **Step 1:** Calculate the value of $\frac{b}{2}$.
>
> **Step 2:** Square that value.
>
> **Step 3:** Add that number to **both** sides of the equation.
>
> **Step 4:** Use factoring and the Square Root Property to find the solutions.

EXAMPLE: Solve $x^2 + 18x = 0$ by using the Completing the Square method.

Since the equation is $x^2 + 18x = 0$, this means that $b = 18$:

Step 1: Calculate the value of $\frac{b}{2}$: $\left(\frac{18}{2}\right) = 9$

Step 2: Square that value: $(9)^2 = 81$

Step 3: Add that number to **both** sides of the equation:

$x^2 + 18x + 81 = 0 + 81$

$x^2 + 18x + 81 = 81$

Step 4: Use factoring and the Square Root Property:

$x^2 + 18x + 81 = 81$

$(x + 9)^2 = 81$ Factor the LHS into a perfect square.

$\sqrt{(x+9)^2} = \pm\sqrt{81}$ Take the square root of both sides and include the ± sign on one side.

$x + 9 = \pm 9$

$x = -9 \pm 9$

$x = -9 + 9$ or $x = -9 - 9$

$x = 0$ or $x = -18$

> We could have also solved the problem by using factoring.

EXAMPLE: Solve $x^2 - 5x = 0$ by using the Completing the Square method.

Since the equation is $x^2 - 5x = 0$, this means that $b = -5$:

Step 1: Calculate the value of $\frac{b}{2}$: $\left(-\frac{5}{2}\right) = -\frac{5}{2}$

Step 2: Square that value: $\left(-\frac{5}{2}\right)^2 = \frac{25}{4}$

Step 3: Add that number to **both** sides of the equation:

$$x^2 - 5x + \frac{25}{4} = 0 + \frac{25}{4}$$

$$x^2 - 5x + \frac{25}{4} = \frac{25}{4}$$

Step 4: Use factoring and the Square Root Property:

$$x^2 - 5x + \frac{25}{4} = \frac{25}{4}$$

$$\left(x - \frac{5}{2}\right)^2 = \frac{25}{4}$$ Factor the LHS into a perfect square.

$$\sqrt{\left(x - \frac{5}{2}\right)^2} = \pm\sqrt{\frac{25}{4}}$$ Take the square root of both sides and include the ± sign on one side.

$$x - \frac{5}{2} = \pm\frac{5}{2}$$

$$x = \frac{5}{2} + \frac{5}{2} \quad \text{or} \quad x = \frac{5}{2} - \frac{5}{2}$$

$$x = 5 \quad \text{or} \quad x = 0$$

EXAMPLE: Solve $x^2 - 14x = -11$ by using the Completing the Square method.

Since the equation is $x^2 - 14x = -11$, this means that $b = -14$:

Step 1: Calculate the value of $\frac{b}{2}$: $\left(\frac{-14}{2}\right) = -7$

Step 2: Square that value: $(-7)^2 = 49$

Step 3: Add that number to **both** sides of the equation:

$x^2 - 14x + 49 = -11 + 49$

$x^2 - 14x + 49 = 38$

Step 4: Use factoring and the Square Root Property:

$x^2 - 14x + 49 = 38$

$(x - 7)^2 = 38$ Factor the LHS into a perfect square.

$x - 7 = \pm\sqrt{38}$ Take the square root of both sides and include the ± sign on one side.

$x = 7 \pm \sqrt{38}$

Before you use the Completing the Square method, make sure that you first rewrite the equation into the form $x^2 + bx = c$.

EXAMPLE: Solve $2x^2 + 12x = 10$ by using the Completing the Square method.

First, we rewrite the equation $2x^2 + 12x = 10$ into the form $x^2 + bx = c$:

$2x^2 + 12x = 10$ Divide all the terms by 2.

$x^2 + 6x = 5$

Since the equation is $x^2 + 6x = 5$, this means that $b = 6$:

Step 1: Calculate the value of $\dfrac{b}{2}$: $\left(\dfrac{6}{2}\right) = 3$

Step 2: Square that value: $(3)^2 = 9$

Step 3: Add that number to **both** sides of the equation:

$x^2 + 6x + 9 = 5 + 9$

$x^2 + 6x + 9 = 14$

Step 4: Use factoring and the Square Root Property:

$x^2 + 6x + 9 = 14$

$(x + 3)^2 = 14$ — Factor the LHS into a perfect square.

$x + 3 = \pm\sqrt{14}$ — Take the square root of both sides and include the ± sign on one side.

$x = -3 \pm \sqrt{14}$

EXAMPLE: Solve $-3x^2 - x + 10 = 0$ by using the Completing the Square method.

First, rewrite the equation $-3x^2 - x + 10 = 0$ into the form $x^2 + bx = c$:

$-3x^2 - x + 10 = 0$

$-3x^2 - x = -10$

$x^2 + \dfrac{1}{3}x = \dfrac{10}{3}$

Since the expression is $x^2 + \frac{1}{3}x = \frac{10}{3}$, this means that $b = \frac{1}{3}$:

Step 1: Calculate the value of $\frac{b}{2}$: $\left(\dfrac{\frac{1}{3}}{2}\right) = \frac{1}{6}$

Step 2: Square that value: $\left(\frac{1}{6}\right)^2 = \frac{1}{36}$

Step 3: Add that number to **both** sides of the equation:

$$x^2 + \frac{1}{3}x + \frac{1}{36} = \frac{10}{3} + \frac{1}{36}$$

$$x^2 + \frac{1}{3}x + \frac{1}{36} = \frac{120}{36} + \frac{1}{36}$$

$$x^2 + \frac{1}{3}x + \frac{1}{36} = \frac{121}{36}$$

Step 4: Use factoring and the Square Root Property:

$$x^2 + \frac{1}{3}x + \frac{1}{36} = \frac{121}{36}$$

$$\left(x + \frac{1}{6}\right)^2 = \frac{121}{36} \qquad \text{Factor the LHS into a perfect square.}$$

$$x + \frac{1}{6} = \pm\frac{11}{6} \qquad \text{Take the square root of both sides}$$
and include the $\pm$ sign on one side.

$$x = -\frac{1}{6} + \frac{11}{6} \quad \text{or} \quad x = -\frac{1}{6} - \frac{11}{6}$$

$$x = \frac{10}{6} = \frac{5}{3} \quad \text{or} \quad x = -\frac{12}{6} = -2$$

For problems 1 through 3, find the number that should be added to the expression to obtain a perfect square.

1. $x^2 + 22x$

2. $x^2 - 2x$

3. $x^2 + 7x$

For problems 4 through 8, solve each of the quadratic equations by using the Completing the Square method.

4. $x^2 + 10x = 4$

5. $x^2 - 18x = -57$

6. $3x^2 + 12x = 21$

7. $4x^2 = 8 - 40x$

8. $-2x^2 + 7x + 4 = 0$

CHECK YOUR ANSWERS

1. 121

2. 1

3. $\dfrac{49}{4}$

4. $x = -5 \pm \sqrt{29}$

5. $x = 9 \pm 2\sqrt{6}$

6. $x = -2 \pm \sqrt{11}$

7. $x = -5 \pm 3\sqrt{3}$

8. $x = -\dfrac{1}{2}, 4$

Chapter 65

SOLVING QUADRATIC EQUATIONS WITH THE QUADRATIC FORMULA

Not all quadratic equations can be solved by factoring, and not all quadratic equations can be solved by using the Square Root Property.

But all quadratic equations can be solved using the Completing the Square method.

All quadratic equations can also be solved by using the QUADRATIC FORMULA.

> Quadratic Formula:
>
> For a quadratic equation $ax^2 + bx + c = 0$, the solution is: $x = \dfrac{-b \pm \sqrt{b^2 - 4ac}}{2a}$.

EXAMPLE: Solve the equation $x^2 + 6x + 5 = 0$ by using the quadratic formula.

$x^2 + 6x + 5 = 0$ Substitute $a = 1$, $b = 6$, and $c = 5$ into the quadratic formula.

$$x = \frac{-6 \pm \sqrt{6^2 - 4 \cdot 1 \cdot 5}}{2 \cdot 1}$$

$$x = \frac{-6 \pm \sqrt{16}}{2}$$

$$x = \frac{-6 \pm 4}{2}$$

$$x = \frac{-6 + 4}{2} \quad \text{or} \quad x = \frac{-6 - 4}{2}$$

$$x = \frac{-2}{2} \quad \text{or} \quad x = \frac{-10}{2}$$

Factoring or Completing the Square could also have been used to solve this problem.

$x = -1 \quad \text{or} \quad x = -5$

EXAMPLE: Solve the equation $2x^2 - 7x + 3 = 0$ by using the quadratic formula.

$2x^2 - 7x + 3 = 0$ Substitute $a = 2$, $b = -7$, and $c = 3$ into the quadratic formula.

$$x = \frac{-(-7) \pm \sqrt{(-7)^2 - 4 \cdot 2 \cdot 3}}{2 \cdot 2}$$

$$x = \frac{7 \pm \sqrt{25}}{4}$$

$$x = \frac{7 \pm 5}{4}$$

$$x = \frac{7+5}{4} \quad \text{or} \quad x = \frac{7-5}{4}$$

$$x = \frac{12}{4} \quad \text{or} \quad x = \frac{2}{4}$$

$$x = 3 \quad \text{or} \quad x = \frac{1}{2}$$

Factoring or Completing the Square could also have been used to solve this quadratic equation.

EXAMPLE: Solve the equation $2x^2 + 4x - 5 = 0$ by using the quadratic formula.

$2x^2 + 4x - 5 = 0$

Substitute $a = 2$, $b = 4$, and $c = -5$ into the quadratic formula.

$$x = \frac{4 \pm \sqrt{4^2 - 4(2)(-5)}}{2(2)}$$

$$x = \frac{-2 \pm \sqrt{14}}{2}$$

The Completing the Square method could also have been used to solve this quadratic equation.

Make sure that the equation is first in the form $ax^2 + bx + c = 0$ before using the quadratic formula.

EXAMPLE: Solve the equation $(3x - 1)^2 = 4$ by using the quadratic formula.

$(3x - 1)^2 = 4$

Rewrite the equation into the form $ax^2 + bx + c = 0$.

$9x^2 - 6x + 1 = 4$

$9x^2 - 6x - 3 = 0$

Substitute $a = 9$, $b = -6$, and $c = -3$ into the quadratic formula.

$x = \dfrac{-(-6) \pm \sqrt{(-6)^2 - 4 \cdot 9 \cdot (-3)}}{2 \cdot 9}$

$x = \dfrac{6 \pm \sqrt{144}}{18}$

$x = \dfrac{6 \pm 12}{18}$

$x = \dfrac{6 + 12}{18}$ or $x = \dfrac{6 - 12}{18}$

$x = \dfrac{18}{18}$ or $x = \dfrac{-6}{18}$

We could have also used the Square Root Property to solve this quadratic equation.

$x = 1$ or $x = -\dfrac{1}{3}$

CHECK YOUR KNOWLEDGE

For problems 1 through 8, solve using the quadratic formula.

1. $x^2 + 4x - 5 = 0$

2. $x^2 + 8x + 12 = 0$

3. $2x^2 + 5x - 12 = 0$

4. $3x^2 + 4x - 4 = 0$

5. $x^2 - 3x - 7 = 0$

6. $x^2 + 7x + 2 = 0$

7. $4x^2 - x - 6 = 0$

8. $2x^2 = -5x + 6$

For problems 9 and 10, solve and state the method you used.

9. $x^2 - 3x - 10 = 0$

10. $2x^2 - x + 4 = 9$

ANSWERS   577

1. $x = 1, -5$

2. $x = -2, -6$

3. $x = -4, \dfrac{3}{2}$

4. $x = \dfrac{2}{3}, -2$

5. $x = \dfrac{3 \pm \sqrt{37}}{2}$

6. $x = \dfrac{-7 \pm \sqrt{41}}{2}$

7. $x = \dfrac{1 \pm \sqrt{97}}{8}$

8. $x = \dfrac{-5 \pm \sqrt{73}}{4}$

9. Factoring, Completing the Square, the Quadratic Formula

10. Completing the Square, the Quadratic Formula

Chapter 66

THE DISCRIMINANT AND THE NUMBER OF SOLUTIONS

Quadratic equations can have 0, 1, or 2 solutions. The expression $b^2 - 4ac$ can be used when solving quadratic equations to determine the possible types of answers. This expression is called the DISCRIMINANT.

The formula to find the Discriminant (D) is: $b^2 - 4ac$

For the graph of the quadratic equation:
- If $D > 0$, the quadratic equation, and the corresponding graphed parabola, has 2 solutions.
- If $D = 0$, the quadratic equation, and the corresponding graphed parabola, has 1 solution.
- If $D < 0$, the quadratic equation, and the corresponding graphed parabola, has 0 solutions.

EXAMPLE: Find the value of the discriminant for the equation $x^2 - 6x + 5 = 0$.

Then determine the number of solutions for the quadratic equation.

Since $a = 1$, $b = -6$, and $c = 5$, the value of the discriminant is:

$D = b^2 - 4ac$

$= (-6)^2 - 4 \cdot 1 \cdot 5$

$= 36 - 20$

$= 16$

Since $D > 0$, the parabola has 2 solutions.

EXAMPLE: Find the value of the discriminant for the equation $\frac{1}{2}x^2 - 8x + 32 = 0$.

Then determine the number of solutions that the parabola has.

Since $a = \dfrac{1}{2}$, $b = -8$, and $c = 32$, the value of the discriminant is:

$D = b^2 - 4ac$

$= (-8)^2 - 4 \cdot \left(\dfrac{1}{2}\right) \cdot (32)$

$= 64 - 64$

$= 0$

Since $D = 0$, the parabola has 1 solution.

We can verify this by solving the quadratic equation.

$\dfrac{1}{2}x^2 - 8x + 32 = 0$ 　　　　Substitute $a = \dfrac{1}{2}$, $b = -8$, and $c = 32$ into the Quadratic Formula.

$x = \dfrac{-(-8) \pm \sqrt{(-8)^2 - 4 \cdot \left(\frac{1}{2}\right) \cdot (32)}}{2 \cdot \left(\frac{1}{2}\right)}$

$= \dfrac{8 \pm \sqrt{64 - 64}}{1}$

$= \dfrac{8 \pm \sqrt{0}}{1}$

$= 8$

Therefore, the equation has 1 solution.

EXAMPLE: Find the value of the discriminant for the equation $-2x^2 + 7x = 8$.

Then determine the number of solutions for the quadratic equation.

Rewrite the equation into the form $ax^2 + bx + c = 0$,

$-2x^2 + 7x = 8$

$-2x^2 + 7x - 8 = 0$

Since $a = -2$, $b = 7$, and $c = -8$, the value of the discriminant is:

$D = b^2 - 4ac$

$= 7^2 - 4 \cdot (-2) \cdot (-8)$

$= 49 - 64$

$= -15$

Since $D < 0$, the quadratic equation has 0 solutions.

We can verify this by trying to solve the quadratic equation.

$-2x^2 + 7x - 8 = 0$ Substitute $a = -2$, $b = 7$, and $c = -8$ into the quadratic formula.

$$x = \frac{-7 \pm \sqrt{7^2 - 4 \cdot (-2) \cdot (-8)}}{2 \cdot (-2)}$$

$$= \frac{-7 \pm \sqrt{49 - 64}}{-4}$$

$$= \frac{-7 \pm \sqrt{-15}}{-4}$$

However, $\sqrt{-15}$ is not a real number.

Therefore, the equation has 0 solutions.

For problems 1 through 8, find the value of the discriminant. Then determine the number of solutions for the quadratic equation.

1. $x^2 + 6x + 3 = 0$

2. $x^2 + 6x + 11 = 0$

3. $x^2 + 6x + 9 = 0$

4. $3x^2 - 5x - 7 = 0$

5. $-3x^2 - 5x - 7 = 0$

6. $-3x^2 - 5x + 7 = 0$

7. $-\dfrac{1}{2}x^2 = -64$

8. $3x^2 + 75 = 30x$

For problems 9 and 10, find the value of the discriminant. Then determine the number of solutions for the quadratic equation. Verify your answer by finding the solution(s) to the equation.

9. $x^2 + 5x - 6 = 0$

10. $8 = 6x - 3x^2$

CHECK YOUR ANSWERS

1. D = 24; has 2 solutions.

2. D = -8; has 0 solutions.

3. D = 0; has 1 solution.

4. D = 109; has 2 solutions.

5. D = -59; has 0 solutions.

6. D = 109; has 2 solutions.

7. D = 128; has 2 solutions.

8. D = 0; has 1 solution.

9. D = 49; has 2 solutions: $x = -6$ or $x = 1$.

10. D = -60; has 0 solutions.

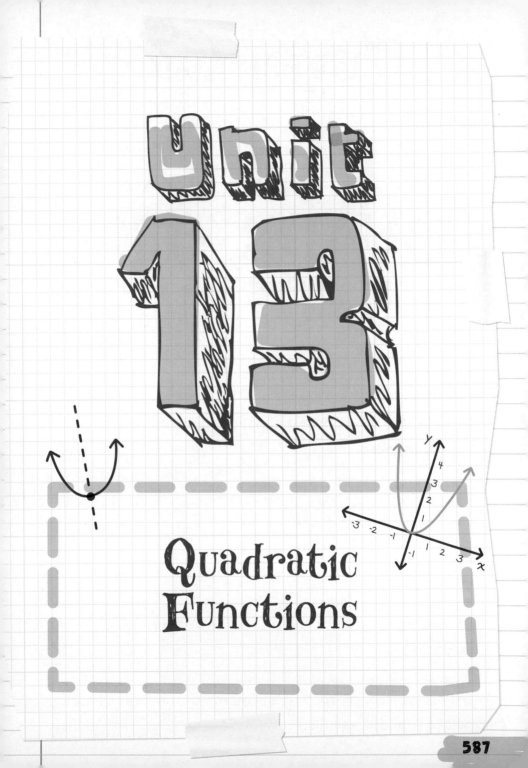

Unit 13

Quadratic Functions

Chapter 67

GRAPHING QUADRATIC FUNCTIONS

A **QUADRATIC FUNCTION** is a function that can be written in the standard form:

$$y = ax^2 + bx + c,$$
where $a \neq 0$

Every quadratic function has a U-shaped graph called a **parabola**.

There are several characteristics of the graph that we can calculate from the equation.

DIRECTION

Most parabolas open up either upward or downward.
The parabola opens upward if the value of **a** is positive.
The parabola opens downward if the value of **a** is negative.

- If $a > 0$, then the parabola opens **UPWARD**. This graph of $y = x^2$ opens upward because $a = 1$.

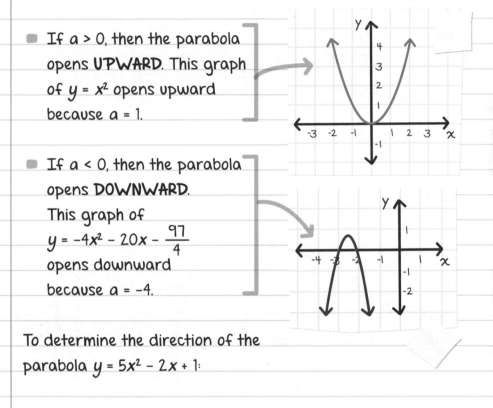

- If $a < 0$, then the parabola opens **DOWNWARD**. This graph of $y = -4x^2 - 20x - \dfrac{97}{4}$ opens downward because $a = -4$.

To determine the direction of the parabola $y = 5x^2 - 2x + 1$:

Write the formula $y = ax^2 + bx + c$.

Write the values for each variable:

$a = 5$, $b = -2$, and $c = 1$

$a > 0$, so the parabola opens upward.

Determine the direction of the parabola $y = -\frac{3}{2}(x - 8)^2$.

Rewrite the equation into the form $y = ax^2 + bx + c$,

$$y = -\frac{3}{2}(x - 8)^2$$

$$= -\frac{3}{2}(x^2 - 16x + 64)$$

$$= -\frac{3}{2}x^2 + 24x - 96$$

Since $a = -\frac{3}{2}$, this means that $a < 0$, so the parabola opens downward.

VERTEX

The **VERTEX** of the parabola is the "tip" of the parabola.

You can find the coordinates of the vertex of the graph of $y = ax^2 + bx + c$.

- The x-coordinate of the vertex is at: $-\frac{b}{2a}$.

- The y-coordinate of the vertex is found by substituting the value of the x-coordinate back into the equation.

EXAMPLE: Find the coordinates of the vertex of the graph of $y = x^2 + 6x - 7$.

Step 1: Find the x-coordinate by using the formula $x = -\dfrac{b}{2a}$.

Since $a = 1$, $b = 6$, and $c = -7$, the x-coordinate of the vertex is: $x = -\dfrac{b}{2a} = -\dfrac{6}{2 \cdot 1} = -3$.

Step 2: Find the y-coordinate by substituting the value of the x-coordinate back into the equation.

Since the x-coordinate is $x = -3$, the y-coordinate is: $y = (-3)^2 + 6(-3) - 7 = -16$.

Therefore, the coordinates of the vertex are: $(-3, -16)$.

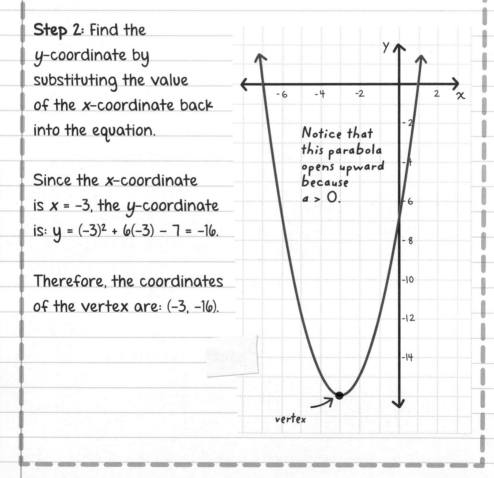

Notice that this parabola opens upward because $a > 0$.

vertex

EXAMPLE: Find the coordinates of the vertex of the graph of $y = -4\left(x - \dfrac{3}{2}\right)^2 + 5$.

Rewrite the equation into the form $y = ax^2 + bx + c$.

$$y = -4\left(x - \frac{3}{2}\right)^2 + 5$$

$$= -4\left(x^2 - 3x + \frac{9}{4}\right) + 5$$

$$= -4x^2 + 12x - 9 + 5$$

$$= -4x^2 + 12x - 4$$

Step 1: Find the x-coordinate by using the formula $x = -\dfrac{b}{2a}$.

Since $a = -4$, $b = 12$, and $c = -4$, the x-coordinate of the vertex is: $x = -\dfrac{b}{2a} = -\dfrac{12}{2 \cdot (-4)} = \dfrac{3}{2}$

Step 2: Find the y-coordinate by substituting the value of the x-coordinate back into the equation.

Since the x-coordinate is $x = \dfrac{3}{2}$, the y-coordinate is:

$$y = -4\left(\left(\frac{3}{2}\right) - \frac{3}{2}\right)^2 + 5 = 5$$

Therefore, the coordinates of the vertex are:

$\left(\dfrac{3}{2}, 5\right)$.

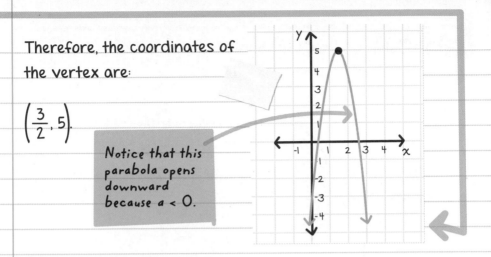

Notice that this parabola opens downward because $a < 0$.

VERTEX FORM

The standard form of a quadratic equation is: $y = ax^2 + bx + c$. Another form of writing a quadratic equation is the **vertex form**. In both the standard form and vertex form y is the y-coordinate, x is the x-coordinate and a is the constant that tells when the parabola is facing up (> 0) or down (< 0).

Vertex Form

$$y = a(x - h)^2 + k,$$

where (h, k) are the coordinates of the vertex.

EXAMPLE: Find the coordinates of the vertex of the quadratic equation $y = 7(x - 3)^2 + 8$.

Since $a = 7$, $h = 3$, and $k = 8$, the coordinates of the vertex are: $(h, k) = (3, 8)$.

EXAMPLE: Find the coordinates of the vertex of the quadratic equation $y = -\frac{1}{2}(x + 7)^2 + \frac{3}{4}$.

Don't forget to include the negative sign.

Since $a = -\frac{1}{2}$, $h = -7$, and $k = \frac{3}{4}$, the coordinates of the vertex are:

$$(h, k) = \left(-7, \frac{3}{4}\right)$$

To rewrite a quadratic equation from standard form to vertex form, use the Completing the Square method, because the vertex form contains a perfect square.

EXAMPLE: Rewrite the equation $y = x^2 + 10x - 7$ into vertex form.

$y = x^2 + 10x - 7$ Rewrite the equation so the RHS has the form $x^2 + bx$.

$y + 7 = x^2 + 10x$

This means that $b = 10$:

Step 1: Calculate the value of $\dfrac{b}{2}$: $\dfrac{10}{2} = 5$

Step 2: Square that value: $5^2 = 25$

Step 3: Add that number to **both** sides of the equation:

$y + 7 + 25 = x^2 + 10x + 25$

$y + 32 = x^2 + 10x + 25$

Step 4: Factor the RHS and then solve for y:

$y + 32 = (x + 5)^2$

$y = (x + 5)^2 - 32$

EXAMPLE: Rewrite the equation $y = 3x^2 - 6x + 7$ into vertex form and name the coordinates of the vertex.

$y = 3x^2 - 6x + 7$

$y - 7 = 3x^2 - 6x$

$\dfrac{1}{3}y - \dfrac{7}{3} = x^2 - 2x$

This means that $b = 2$:

Step 1: Calculate the value of $\frac{b}{2}$: $\frac{-2}{2} = -1$

Step 2: Square that value: $(-1)^2 = 1$

Step 3: Add that number to **both** sides of the equation:

$$\frac{1}{3}y - \frac{7}{3} + 1 = x^2 - 2x + 1$$

$$\frac{1}{3}y - \frac{4}{3} = (x - 1)^2$$

Step 4: Factor the RHS and then solve for y:

$$\frac{1}{3}y = (x - 1)^2 + \frac{4}{3}$$

$$y = 3(x - 1)^2 + 4$$

Therefore, the coordinates of the vertex are:
(1, 4).

MAXIMUM/MINIMUM

If a parabola opens **upward**,
it has a MINIMUM VALUE,
and that minimum value is
at the **vertex**.

The minimum
value of an
upward-opening
parabola is at
the vertex.

If a parabola opens
downward, it has a
MAXIMUM VALUE, and
that maximum value is
at the **vertex**.

The maximum
value of a
downward-
opening parabola
is at the vertex.

The maximum/minimum value
is always the **y-coordinate** of the vertex.

To find the maximum/minimum value of a quadratic equation:

Step 1: Determine if the parabola opens upward or downward.

    upward = minimum value

    downward = maximum value

Step 2: Find the coordinates of the vertex.

    The y-coordinate of the vertex is the minimum/maximum
    value.

EXAMPLE: Find whether $y = x^2 - 8x + 3$ has a maximum value or a minimum value. Then find that value.

Step 1: Since $a = 1$, this means that $a > 0$, so the parabola opens upward. The parabola has a **MINIMUM value** at the vertex.

Step 2: Since $a = 1$, $b = -8$, and $c = 3$, the x-coordinate of the vertex is:
$$x = -\frac{b}{2a} = -\frac{-8}{2 \cdot 1} = 4.$$

Substitute $x = 4$ into the equation. The y-coordinate of the vertex is:
$$y = (4)^2 - 8(4) + 3$$
$$= 16 - 32 + 3 = -13.$$

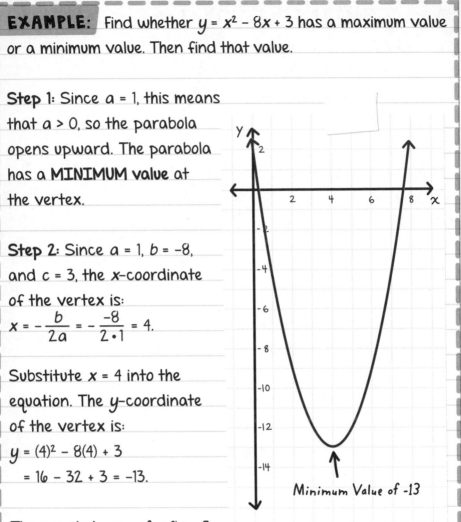

Minimum Value of -13

The parabola $y = x^2 - 8x + 3$ has a **MINIMUM VALUE** of -13.

AXIS OF SYMMETRY

All parabolas are SYMMETRICAL.

axis of symmetry

This means that if we draw a vertical line down the center of the parabola, the left side and right side would be mirror images of each other.

That vertical line is called the AXIS OF SYMMETRY.

The equation of the axis of symmetry is $x = -\dfrac{b}{2a}$.

> This is the same value as the x-coordinate of the vertex, because the axis of symmetry goes through the vertex.

EXAMPLE: Find the equation of the axis of symmetry of the parabola $y = -\dfrac{1}{2}(x - 1)(x + 8)$.

Rewrite the equation into the form $y = ax^2 + bx + c$.

$$y = -\frac{1}{2}(x - 1)(x + 8)$$

$$= -\frac{1}{2}(x^2 + 7x - 8)$$

$$= -\frac{1}{2}x^2 - \frac{7}{2}x + 4$$

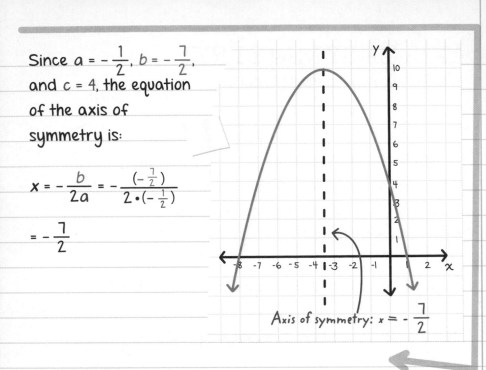

Since $a = -\dfrac{1}{2}$, $b = -\dfrac{7}{2}$, and $c = 4$, the equation of the axis of symmetry is:

$$x = -\frac{b}{2a} = -\frac{\left(-\frac{7}{2}\right)}{2 \cdot \left(-\frac{1}{2}\right)}$$

$$= -\frac{7}{2}$$

Axis of symmetry: $x = -\dfrac{7}{2}$

INTERCEPTS

INTERCEPTS are the points where the parabola *intersects*—or intercepts—the *x*-axis and the *y*-axis. They are expressed as numbers or coordinates.

The *x*-intercept is where the parabola intersects the *x*-axis. The *y*-intercept is where the parabola intersects the *y*-axis.

- To find any *y*-intercept, substitute 0 for *x* and then solve for *y*.

- To find any *x*-intercept, substitute 0 for *y* and then solve for *x*.

An x-intercept is also known as a ZERO or a ROOT.

EXAMPLE: Find all the intercepts of the parabola $y = x^2 + 3x - 10$.

Find the y-intercept by substituting 0 for x:

$y = x^2 + 3x - 10$
$= (0)^2 + 3(0) - 10$
$= -10$

Therefore, the y-intercept is -10 or $(0, -10)$.

Find the x-intercepts by substituting 0 for y:

$y = x^2 + 3x - 10$

$(0) = x^2 + 3x - 10$ Use factoring or Completing the Square or the Quadratic Formula to find the solutions.

$0 = (x + 5)(x - 2)$

$x = -5, 2$

Therefore, the
x-intercepts are:
-5 and 2 or
(-5, 0) and (2, 0).

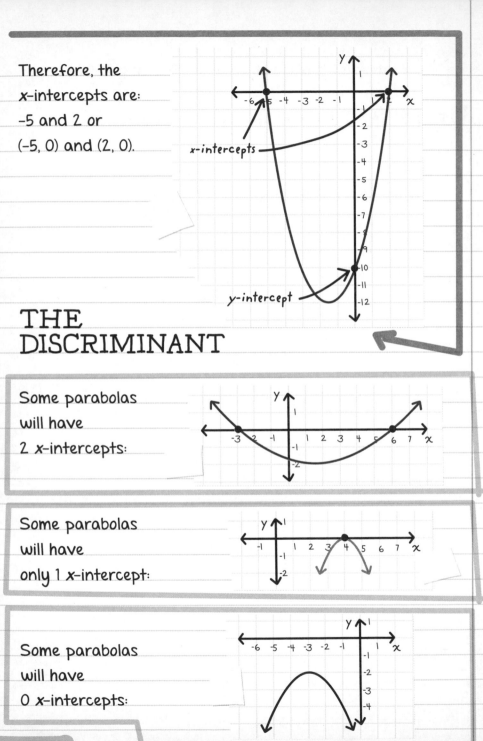

THE DISCRIMINANT

Some parabolas
will have
2 x-intercepts:

Some parabolas
will have
only 1 x-intercept:

Some parabolas
will have
0 x-intercepts:

We can find the amount of x-intercepts (or roots) by analyzing the value of the **DISCRIMINANT**: $D = b^2 - 4ac$

- If $D > 0$, the parabola has 2 x-intercepts.

- If $D = 0$, the parabola has 1 x-intercept.

- If $D < 0$, the parabola has 0 x-intercepts.

EXAMPLE: For the parabola $y = 3x^2 - 6x + 5$, find the value of the discriminant.

Then determine the amount of x-intercepts that the parabola has.

Since $a = 3$, $b = -6$, and $c = 5$,
the value of the discriminant is:

$D = b^2 - 4ac$

$= (-6)^2 - 4 \cdot 3 \cdot 5$

$= 36 - 60 = -24$

Since $D < 0$, the parabola has
0 x-intercepts.

To graph a quadratic equation, take all the different characteristics of a parabola and connect the points. When graphing a parabola, we should always find:

- The direction of the parabola.

- The coordinates of the vertex.

- The coordinates of the intercepts—y-intercept and x-intercept(s).

The discriminant will tell how many x-intercepts there are.

EXAMPLE: Graph $y = x^2 - 4x - 5$.

Find the direction of the parabola:

$a = 1$, and since $a > 0$, the parabola opens **upward**.

Find the coordinates of the vertex:

Since $a = 1$, $b = -4$, and $c = -5$, the x-coordinate of the vertex is:

$$x = -\frac{b}{2a} = -\frac{-4}{2 \cdot 1} = 2$$

Substitute $x = 2$ into the equation. The y-coordinate of the vertex is: $y = (2)^2 - 4(2) - 5 = 4 - 8 - 5 = -9$

Therefore, the coordinates of the **vertex** are: $(2, -9)$

Find the y-intercept by substituting 0 for x:

$y = x^2 - 4x - 5$
$= (0)^2 - 4(0) - 5$
$= -5$

Therefore, the y-intercept is -5 or $(0, -5)$.

Find the number of x-intercepts by calculating the discriminant.

Since $a = 1$, $b = -4$, and $c = -5$, the value of the discriminant is: $D = b^2 - 4ac$.

$= (-4)^2 - 4 \cdot 1 \cdot (-5) = 16 + 20 = 36$

Since $D > 0$, the parabola has 2 x-intercepts.

Find the x-intercepts by substituting 0 for y:

$y = x^2 - 4x - 5$

$(0) = x^2 - 4x - 5$ Use factoring to find the solutions.

$0 = (x - 5)(x + 1)$

$x = 5, -1$

Therefore, the x-intercepts are: 5 and –1 or (5, 0) and (–1, 0).

Graph the points and connect them by drawing a parabola.

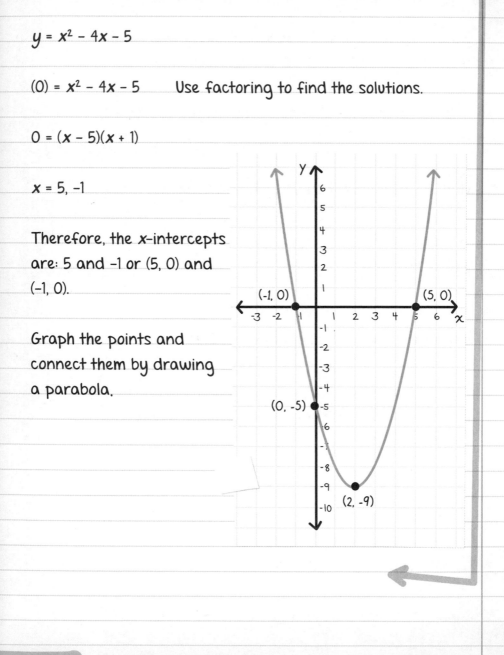

CHECK YOUR KNOWLEDGE

For problems 1 through 3, find the following characteristics of each parabola:

- the direction

- the coordinates of the vertex

- whether the parabola has a maximum or minimum value

- the equation of the axis of symmetry

- the value of the discriminant

- the coordinates of all intercepts

1. $y = x^2 - 6x + 8$

2. $y = -x^2 + 2x + 3$

3. $y = 2x^2 + 8x - 10$

For problem 4, rewrite the quadratic equation into vertex form. Then state the coordinates of the vertex.

4. $y = 4x^2 + 12x - 7$

5. Draw the graph of $y = x^2 - 2x - 8$.

6. Draw the graph of $y = -2x^2 - 8x - 3$.

CHECK YOUR ANSWERS

1. direction: upward
   vertex: (3, –1)
   the parabola has a minimum value
   axis of symmetry: $x = 3$
   discriminant: $D = 4$
   y-intercept: (0, 8); x-intercepts: (4, 0) and (2, 0)

2. direction: downward
   vertex: (1, 6)
   the parabola has a maximum value
   axis of symmetry: $x = 1$
   discriminant: $D = 16$
   y-intercept: (0, 3); x-intercepts: (3, 0) and (–1, 0)

3. direction: upward
   vertex: (–2, –18)
   the parabola has a minimum value
   axis of symmetry: $x = -2$
   discriminant: $D = 144$
   y-intercept: (0, –10); x-intercepts: (–5, 0), and (1, 0)

4. $y = 4\left(x + \dfrac{3}{2}\right)^2 - 16$; vertex is $\left(\dfrac{3}{2}, -16\right)$

5.

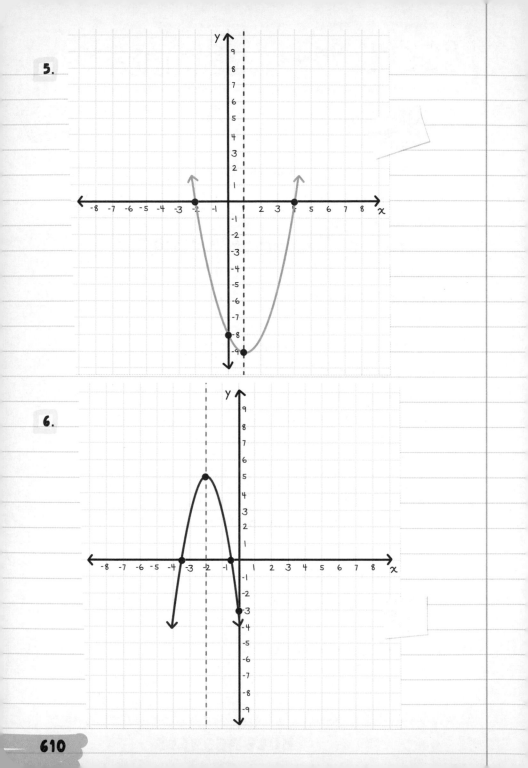

6.

Chapter 68

SOLVING QUADRATIC EQUATIONS BY GRAPHING

When we graph the quadratic equation $y = ax^2 + bx + c$, the x-intercepts are where the parabola crosses the x-axis and the intercepts have a y-value of 0.

This is why the x-intercepts represent the **roots** or the **solution** of the quadratic equation.

$0 = ax^2 + bx + c$ or $ax^2 + bx + c = 0$

Notice that y has been replaced with 0.

EXAMPLE: Find the solutions of $-\frac{2}{3}x^2 - \frac{2}{3}x + 4 = 0$.

Use the graph of $y = -\frac{2}{3}x^2 - \frac{2}{3}x + 4$, shown.

The solutions of $-\frac{2}{3}x^2 - \frac{2}{3}x + 4 = 0$ are the x-intercepts of the equation $y = -\frac{2}{3}x^2 - \frac{2}{3}x + 4$.

Since the x-intercepts of the graph are −3 and 2, the solutions are: $x = -3$ and $x = 2$.

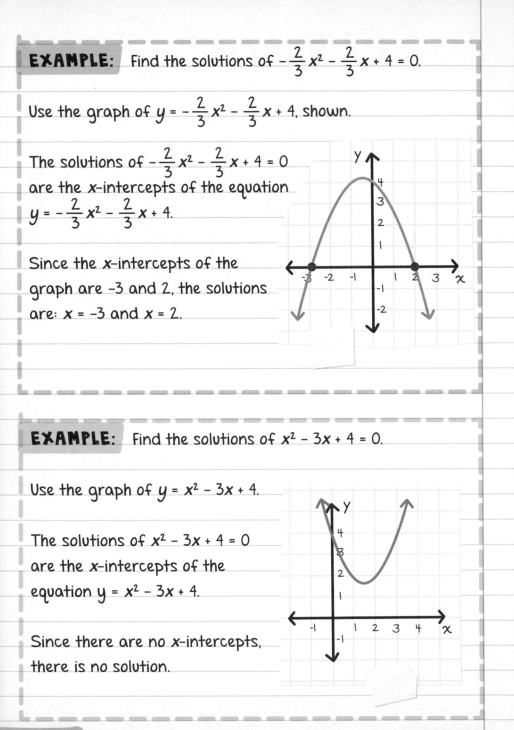

EXAMPLE: Find the solutions of $x^2 - 3x + 4 = 0$.

Use the graph of $y = x^2 - 3x + 4$.

The solutions of $x^2 - 3x + 4 = 0$ are the x-intercepts of the equation $y = x^2 - 3x + 4$.

Since there are no x-intercepts, there is no solution.

EXAMPLE: The vertex of a parabola is at (-4, -3). One of the roots of the quadratic equation is (-6, 0). Find the other root of the quadratic equation.

Graph the vertex and the root, where the axis of symmetry runs through the vertex.

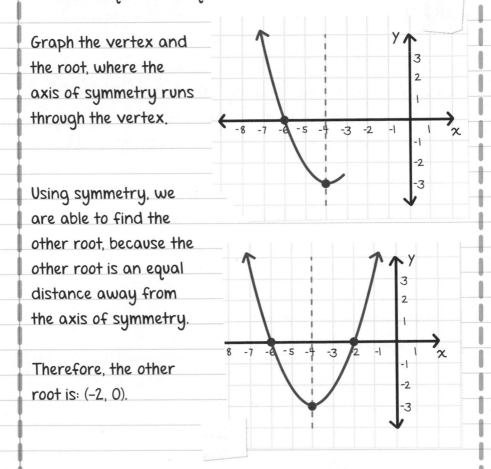

Using symmetry, we are able to find the other root, because the other root is an equal distance away from the axis of symmetry.

Therefore, the other root is: (-2, 0).

There are real-life applications to finding solutions to quadratic equations.

EXAMPLE: Jamie kicks a soccer ball into the air, away from her. The path that the ball takes is in the shape of a parabola and is represented by the equation $y = 2x^2 + 9x$, where x represents how far away the soccer ball travels (in meters), and y represents how high the soccer ball travels above the ground (in meters). How far away is the soccer ball when it hits the ground?

Since we are examining the moment when the soccer ball hits the ground, this means that the height of the soccer ball above the ground is $y = 0$.

This is like finding the x-intercept of the graph of a quadratic equation.

Setting $y = 0$ for $y = 2x^2 + 9x$:

$(0) = 2x^2 + 9x$ Use factoring.

$0 = -x(2x - 9)$ Apply the Zero-Product Principle.

$x = 0$ or $2x - 9 = 0$

$x = 0$ or $x = \dfrac{9}{2}$

There are two answers: 0 meters away, or $\dfrac{9}{2} = 4.5$ meters away.

The first answer doesn't make sense (it represents where the ball is before it is kicked), so the answer is: $\dfrac{9}{2} = 4.5$ meters away.

1. Find the solution(s) of
   $-x^2 + 6x - 5 = 0$, using this
   graph of $y = -x^2 + 6x - 5$.

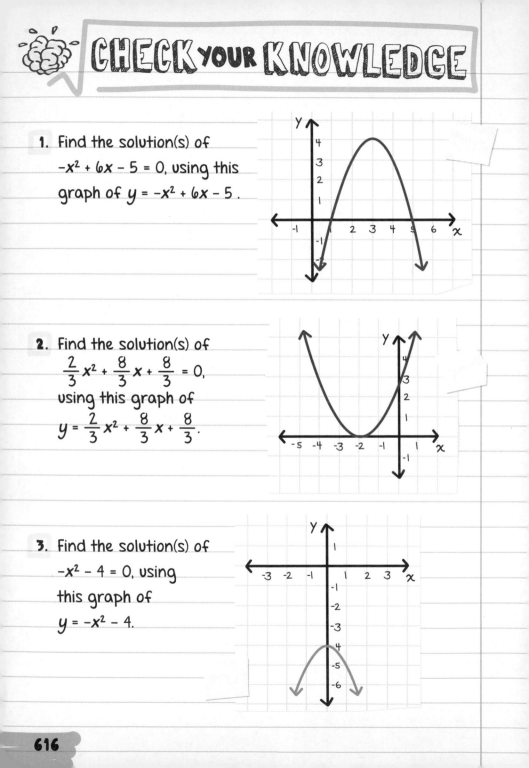

2. Find the solution(s) of
   $\frac{2}{3}x^2 + \frac{8}{3}x + \frac{8}{3} = 0$,
   using this graph of
   $y = \frac{2}{3}x^2 + \frac{8}{3}x + \frac{8}{3}$.

3. Find the solution(s) of
   $-x^2 - 4 = 0$, using
   this graph of
   $y = -x^2 - 4$.

4. Find the solution(s) of $\frac{1}{8}x^2 + \frac{1}{4}x - 3 = 0$, using this graph of $y = \frac{1}{8}x^2 + \frac{1}{4}x - 3$.

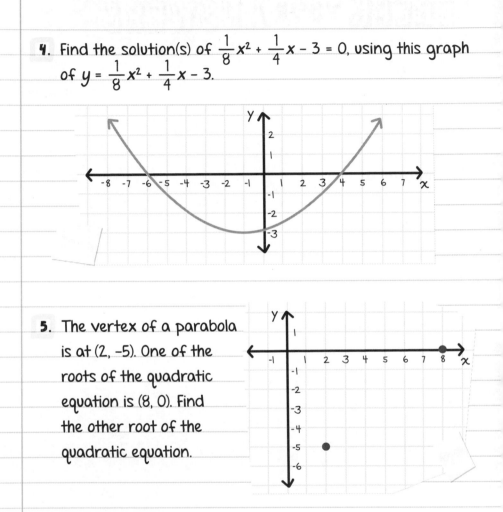

5. The vertex of a parabola is at (2, –5). One of the roots of the quadratic equation is (8, 0). Find the other root of the quadratic equation.

6. A cannonball is fired. The path the ball takes is in the shape of a parabola and is represented by the equation $y = -4x^2 + 31x$, where x represents how far away the cannonball travels (in miles) and y represents how high the cannonball travels above the ground (in miles). How far away is the cannonball when it hits the ground?

ANSWERS

CHECK YOUR ANSWERS

1. $x = 1$ or $x = 5$

2. $x = -2$

3. No solution

4. $x = -6$ or $x = 4$

5. $(-6, 10)$

6. 7.75 miles away

★INDEX★

GOODBYE, ALGEBRA. . .
HELLO, GEOMETRY!

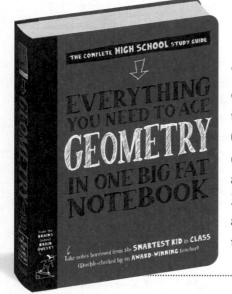

This BIG FAT NOTEBOOK covers everything you need to know during a year of GEOMETRY class, breaking down one big fat subject into accessible units, from the basics like points, lines, planes, and angles to the beginning of trigonometry.

P.S. Are you one of those brainiacs taking Algebra in middle school? Don't forget to ace the rest of your classes with the original **BIG FAT NOTEBOOKS** series:

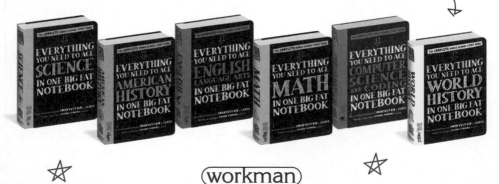